Migrating Linux to Microsoft Azure

A hands-on guide to efficiently relocating your Linux workload to Azure

Rithin Skaria

Toni Willberg

BIRMINGHAM–MUMBAI

Migrating Linux to Microsoft Azure

Authors: Rithin Skaria, Toni Willberg

Technical Reviewers: Marin Nedea, Micha Wets

Managing Editors: Neha Pande, Mamta Yadav

Acquisitions Editors: Saby Dsilva, Ben Renow-Clarke

Production Editor: Deepak Chavan

Editorial Board: Vishal Bodwani, Edward Doxey, Ben Renow-Clarke, Arijit Sarkar, and Dominic Shakeshaft

First Published: July 2021

Production Reference: 1150721

ISBN: 978-1-80107-172-7

Published by Packt Publishing Ltd.
Livery Place, 35 Livery Street,
Birmingham, B3 2PB, UK.

www.packt.com

Table of Contents

Preface   i

Chapter 1: Linux: History and future in the cloud   1

A brief history of Linux 3

    Unix 3

    Linux 3

    Linux version history 4

    Linux evolution and distributions 5

Typical Linux use cases in IT infrastructure 6

    Workstations 6

    Application servers 7

    Database servers 8

    Virtualization 8

    Containers 9

    Cloud computing 11

    Container orchestration 12

    Big data 13

Challenges in on-premises infrastructure 14

Cloud economics 15

    Scale comes with benefits 16

    Many services available 16

Benefits of migrating to Azure 17

The journey from Linux to Azure 18

    Clustering 19

    Subscription portability 23

Summary 24

Chapter 2: Understanding Linux distributions   27

Linux licensing and open-source business models 28

    Open-source licenses 28

    Enterprise agreements 29

    Linux subscriptions 29

Popular Linux distributions 30

Linux on Azure 32

    Benefits of Linux on Azure 33

    Linux support scope 35

    Licensing on Azure 36

    Available distros 46

Summary 55

Chapter 3: Assessment and migration planning   57

Popular workloads on Linux 58

    LAMP 59

    Database servers 60

    HPC, clustering, and SAP 61

    Shared storage 61

Pre-project preparations 63

    Identifying relevant roles and responsibilities 63

    Cloud governance and operations 66

Migration assessment 67

   Preparing a cloud migration plan 67

   Discovery and evaluation 68

   Involving key stakeholders 69

   Estimating the savings 69

   Identifying tools 70

Assessing tooling 70

   Azure Migrate 71

   Service Map 71

   Azure TCO calculator 73

Hands-on assess lab 75

   Prerequisites 76

   Setting up the Azure Migrate project 76

   Setting up and registering the Azure Migrate appliance 80

   Verifying discovered VMs in the portal 85

   Running an assessment 86

   Reviewing the assessment 89

   Dependency analysis 90

Summary 95

Chapter 4: Performing migration to Azure   97

Hands-on migration lab 99

   Migrating servers to Azure 99

   Migrating databases 117

Summary 133

Chapter 5: Operating Linux on Azure   135

Optimize 136

    Azure Cost Management 136

    Azure Advisor 138

Manage and Secure 139

    Linux Agent for Azure 139

    Extensions 141

    Data protection 143

    Azure Disk Encryption 144

    Updating Linux on Azure 145

    Azure Update Management 147

Hands-on managing Linux on Azure 148

    Creating a Log Analytics workspace 150

    Onboarding an Azure virtual machine 152

    Data collection 154

    Querying data 156

Summary 159

Chapter 6: Troubleshooting and problem solving   161

Remote connectivity and VM start issues 162

    Run commands without a network connection 164

    Boot diagnostics and serial console access 166

    Common boot problems 167

Common Linux runtime challenges 169

    SELinux 169

    Storage configuration issues 171

    Disk encryption problems 173

    Resizing disks 173

    Performance issues and analysis 176

Azure diagnostics tooling – a summary 179

Opening support requests 180

Summary 183

New horizons for Linux in Azure 184

Index   187

Preface

About

This section briefly introduces the authors and reviewers, the coverage of this book, the technical skills you'll need to get started, and the hardware and software needed to complete all of the topics.

About Migrating Linux to Microsoft Azure

With cloud adoption at the core of digital transformation for organizations, there has been a lot of demand to deploy and host enterprise business workloads in the cloud. *Migrating Linux to Microsoft Azure* offers a series of actionable insights into deploying Linux workloads to Azure.

You will begin by learning about the history of IT, operating systems, Unix, Linux, and Windows, before moving on to look at the cloud and what things were like before virtualization. This will enable those not very familiar with Linux to learn the terms required to grasp the upcoming chapters. Furthermore, you will explore popular Linux distributions including RHEL 7, RHEL 8, SLES, Ubuntu Pro, CentOS 7, and more.

As you progress, you will dive into the technical details of Linux workloads such as LAMP, Java, and SAP. You will learn how to assess your current environment and plan migrating to Azure through cloud governance and operations planning.

Finally, you will go through the execution of a real migration project and learn how to analyze, debug, and recover from some common problems that Linux on Azure users have encountered.

By the end of Linux book, you will be proficient in performing the effective migration of Linux workloads to Azure for your organization.

About the authors

Rithin Skaria is an open-source evangelist with over 9 years of experience in managing open-source workloads on Azure, AWS, and OpenStack. He is currently working for Microsoft as a Customer Engineer and is part of several open-source community activities conducted within Microsoft. He has played a vital role in several open-source deployments and the administration and migration of these workloads to the cloud. He also co-authored *Linux Administration on Azure, Second Edition* and *Azure For Architects, Third Edition* both published by Packt. Connect with him on LinkedIn at `@rithin-skaria`.

Toni Willberg is a Linux on Azure subject matter expert with 25 years of professional IT experience. He has worked with Microsoft and Red Hat as a solution architect, helping clients and partners in their open-source and cloud journeys. He has been involved in the technical reviews of various books published by Packt.

Currently, Toni holds the position of Head of Cloud Business Unit at Iglu, a managed service provider company offering professional public cloud projects and services. Connect with him on Twitter at `@ToniWillberg`.

About the reviewers

Marin Nedea is an experienced Linux Escalation Engineer, a mentor, and a certified Azure Linux Trainer, ITIL, and KT practitioner, with a history of more than 15 years in the IT services industry. He has strong theoretical and practical knowledge regarding replication, clustering, and high availability, as well as expertise in on-premises datacenters, virtualization, IBM Cloud, and Azure cloud technologies. Although he is an IT professional, his studies are in Psychology of Educational Sciences at Spiru Haret University in Bucharest, Romania. You can follow on LinkedIn at @Marin Nedea.

Micha Wets is a Microsoft MVP who enjoys talking about Azure, Powershell, and automation and has previously spoken at Microsoft conferences, international events, Microsoft webinars, workshops, and much more. He has over 15 years of experience as a DevOps engineer and has in-depth knowledge concerning hybrid and public clouds.

Today, Micha mainly focuses on Azure, Powershell, automation, Azure DevOps, GitHub Actions, and Windows Virtual Desktop environments, and he is particularly knowledgeable when it comes to migrating those environments to Azure. Micha is the founder of Cloud.Architect and you can follow him on Twitter at @michawets.

Learning objectives

- Explore the terminology and technology of various Linux distributions
- Understand the technical support co-operation between Microsoft and commercial Linux vendors
- Assess current workloads by using Azure Migrate
- Plan cloud governance and operations
- Execute a real-world migration project
- Manage projects, staffing, and customer engagement

Audience

This book is intended to benefit cloud architects, cloud solution providers, and any stakeholders dealing with the migration of Linux workloads to Azure. Basic familiarity with Microsoft Azure would be a plus.

Approach

Migrating Linux to Microsoft Azure uses an ideal blend of theoretical explanations and hands-on examples to help you prepare for real-world migration challenges faced by businesses today.

Hardware and software requirements

Hardware requirements

For the optimal lab experience, we recommend the following hardware configuration:

- Windows Server 2016 with a Hyper-V role installed and at least 8 GB RAM and 8 cores for the Assess and Migration Lab

Software requirements

We also recommend that you have the following software configuration in advance:

- Azure subscription
- Azure CLI

Conventions

Code words in the text, database names, folder names, filenames, and file extensions are shown as follows.

"You can either download it in Linux using the wget command or download it to your computer and transfer it to a Linux machine using SFTP/SCP."

Here's a sample block of code:

```
wget --content-disposition https://aka.ms/dependencyagentlinux -O
InstallDependencyAgent-Linux64.bin

sh InstallDependencyAgent-Linux64.bin
```

As Azure is evolving at a very rapid pace, it is possible that some of the views or features you see in the Azure Portal are different from the screenshots seen in this book. We have tried to make sure that the screenshots and all the technical facts in this book are correct at the time of writing. We have provided links to the official documentation throughout this book. If you're unsure, check the documentation for the latest usage guidance.

Downloading resources

We also have other code bundles from our rich catalog of books and videos available at https://github.com/PacktPublishing/. Check them out!

1

Linux: History and future in the cloud

"Microsoft ♡ Linux" was written on the closing slide of a presentation given by Microsoft CEO Satya Nadella in 2015. This announced a wave of changes that were going to happen, and Satya Nadella wanted to address Microsoft's interest in Linux and **Open-Source Software (OSS)** technologies. Everyone felt that there was some contradiction here, wondering why Microsoft was working with OSS technologies. Wired magazine reported that Nadella is not interested in fighting old battles–especially, when, like it or not, Linux has become a vital part of today's business technology. "If you don't jump on the new," Nadella told Wired, "you don't survive."

At the time of writing, more than 50% of Microsoft Azure is ruled by Linux. There are a lot of misconceptions around migrating existing Linux workloads to Microsoft Azure and this book will help in understanding the complexities, simplifying the migration process.

We will start off with a brief history of Linux and the events that led to its development. Along with that, we will talk about some of the competitors of Linux and the use cases for both Linux and these competitors. We will cover some of the key roles that Linux servers play in IT infrastructure, touching on why the cloud is better for running these workloads compared to on-premises solutions. As most organizations are going with a cloud transformation strategy, the demand for virtual machines, containers, container orchestration solutions, big data, and so on is increasing, and Microsoft Azure provides a platform to run all these mission-critical workloads.

In order to understand the complexity of migrating Linux workloads to Azure, you need to understand the history of IT, operating systems, Unix, Linux, and Windows, before the cloud and virtualization. This chapter will provide some important background information about Linux to enable those who are not very familiar with it to learn the terminology.

The public cloud has many benefits over self-hosted environments. We will talk about them, particularly covering how Azure is designed to support Linux workloads.

While we will briefly mention some typically difficult aspects of Linux systems, you will also learn that Azure is evolving rapidly. Azure now has out-of-the-box features that will make Linux sysadmins' lives much easier.

This chapter covers the following key topics:

- Brief history and evolution of Linux
- Use cases of Linux in IT infrastructure
- Challenges in on-premises infrastructure
- Cloud economics
- Advantages of migrating to Azure
- Simplifying the complexity associated with migration

Let's get started with a brief history of Linux.

A brief history of Linux

Before we talk about the history of Linux, it's a good idea to start with the events that led to its development. You might have seen pictures of old computers that were as big as a car or a house. It's hard to imagine how cumbersome it would be to handle a system this big now that we live in a world of handheld devices and thin clients. It's not just the massive size; the different operating systems that used to run on these devices made things more complicated. Every piece of software was designed to serve a single purpose and was impossible to run on another computer. In short, we had a compatibility issue. On top of these problems, the cost of buying these computers was huge. Purchasing a computer was not a dream that came true for normal people.

Unix

The aforementioned shortcomings led to the development of a project called **Unix**, which was started in the mid-1970s by a group of developers at Bell Laboratories. The main intention of this project was to make a common software for all computers, rather than having individual pieces of software for each computer. The project used the C language instead of assembly language; it was indeed refined and uncomplicated.

The Unix operating system was widely adopted by government organizations, universities, and schools. It existed for many systems, ranging from personal computers all the way to supercomputers. Though the advent of Unix resolved some issues, it hadn't dealt with the pricing problem; these systems were still expensive.

During the early 1980s, organizations began developing their own versions of Unix. As a result of the multiple development branches, we ended up with lots of different versions, or dialects. Every developer and organization wanted to create a free Unix-like operating system and, in 1983 at MIT, Richard Stallman developed the GNU project. The goal of this project was to create a free operating system (in the sense of licensing, and not necessarily cost). This project didn't gain much popularity, as expected; nevertheless, GNU tools were adopted by Linux when it came into existence.

Linux

In 1991, Linus Torvalds developed Linux as a freely distributable Unix while he was a student at the University of Helsinki, Finland. Linus was motivated by Andrew Tanenbaum's Minix operating system, which was another free Unix for PCs. Linus wanted to author a freely available academic version of Unix that could run on Intel 386-based PCs for Minix users who wanted to get more out of their computers. The project was initially named "Freax," a fun project that ended up as one of the biggest revolutions in the history of computers with the name "Linux." On a public forum (comp. os.minix) during the initial days of Linux, Linus referred to his work as "a better Minix than Minix." Quoting his own words:

"After that it was plain sailing: hairy coding still, but I had some devices, and debugging was easier. I started using C at this stage, and it certainly speeds up development. This is also when I start to get serious about my megalomaniac ideas to make "a better Minix than Minix." I was hoping I'd be able to recompile gcc under Linux some day...

"Two months for basic setup, but then only slightly longer until I had a disk driver (seriously buggy, but it happened to work on my machine) and a small filesystem. That was about when I made 0.01 available [around late August of 1991]: it wasn't pretty, it had no floppy drive, and it couldn't do much of anything. I don't think anybody ever compiled that version. But by then I was hooked, and didn't want to stop until I could chuck out Minix."

If only he had guessed how widely adopted Linux would be 30 years on.

Linux version history

For the first version of Linux (v0.01), there were no executables. To play with this version, you needed a Minix machine to compile, as the intention was to make the Minix system better. In 1991, v0.02 was launched and is now referred to as the first official version of Linux. The current Linux systems that we see have immense provisions for a variety of things, such as user support, documentation, and software repositories. However, this was not the case during the early stages of Linux. In v0.02, Bash (GNU Bourne Again Shell) and gcc (GNU compiler) were the only things that were running, and the main focus was kernel development.

After v0.02 came v0.03, and so on; revisions were made until Linux reached v0.95 in 1992, with the goal of a bug-free v1.0. After two years with a couple of revisions in between, v1.0 came out in March 1994. After 25+ years of v1.0, we are currently in v5.x and, at the time of writing, the last version released is v5.9. We are expecting v5.10 soon.

As mentioned earlier, Linux adopted GNU tools, and these tools played an inevitable role in the making of Linux. Without these, Linux might not have made the impact that we see today. Along with GNU, **Berkeley Software Distribution (BSD)** played a role in making Linux popular. Though BSD was not initially adopted in the early stages of Linux, later versions had tools that were ported from BSD. The networking daemon and several other utilities are perfect examples of BSD's contributions to Linux that have made it the subject of admiration.

Linux evolution and distributions

Linux evolved over these years and the fun project started by Linus Torvalds is now used by millions of computers, smartphones, servers, and even supercomputers across the globe. Today, Linux is capable of running web, mail, emacs, the X Windows System... the list goes on. Linux not only dominates on-premises but has a major share of the workload in Azure too. Currently, we have a lot of Linux flavors tailored for enterprise use as well as personal use.

As already stated, Linux isn't something that is developed by a single organization. It is a combination of different parts or modules, such as the kernel, GNU shell utilities, the X server, the desktop environments, system services, daemons, and Terminal commands—all of these come from different developers and they are developed independently. If you want, you can take source code for the kernel, shell, and other components and assemble it. There are projects such as **Linux from Scratch (LFS)** and **Beyond Linux from Scratch (BLFS)** where users can download these pieces of software that are licensed under open-source software, compile them, and make their own Linux flavor.

Although exciting, the amount of work needed for this is heavy and you have to invest a lot of time for these components to work together properly. Linux distributions (often referred to as **distros**) make this hectic task easier. Distros will take all the code from the repositories and compile them, finally creating a single operating system that you can boot up on your computer. Examples of distros include Ubuntu, Fedora, CentOS, RHEL, Mint, and SUSE Linux. Some distros, such as RHEL, SUSE, and Ubuntu, have an enterprise server–grade version as well, which is used by organizations to host their mission-critical workloads.

Linux for Enterprise is a new realm altogether. It began with Red Hat, which used to have a monopoly. However, more competitors soon appeared, including Canonical and SUSE, as well as the non-commercial CentOS. Azure supports all of the preceding enterprise-grade Linux operating systems, so each and every organization can migrate their Linux workloads to Azure.

Before we talk about the benefits of moving workloads to Azure, let's understand the common use case scenarios for these Linux servers in IT infrastructure, along with some of the challenges associated with on-premises approaches.

Typical Linux use cases in IT infrastructure

As mentioned in the previous section, A *brief history of Linux*, the customer base for the Linux operating system is very large for on-premises environments as well as the cloud. In this section, we will talk about some use cases of Linux in IT infrastructure. Some things have been relevant since the beginning of Linux adoption (files, the web, databases, and so on), while others have been adopted recently with the introduction of new technologies (containerization and container orchestration, for example). These use cases will be added to and evolve over time.

Workstations

There is a large subset of consumers who prefer to use Linux as a daily commuter on their personal computers. This area was mainly monopolized by Windows and macOS, but things changed a lot when Linux came to the stage. Traditionally, Linux was an all-time favorite for coders and programmers, providing more customization options for the general consumer than Windows or macOS. For this reason, Linux became the preferred option for millions of people across the globe:

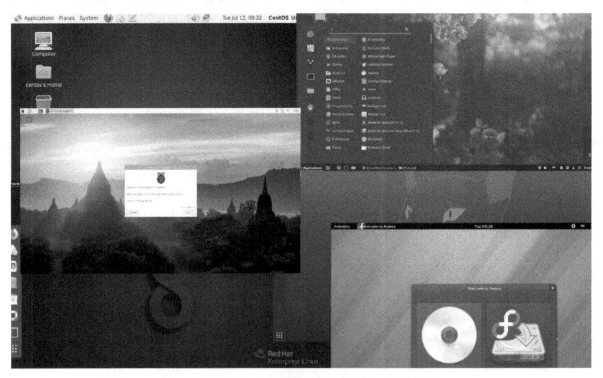

Figure 1.1: Different workstation distros and GUIs

Currently, we have flavors such as Ubuntu, Fedora Workstation, Linux Mint, Elementary OS, CentOS, and Arch Linux. *Figure 1.1* shows how the **Graphical User Interface (GUI)** appears in different workstation distros.

Application servers

An application server is computer software that is bundled together to facilitate business logic. If we take a three-tier application, the application server is the component that comprises the GUI, the business logic, and the database server. The majority of application servers support the Java platform, some examples being JBoss, Jetty, JOnAS, Apache Geronimo, and Glassfish:

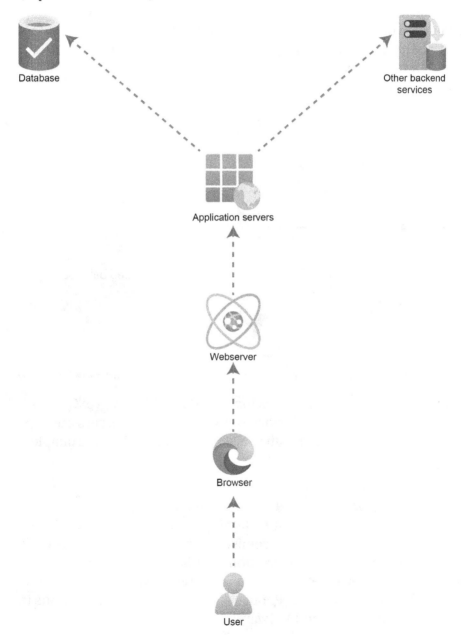

Figure 1.2: Coupling of application servers with other services to provide end-to-end solutions

In *Figure* 1.2, you can see how the application servers are coupled with other services, including the front-end and back-end services. An application server handles connections between the user requests that originate from the front-end and back-end services, such as databases and other logic.

Database servers

Linux has been the home of databases for a very long time now. We can install relational and non-relational databases on Linux as per our data requirements. The term **database server** refers to the combination of a database application and memory allocated for data storage. These databases can be used to record transactions in a similar way to how SQL Server works on Microsoft Windows:

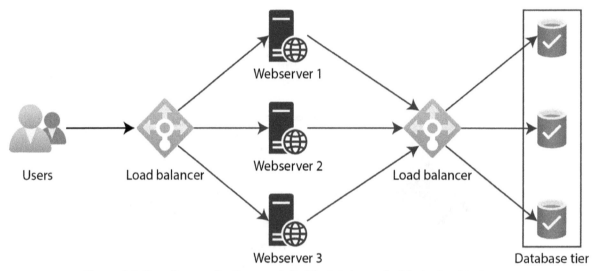

Figure 1.3: Two-tier application model with databases behind a load balancer

Some commonly used database services include MariaDB, PostgreSQL, MySQL, and MongoDB. In most scenarios, the databases hosted in Linux servers are kept behind a load balancing solution to provide high availability. *Figure* 1.3 is an example of this.

Virtualization

The purpose of virtualization is to create virtual machines using specialized software called **hypervisors**. Most of you might be familiar with the term **virtual machines (VMs)**, as this is quite common in on-premises environments as well as in the cloud. The purpose of making Linux a virtualization host is the same as installing a Windows Server instance with the Hyper-V role. VMs are often created for the isolation of workloads and for testing purposes. Popular Linux virtualization solutions include KVM, RHEV, Xen, QEMU, VirtualBox, and VMware:

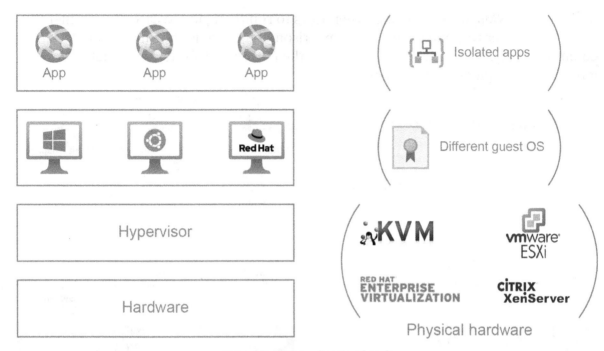

Figure 1.4: Virtualization levels

As shown in *Figure* 1.4, the hypervisor is installed on the hardware and different VMs are created using hypervisors. Each of these VMs is isolated from the operating system and can host different applications.

Containers

We just discussed VMs and their creation using hypervisors installed on our Linux servers. The footprint of these servers will be large and will often contain some stock libraries and binaries that we do not require. This leads to a waste of compute resources; with all VMs being deployed, your host capacity will soon be exhausted. With the introduction of containers, things have changed, and we don't need to deploy the entire VM to host a dedicated service.

A container is just a software package that contains the code, binaries, and libraries required for a specific task. For example, to run a web server, we could deploy a VM and install NGINX on it. The resource consumption for the VM would be high and encompass a lot of services that we do not need. We could instead use containers, so the image would only have code to run the NGINX server, and nothing else. This would mean a lightweight image and quick deployment.

In the case of VMs, we were using hypervisors to run them; in the case of containers, we use container runtime engines. A comparison of the two is shown in *Figure* 1.5. Some common examples include Docker (which is the most used), Runc, Rkt (which is no longer in development), and Mesos:

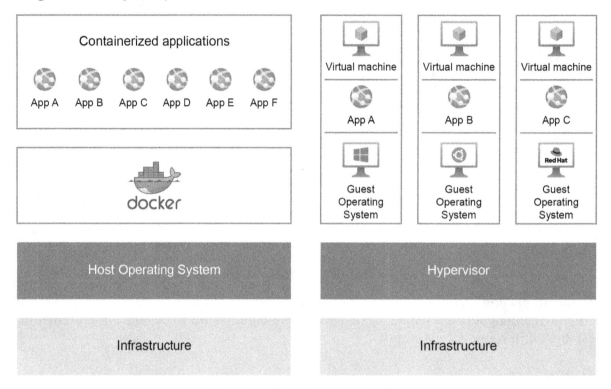

Figure 1.5: Containers versus VMs

Currently, we have container images available for each and every service, including NGINX, MySQL, and Apache. All major software packages have been ported.

Cloud computing

Linux can be used to host cloud operating system solutions such as OpenStack. We can install OpenStack on our Linux server to host a cloud environment (both private and public) to manage large pools of underlying resources including compute, storage, and network. Think of this as the Azure Stack, where you can run Azure in your own datacenter. In a similar way, you can host a cloud environment in your datacenter for your users to deploy services using OpenStack, which is running on Linux:

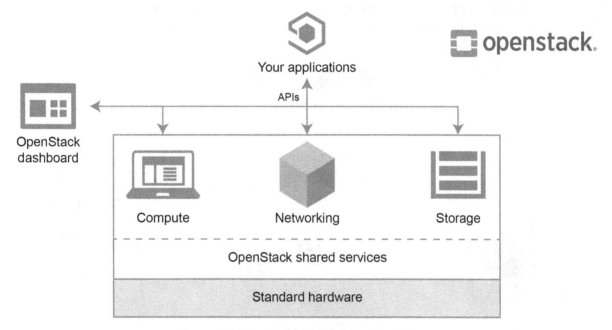

Figure 1.6: OpenStack running on top of Linux

OpenStack exposes a lot of APIs using which users can track, manage, and monitor their deployment. *Figure 1.6* displays the basic architecture of how OpenStack runs on top of Linux to serve as a platform for deployments.

Container orchestration

With the introduction of containers, many organizations are moving from a monolithic architecture to a microservice architecture. As the number of containers increases, it's not easy to manage them on a large scale. That is where container orchestration tools such as Kubernetes come into the picture. We can install the Kubernetes service on a Linux machine and add Linux and Windows worker nodes to it. The master will be running on a Linux server and this will act as a management plane for the cluster. *Figure* 1.7 shows a high-level representation of how Linux nodes are added to the Kubernetes master. In a similar fashion, we can also create a pool of Windows nodes and add it to the Kubernetes cluster:

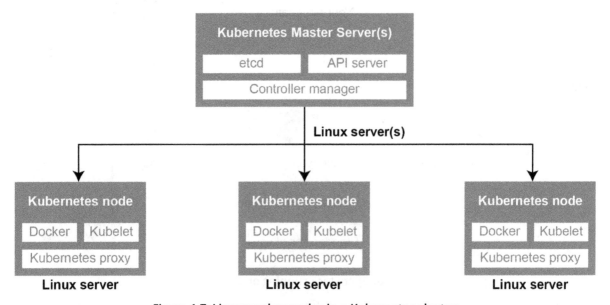

Figure 1.7: Linux worker nodes in a Kubernetes cluster

Another distribution of Kubernetes is OpenShift, developed by Red Hat. There are many Kubernetes distributions published by different vendors, all meant for container orchestration. In fact, there are dedicated Linux distributions that have been developed with Kubernetes in mind, such as k3OS from Rancher. Container orchestration is a booming and ever-growing sector, and we could even write a whole book on this topic alone.

Big data

We started with simple examples and have expanded our horizons all the way to complex scenarios, such as big data on Linux. You can install tools such as Apache Hadoop on Linux and then perform big data analysis. We don't really see this scenario in every organization due to varying availability and support for managed cloud services such as Azure Synapse Analytics or Azure HDInsight. Nevertheless, if you would like to implement big data analytics on Linux, it's possible. *Figure 1.8* shows the extensive list of tools that are used by data scientists and big data analysts, and all of these can be installed on Linux:

Figure 1.8: Tools used for big data analytics

As mentioned earlier, using Linux for big data analytics is a seldom seen scenario, however, some customers to prefer to install certain analytics tools like Splunk on Linux.

In this section, we've talked about some common scenarios, but this doesn't mean that the use cases are confined to these only. With the introduction of new technologies almost daily, the potential use cases will keep on expanding. We explored these particular ones to demonstrate that Linux can handle wide-ranging scenarios, from basic functionality such as workstations all the way to container orchestration and big data.

Even though on-premises infrastructure can also support all these scenarios, there are some disadvantages to this approach. This is the driving force behind the cloud journey of each and every organization. Let's see what these challenges are and how the cloud mitigates them.

Challenges in on-premises infrastructure

Hosting an infrastructure on-premises is quite challenging because of the requirement for qualified personnel and complex networking. The traditional approach has persisted for a long time. With the introduction of cloud computing, organizations started to recognize how the challenges they faced for decades could be resolved by cloud computing. Before we take a look at the benefits of cloud computing, let's understand the root cause of these on-premises challenges:

- **Scaling**: This is one of the primary challenges. It is really hard to implement a solution that can scale in and out based on varying traffic. You can add more servers (physical or virtual) whenever there is a need for more resources and terminate them when they are no longer needed. However, resource utilization in this scenario is not optimized. With the introduction of the cloud, scaling is very easy; you just have to specify the scaling conditions (CPU %, memory %, and so on), and the cloud provider will take care of the scaling itself. You never know where your business is going to be next year and Microsoft Azure can help you scale your infrastructure alongside your business.

- **Agility**: Agility is the ability to react quickly. In Microsoft Azure, you can allocate and deallocate resources quickly, responding to changes in your business needs. All services are provided as on-demand self-service, which means that if you need a new server, it can be deployed in seconds. In on-premises, if we need a new physical server, the process for getting one is very involved. You might need to ask your hardware provider to ship the hardware, license it, patch it, and then install all the required software to make it suitable for running your workload. So, we are looking at a timeline of around 2-3 weeks at a minimum, which is in contrast to the agility offered by Microsoft Azure. Even if you are deploying a new VM on-premises, you need to make sure that your host machine has enough resources for the new VM, or else you may have to buy a new server.

- **Skills**: The skills required to manage your own datacenter are very demanding and it's very hard to find professionals to take care of it. Along with infrastructure management, you have to think about the security aspect of the datacenter as well. For that, you might need to hire more security professionals to make your datacenter more secure. An increase in the headcount of employees is another cost to the organization.

- **Security**: In the previous point, we noted that hiring more professionals increases the cost to the organization. Even after successful hiring, with ever-changing and ever-evolving threats, it's hard to train employees on every possible set of security threats. Managing security and how to react to new threats is still a challenge in on-premises environments. Most organizations implement preventive measures only after they have been hit by a threat. After the incident, you will need to hire cyber forensic professionals to conduct an investigation, which again is an additional expense to the organization.

These are some of the main reasons why it can be challenging to work on-premises. With the introduction of the cloud, organizations can focus more on achieving business goals rather than wasting time on racking and stacking, software patching, and other time-consuming IT management chores.

In the next section, we'll cover cloud economics, where we'll take a deep dive into the advantages of the cloud and how both the aforementioned and other unmentioned challenges can be resolved.

Cloud economics

Owning a datacenter is not a core business of typical companies. While it might be tempting for the IT department to own physical servers that they can set up and physically interact with themselves, it probably is not something your **Chief Financial Officer (CFO)** wants to do. Owning servers not only shows up in the balance sheets as capital expenses, but the costs of the facilities, electricity, insurance, and so on also add up in terms of total operational costs. If you ask any IT manager how much it costs to buy, set up, operate, and dispose of the infrastructure needed to host one application for a year on their own datacenter, they most probably won't know or even dare to guess.

Outsourcing your infrastructure to a hosting provider sounds like a good idea after you realize how expensive it is to operate a datacenter yourself. A multi-customer datacenter is certainly more cost-effective compared to a single-customer datacenter. Adding scale makes it easier to save costs by sharing parts of the infrastructure between all or many customers. At the end of 2020, there were thousands or tens of thousands of professionally run, shared hosting datacenters around the world—how do we know which one to choose and which will be out of business next year?

The size and the complexity of business software have increased, together with the amount of data collected and processed by applications. This creates more and more demand for compute power and storage, which naturally increases the infrastructure costs. Constantly increasing the cost of the hosted environment is not something your CFO will tolerate over an extended period.

Scale comes with benefits

Many hosted datacenter providers are migrating their own infrastructure to public clouds partly for the same reasons as their customers: public cloud infrastructures have become so massive in terms of the number of regions, datacenters, and servers that the scale and features for optimizing cost are really difficult to compete with. With traditional datacenters and hosting providers, it is usually not possible to pay only for times when you actually need the capacity, for example, during office hours.

Public clouds can offer consumption-based pricing due to their massive scale. They can share regional and global resources with all of their customers. Additionally, they are able to make massive investments in their infrastructure and use custom-made components. In many cases, they can also optimize operating costs by choosing locations with favorable conditions, such as a cold climate, which helps in cooling a datacenter; what's more, the heat generated by the datacenter can be used to heat nearby homes.

Another benefit of public clouds worth mentioning is the security aspect. Let's take a look at Azure: it uses Microsoft's global network for all connectivity inside and outside of Azure. Microsoft operates various other cloud-based services, such as Microsoft 365 and Xbox, which receive lots of unwanted traffic from the internet. This has its benefits; for example, some badly behaved Xbox user trying to conduct a DDoS attack on another Xbox user will be noticed by Microsoft, and Microsoft can remediate the attack globally, making sure, for example, that Azure is not affected.

By using public clouds, you save time and money by not having to employ your own datacenter team, or by not having to pay a hosting provider to do so. It also gives you almost unlimited scalability up and down, without having to commit to long-term contracts.

Migrating to public clouds does not mean you need to do it all at once. You may choose a hybrid approach where you leave some applications and data behind and just create a connection between the environments.

Many services available

To better understand the migration strategies, it is useful to understand the various cloud services available.

Cloud services such as Outlook and Gmail, or OneDrive and Google Drive, are good examples of **Software as a Service (SaaS)**. Most cloud services targeted at consumers, such as Facebook, Instagram, and WhatsApp, also fall into this category.

From the user's point of view, these solutions are just "there" and can be used without much initial effort. The same applies to typical business solutions such as Salesforce CRM or Microsoft 365. You cannot install these yourself even if you wanted; they always come as a turnkey service and you do not have any visibility into the underlying infrastructure.

Platform as a Service (PaaS) solutions differ from SaaS in a couple of ways; they need some kind of installation work and an infrastructure where they can be installed. While the installation is automatic, you may need to manage some parts of the infrastructure yourself. Examples of such services include **Azure Kubernetes Service (AKS)** and **Azure Red Hat OpenShift (ARO)**.

In the context of migrating Linux servers to Azure, we are focusing on **Infrastructure as a Service (IaaS)**, which means that you only get the lower-level infrastructure components as a service. Everything else is your own responsibility, including configuring the storage and network and operating the operating system yourself. This type of cloud service is similar to typical VM-hosting services offered by hosting companies.

Benefits of migrating to Azure

Typical Linux deployments in on-premises environments are based on VMs, and migrating them to Azure falls into the realm of IaaS, so they will still be VMs after the migration. For sysadmins, this means the same skills they already have and the same familiar management tools are still useful on Azure.

In the early days of Azure, some services were not designed for Linux use, and users sometimes got frustrated by the complexity of using Linux on Azure. Being originally named Microsoft Azure gives a hint as to what use cases it was designed for. Since then, Azure has evolved and it has been developed to be more and more Linux-friendly.

> **Note**
>
> Linux has rapidly gained popularity in Azure. In 2015, Mark Russinovich, the CTO of Azure, said that one in four VM instances in Azure runs Linux. In 2018, Microsoft Cloud EVP Scott Guthrie revealed in an interview by ZDnet that about half of Azure VMs run Linux.
>
> (https://www.zdnet.com/article/mark-russinovich-the-microsoft-azure-cloud-and-open-source/ and https://www.zdnet.com/article/linux-now-dominates-azure/)

At the time of writing in 2021, Microsoft has already become well known for its love of Linux and open source. Microsoft is supporting many open-source projects, initiatives, and foundations, such as the Linux Foundation. According to their website (https:// opensource.microsoft.com/program/), Microsoft already uses over 150,000 open-source components while building their products and services.

Today, more and more customers are migrating their existing workloads to Azure. As mentioned earlier, many of these workloads are Linux-based. To facilitate these migrations, Microsoft has developed many tools and services with Linux users in mind. We will cover these in more detail later in this book.

Microsoft has partnered with all the major Linux vendors to help their customers move workloads to Azure. These partnerships have the aim of developing new features and ensuring that existing features are better integrated, not to forget providing monetary benefits in the shape of the ability to continue to use existing commercial on-premises contracts in Azure.

Enterprise Linux companies such as Red Hat and SUSE are very popular in the world of on-premises IT infrastructure, and they have both worked with Microsoft to create unified global support services to ensure that their customers can migrate to Azure without hassle.

Community Linux distributions such as CentOS and Ubuntu are very popular in Azure, and there are many companies offering commercial Linux support, including Canonical, with its Ubuntu Pro offering.

The journey from Linux to Azure

In this section, we'll cover some aspects of typical Linux environments that we should know about when we are considering migration to Azure. We'll go through some key features and discuss the solutions available on Azure. We will also provide links to related Azure documentation throughout this section to make your learning curve a bit shallower—the documentation covers Linux on Azure extremely well.

Before going into the technical details, it's good to know that you don't necessarily need to implement everything yourself. Azure Marketplace has lots of Linux-based solutions that may solve your problem in a turnkey fashion.

Azure Marketplace has over 2,000 Linux VM-based images at the time of writing compared to about 800 Windows-based images. Linux is clearly dominating the marketplace. Out of those images, only 14 are from Microsoft; the rest are created and published by third-party ISV companies. For example, if you want to install WordPress on a Linux VM, you need to install Apache, PHP, and MySQL as the database. On the other hand, if you're using a Marketplace image, you'll be able to find customized WordPress images. These images can easily be deployed right from the Marketplace to your Azure subscription without the need to manually install the Apache, PHP, and MySQL services.

You can find Azure Marketplace here: https://azuremarketplace.microsoft.com/marketplace/. The Marketplace images are also available via Azure command-line interfaces. The number of images is increasing as we speak, and it is also possible to publish your own images to Azure Marketplace and make them available to large numbers of customers.

We will begin our discussion by talking about clustering, which is a scenario where there are a lot of gray areas.

Clustering

In plain English, the word "cluster" means group, flock, or assemble. When we say clustering in the IT world, we are expressing the idea of a group of computers (in this context, Linux computers), multiple storage components, and redundant network connections acting together to form a highly available system. Clustering avoids a single point of failure and also provides load balancing along with high availability. Clustering may look complex at first glance as we have to manage multiple computing resources, but this section is all about demystifying the complexity of clustering.

Typical Linux clustering scenarios can be categorized into four types:

- Storage
- High availability
- Load balancing
- High performance

Each of these is implemented with different software and requires its own architecture and configuration. In the next few sections, we will see how Azure addresses each of these four scenarios.

Azure shared disks for storage

Storage clusters in on-premises systems are usually considered to be consistent clustered file systems between multiple nodes. The technology used for file system clusters is very often GlusterFS, GFS2, or OCFS2 when using a software solution. For block-level storage sharing, it's very common to use DRBD. Using these solutions on Azure is not straightforward—setting them up properly even on an on-premises system requires a highly skilled sysadmin.

For shared block storage, you can use Azure shared disks. This is quite a recent feature that allows you to attach a managed disk to multiple VMs at the same time. This solves many issues associated with storage clustering. **SCSI Persistent Reservations (SCSI PR)** is an industry standard that was used by applications in on-premises environments running on a **Storage Area Network (SAN)**. The same SCSI PR facilitates reservations that will be used by the VMs to read or write data to their attached disk. Shared managed disks need to use cluster manager tools such as Pacemaker, which will handle cluster node communication and write locking. Pacemaker is required in clustering as shared managed disks don't offer fully managed file systems that can be accessed via SMB/NFS.

One disadvantage here is that not all tiers of disk types can be used as shared disks. Currently, Ultra SSD and Premium SSD are supported. If you are using Standard HDD or Standard SSD for your VM, in order to fulfill the clustering prerequisites or to overcome the current limitation, you may have to upgrade the disk type to Ultra or Premium SSD.

The documentation on shared disks is available here: https://docs.microsoft.com/azure/virtual-machines/disks-shared. We should note that Azure shared disks are not supported for all Linux distributions.

Azure Files and Azure NetApp Files

A solution for shared file systems is a service called **Azure Files**. It is an easy-to-use cloud file system that allows the mounting of Azure file shares by using the **Server Message Block (SMB)** or **Network File System (NFS)** protocol. NFS is very popular for Linux servers and SMB is typically used with Windows servers. In the *Typical Linux use cases in IT infrastructure* section, we discussed how file servers play a vital role in IT infrastructure; Azure Files is an enterprise-grade cloud version of that. These file shares can be mounted on Linux, Windows, and macOS systems. Azure Files provides a common shared space that can be shared with your on-premises workstations as well as VMs. Being a part of Azure Storage, Azure Files has all the features that Azure Storage supports. When it comes to the NFS share, it has fewer features compared to the SMB share.

Azure Files can be used as a complete replacement for the file server role that we had on our on-premises servers. Since we have the capability to attach to our on-premises server, we can also use Azure Files to move data from on-premises servers to cloud servers with the same file share mounted on both ends. The related documentation is available here: https://docs.microsoft.com/azure/storage/files/storage-files-introduction.

An additional solution for a shared NFS filesystem is called **Azure NetApp Files (ANF)**. This is an enterprise-class high-performance file system service. NetApp is a very popular storage solution typically used in on-premises systems, and it is also now available on Azure. You can read more about the solution here: https://docs.microsoft.com/azure/azure-netapp-files.

ANF supports various performance tiers for storage, depending on your application's IOPS requirement. As this is deeply integrated with the Azure platform, it can be used as a shared file solution for your clustered solutions. Additionally, ANF carries leading industry certifications, which makes it ideal for SAP HANA LOB applications, HPFS, VDI, and HPC. Note that the minimum storage capacity size for ANF is currently 4 TB.

Availability set for high availability

Azure offers very simple availability set functionality that can be used to create simple and easy-to-use HA environments. Availability sets are composed of **Fault Domains (FDs)** and **Update Domains (UDs)**.

FDs are groups of hardware in an Azure datacenter that share common power, cooling, and network connectivity. When we deploy VMs to an availability set, Azure makes sure that they are distributed across three FDs, so that even if the power to **FD 1** goes down, a VM in **FD 2** or **FD 3** can serve customers.

Similarly, we have UDs where the VMs are grouped in a way where the underlying hardware can be rebooted at the same time. When a planned maintenance event happens in an Azure datacenter, only one UD gets rebooted at a time. By default, if you deploy to an availability set, the VMs will be distributed across five FDs. However, if you so wish, you can increase this to up to 20 UDs. *Figure* 1.9 shows how UDs and FDs are mapped in a datacenter:

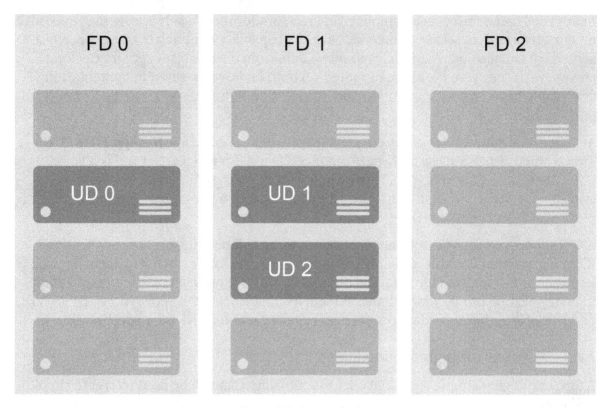

Figure 1.9: FDs and UDs

Availability sets enable you to deploy VMs on Azure in a distributed manner across isolated hardware clusters. A useful tutorial for this feature is available here: https://docs.microsoft.com/azure/virtual-machines/linux/tutorial-availability-sets.

The proximity placement groups feature enables you to keep selected VMs near to one another in terms of distance within an availability set. This reduces network latency, which could impact your applications. See more information about this feature here: https://docs.microsoft.com/azure/virtual-machines/co-location#proximity-placement-groups.

Pacemaker, the software used for clustering on typical on-premises setups, is not often required on Azure. Some legacy solutions ported to Azure, however, are based on Pacemaker and DRBD, for example, the certified SAP on Azure architecture.

Azure layer-4 load balancing

Azure comes with a very useful layer-4 load balancing functionality that can often be used to replace typical on-premises solutions. Load balancing is required to distribute requests and loads between multiple VMs. This tutorial will guide you through the creation and operation of Linux load balancing on Azure: https://docs.microsoft.com/azure/virtual-machines/linux/tutorial-load-balancer.

Many on-premises load balancing solutions are not suitable for moving to the cloud as-is, so it may be beneficial to investigate whether Azure load balancing solves the same need. In particular, if your application architecture is going to be modified during migration, then the current load balancing architecture might not have the features you need or might be unnecessarily expensive when used on Azure.

High-performance computing on Azure

The last clustering type, high-performance computing, or HPC, is a scenario very well suited to Azure. Typical on-premises HPC solutions are extremely expensive, especially when you are not using them, due to the fact that you are paying for the hardware around the clock.

Azure provides both a traditional CPU-based HPC solution and also a very powerful GPU-based highly scalable model. You can use various storage options to share data between the nodes running your workloads. You may also want to reap the benefits of the RDMA-based high-throughput back-end network. Related documentation is available here: https://docs.microsoft.com/azure/architecture/topics/high-performance-computing.

Additionally, there are various third-party HPC solutions available on the Azure Marketplace.

Subscription portability

Very often, the biggest challenge with Azure migrations for Linux is surprisingly not technical. Let's stop here for a moment and think about your Linux licensing and subscriptions, especially if you are using a commercial Linux distribution such as Red Hat Enterprise Linux or SUSE Linux Enterprise Server.

Do you know whether you have simply lifted and shifted your existing VM to the public cloud? Do you need to discuss with your IT procurement or a lawyer the contract terms of Red Hat or SUSE? The correct answer to any question you may have in your mind right now is: *Yes, but check with your IT procurement first.*

Both Red Hat and SUSE allow customers to move their existing enterprise subscriptions to the public cloud, but there are a couple of steps you'll need to take in order to be compliant and to continue to receive support directly from them. In Azure, the Linux VMs created using these migrated subscriptions are **Bring Your Own Subscription (BYOS)**. Red Hat calls the related program **Red Hat Cloud Access**, and SUSE's program is called **SUSE Public Cloud Program**.

Please note that migrating your existing Linux subscriptions to Azure means that you will continue to have a billing relationship with Red Hat or SUSE for VMs utilizing these subscriptions. You can create new Linux VMs on Azure using Microsoft's **Pay as You Go (PAYG)** billing.

Finally, it's useful to learn about Azure Hybrid Benefit, which allows you to change between BYOS and PAYG. This feature is under active development and, at the time of writing, supports only VMs migrated from on-premises to Azure. See more details in the documentation here: https://docs.microsoft.com/azure/virtual-machines/linux/azure-hybrid-benefit-linux.

If you are using community distributions such as CentOS and Ubuntu, none of the preceding should matter to you as those distributions are completely free to use, but at least you learned something new today.

Summary

This chapter started with the history of Linux. The leap that Linux took from being a fun project to being an enterprise-grade operating system was astonishing. Today, Linux is everywhere, from high-end servers to smartphones to smart bulbs. Due to the freedom of customization, there are a lot of variants of Linux, referred to as flavors or distros; there is a distro available for each and every use case. If none of the distros matches your exact requirements and you want to add more features, feel free to customize and build your own Linux. We explored some use case scenarios for Linux and looked at some of the challenges that traditional IT is facing with infrastructure management in on-premises environments.

Every organization runs by numbers. In the Cloud economics section, we examined how running workloads in the cloud can draw profit if we make a CapEx versus OpEx comparison. The upper hand of the cloud not only comes from cost reduction; it's a solution for all the challenges we encountered in on-premises environments. We discussed several advantages, including fault tolerance, high availability, agility, elasticity, and scaling.

It is safe to say that everything you used to do in on-premises environments can be migrated into Azure in one way or another. There's plenty of good-quality documentation available, and third-party ISV solutions can shorten your implementation cycle. There is additional help available from Microsoft partner companies, Microsoft's customer account teams, and also from the Microsoft Fast Track team, which is dedicated to helping customers move to Azure.

The next chapter is where we take a deep dive into these distros, starting with the licensing part, discussing some widely adopted distros and, ultimately, the Linux on Azure experience.

Understanding Linux distributions

Good things come in many flavors, and so do Linux distributions.

To create a successful cloud migration plan, you need a good understanding of the components and variables of the system that you want to migrate to the cloud.

In this chapter, you will learn about the relevant terminology and technical details of various Linux distributions to help you plan successful migrations to Azure. Even though all the distributions are based on the same operating system, each of them has its own small technical details that require detailed knowledge to successfully prepare for a migration. Along with the introduction to the distributions, we will have a look at the licensing options, as well as the differences between free and commercial open-source software. Commercial Linux distributions have various add-on features and support options. We will also cover some typical use cases for different distributions.

The final section of this chapter is *Linux on Azure*, and it starts with a discussion of the Microsoft-endorsed distributions and the scope of support provided by Microsoft. The support is shared between Microsoft and the Linux vendor. We will also cover the licensing models in Azure for Linux virtual machines and what the potential savings for the customer are with each model. We will conclude this chapter with a demonstration using the Azure CLI to find details on VM images; this is useful if you want to see a list of available images on Azure.

This chapter will cover the following topics:

- Linux licensing and open-source business models
- Popular Linux distributions
- Linux on Azure: benefits, licensing models, support

By the end of this chapter, you will have learned the necessary tips and tricks for moving Linux subscriptions to the cloud. Let's start our discussion by exploring Linux licenses.

Linux licensing and open-source business models

This section focuses on commercial Linux distributions. If you are using only free community editions of Linux, such as CentOS or Debian, some of the content may not be applicable to you.

Open-source licenses

How do you make money from something that is free? To answer that, we must look back and see what it means when we say something is open source.

Linux distributions and the Linux kernel are open source, but at the same time, they are covered by copyright laws. To make things very complicated, there are numerous open-source licenses covering different parts of a Linux distribution. Some components may be covered by a **GNU General Public License** (**GPL**), some by an **Apache License** (**APL**), and some by an MIT license. To make this even more complex, it is important to realize that there may be multiple versions of the same license and that they may not all be compatible with each other or with any other license whatsoever.

At this point, it is enough to understand that all Linux distributions are covered by an open-source license. This means you have the right to download the source code of all the software included in a Linux distribution. What you can do with the source code is out of the scope of this book, since we are not creating our own Linux distributions. In this book, we do not have to go into the details of various open-source licenses and copyright laws.

Enterprise agreements

When talking about commercial open source, and specifically commercial Linux distributions, the term **enterprise agreement** is something you will need to familiarize yourself with before thinking about moving your Linux servers to Azure. We might often skip reading the terms and conditions of such agreements before accepting them with a simple click of a mouse, but it's important to read them.

An enterprise agreement for commercial Linux vendors typically states that you agree to pay to use their software according to their latest price lists and to follow the rules of where and how you can use the software. It also says many other things, but since this is not a software procurement book, we will not go into those details. However, it might make sense for you to have a conversation with your software purchasing team to check if they know the contract details.

Linux subscriptions

What proprietary software vendors call "licenses" can be loosely referred to as "subscriptions" in the Linux world. Technically these are, of course, two different things, but in a typical sales conversation, you may hear someone talk about Linux licenses–and as we learned earlier, those are not the licenses you are looking for.

Subscription practically means the right to download, use, and update a commercial Linux distribution. It very often also comes with a technical support service with varying service level agreements. In order to subscribe to such a service, you will need to sign a contract with a commercial Linux vendor on behalf of your employer. This contract is usually referred to as an enterprise agreement, and it typically comes with some additional obligations. One of these obligations is to follow the rules of the service subscription agreement.

For example, the subscription rules for Red Hat Enterprise Linux state that you may only use the software on your own infrastructure. Practically, this also includes hosted environments, which are considered rented infrastructure. Public clouds are not considered as your own infrastructure and you will need to inform Red Hat if you want to move your Linux servers to the public cloud.

SUSE has very similar subscription rules. As mentioned, it is a very good idea to check the contracts with your software purchasing department to ensure that you are following the rules.

With Ubuntu, the concept of subscriptions is a bit different; you do not need a subscription to use it at all. In this case, the subscription refers to a professional support service contract from Canonical, the company behind Ubuntu. In addition to the free Ubuntu Linux, Canonical also offers Ubuntu Pro, their commercial Ubuntu image on Azure.

Figure 2.1 illustrates the differences between licenses, subscriptions, and support contracts of commercial and community Linux distributions:

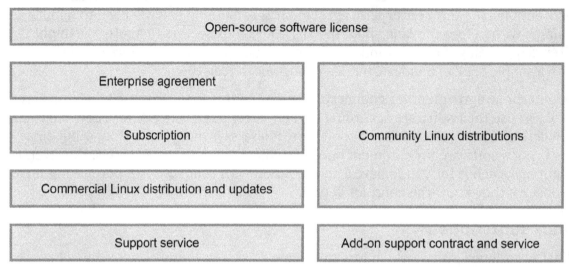

Figure 2.1: The differences between licenses, subscriptions, and contracts

Enough of licenses and subscriptions. Let's take a look at the actual Linux distributions.

Popular Linux distributions

Various Linux server distributions have gained quite a stable market share over the years. Corporate users usually standardize on one or two distributions depending on the business applications they use. Red Hat and SUSE are the two most famous enterprise Linux development companies and vendors and they both have similar offerings around the Linux operating system area. Nowadays, the third commercial Linux vendor, Canonical, is playing in the same category. Their Ubuntu Linux used to be best known as a developer workstation distribution, and it has quickly gained popularity as a production server operating system as well. Coupled with Canonical's commercial support offering, Ubuntu Linux is a great alternative to the two leading enterprise Linux distributions.

Red Hat was founded in 1993 when Bob Young and Marc Ewing joined forces and created *Red Hat Software*. In 1999, Red Hat went public on the **New York Stock Exchange (NYSE)**. Before its acquisition by IBM in 2019, Red Hat had acquired dozens of small open-source companies, such as Cygnus (cross-platform tools), JBoss (Java middleware), Qumranet (the creators of KVM virtualization technology), Makara (a PaaS platform, the first version of OpenShift), ManageIQ (a hybrid cloud orchestrator, the first version of CloudForms), InkTank (the creators of Ceph storage technology), Ansible (a popular automation toolkit), and CoreOS (a small Linux distro for containers).

The complete acquisition list consists of more than 30 companies that most of you have probably not heard of, since the brands have been merged with Red Hat's other product lines. **Red Hat Enterprise Linux (RHEL)** is a very popular platform nowadays, especially for Java middleware JBoss products, as is the commercial Kubernetes packaging, OpenShift, since both are published by Red Hat as well.

SUSE was founded a year before Red Hat, in 1992, and became the first company to market Linux to enterprise customers. Rolard Dyroff, Burchard Steinbild, Hubert Mantel, and Thomas Fehr first named the company *Gesellschaft für Software und Systementwicklung mbH* and used the acronym SuSE, which came from the German phrase *Software- und System-Entwicklung*, meaning *software and systems development*. The first version of their product was an extension of the then-popular Slackware Linux distribution. In 1996, they released their first Linux distribution, based on the already-forgotten Linux distribution Jurix, and deviated from Slackware.

Over the years, SUSE has been acquired and changed names several times, most notably by Novell in 2003 and EQT Partners in 2018. SUSE itself acquired **Hewlett Packard Enterprise's (HPE's)** OpenStack and CloudFoundry assets in 2017, as well as Rancher Labs—a company known for its Kubernetes management platform—in 2020. Today, **SUSE Linux Enterprise Server (SLES)** is a very common platform for SAP system deployments.

For non-commercial use, it seems like Ubuntu is the clear winner if you look at the number of deployments. Ubuntu is based on Debian, once a very popular Linux distribution for server workloads.

CentOS, being fully compatible with RHEL, is also popular since it's typically used by RHEL professionals on their hobbyist projects and other work that doesn't have an enterprise-level budget available.

Over the years, there have been many popular Linux distributions for desktop use, but they have not gained popularity on server use cases. We will not be covering those in the scope of this book since Linux on Azure usually refers to using server operating systems.

In the next section, we will go into the details of using free and commercial Linux distributions on Azure, with a particular focus on RHEL, SLES, and Ubuntu Pro. However, most of the content is applicable to their free versions CentOS, openSUSE, and Ubuntu as well.

Linux on Azure

In *Chapter 1, Linux: History and future in the cloud,* we mentioned that Microsoft came up with the motto "Microsoft ♡ Linux." On Azure, Linux mainly refers to the different Linux distributions that are supported on Azure. Microsoft Azure supports common Linux server distros including RHEL, CentOS, Ubuntu, Debian, SLES, openSUSE, Oracle Linux, and Flatcar Container Linux. You can find the up-to-date list and much more about Linux on Azure at this landing page: https://azure.com/linux.

If the operating system that you are looking for is not on the list or you need to have a customized or pre-configured image, feel free to visit Azure Marketplace where you can browse through hundreds of images that may suit your requirements.

If the Azure Marketplace images do not meet your organization's standards or requirements, you can create and upload your own images to Azure:

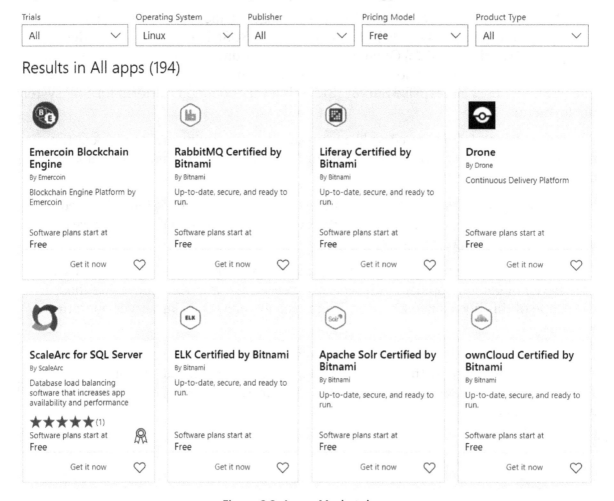

Figure 2.2: Azure Marketplace

Figure 2.2 is a view of Azure Marketplace, showing some of the different types of pre-configured images that are available.

Benefits of Linux on Azure

Deploying in the cloud is no different from what you are used to on-premises; you will be able to work with the Linux OS in the cloud in the same way as with an on-premises server. You can use the commands and tools that you are already acquainted with and add more packages as required.

You can use out-of-the-box features such as cloud-init, Azure Automation Runbooks, and Azure Custom Script Extension for Azure Resource Manager templates to automate configuration management during the deployment phase itself. By using these tools, administrators will be able to save time that would have been spent on lengthy and repetitive configuration management tasks.

As the environment is already set up and ready to log into, you do not have to go through the lengthy installation process that you used to do in the case of on-premises hypervisors while creating VMs. The credentials will be supplied during the Azure VM creation and, once the VM is deployed, you can log in and start using the VM.

Since all deployments are integrated with Azure Monitor, you can monitor all the metrics associated with the VM, such as CPU usage, disk write, disk read, network out, network in, and so on. Azure exposes the Metrics API, so you can further utilize the developed dashboards to monitor the metrics of your mission-critical workloads. Along with the metrics, Azure provides an agent that can be installed on your Linux VMs known as the **OMS agent**. Using this agent, you can ingest syslogs, auth logs, and custom logs such as Apache logs to an Azure Log Analytics workspace. Once the data is ingested, you can use the **Kusto Query Language (KQL)** to analyze the logs.

From a security standpoint, you can improve the security posture of your infrastructure using Azure Security Center. Azure Security Center can detect threats and provide policy insights and recommendations for your deployments.

Additionally, we can now make use of Azure Active Directory Login for Linux VMs. This eradicates the management overhead and security risk of managing local user accounts on each Linux machine; users can sign in to Linux VMs with their corporate credentials.

From this non-exhaustive list of advantages, we see that Linux on Azure offers the best of both worlds; you get all the customization features of Linux and at the same time all the features and benefits provided by Microsoft Azure.

Linux on Azure is very generic; the "on Azure" suffix can apply separately to each distro. For example, you should take "Red Hat on Azure" to mean all the Red Hat products that are supported on Azure. You might think RHEL is the only offering from Red Hat that is available on Azure, but you can also find other products such as Azure Red Hat OpenShift, Red Hat JBoss Enterprise Application Platform, Red Hat Gluster Storage, Red Hat OpenShift Container Platform, Red Hat CloudForms, and Red Hat Ansible Automation. You can see that all the major product lines of Red Hat are available on Azure; this is a clear example of how large organizations promote their products to Microsoft Azure. You will see similar approaches from other vendors, as in "SUSE on Azure" and "Ubuntu on Azure," which stand for the products supported by the respective vendors in Azure.

> **Note**
>
> Check out the product lines available on Azure for the following vendors:
>
> - **Red Hat product lines** available on Azure: https://Azure.com/RedHat
> - **SUSE product lines** available on Azure: https://Azure.com/SUSE
> - **Ubuntu** on Azure: https://Azure.com/Ubuntu

Microsoft recommends using endorsed Linux distributions in Azure to host your production workloads. The rationale for this is that all endorsed images are maintained by the most well-known Linux vendors in the world, such as Red Hat, Canonical, SUSE, and so on; basically, endorsed images are images published by these vendors. The complete Linux support matrix can be reviewed at https://docs.microsoft.com/troubleshoot/azure/cloud-services/support-linux-open-source-technology#linux-support-matrix.

You can also bring your own images to Azure if you do not want to use an endorsed image. You may even customize Azure images using the Azure Image Builder tool, which is based on Hashicorp Packer: https://docs.microsoft.com/azure/virtual-machines/image-builder-overview.

One key point to note here is that Microsoft provides support to endorsed distributions only. Having said that, let's take a look at how the technical support for Linux on Azure is arranged.

Linux support scope

Microsoft provides support for the endorsed Linux distributions on Azure, and if there is a need to engage the vendor, they will be engaged on your behalf depending on the scenario. For example, if there is an issue with the image of Ubuntu 18.04 LTS and Microsoft cannot fix it, they will engage Canonical (the publisher of Ubuntu) to check the scenario. Here are some of the key points that you should keep in mind when engaging Microsoft Support.

Microsoft's technical support team can help you mainly in Linux troubleshooting scenarios—for instance, if you are unable to connect to a Linux VM with SSH, or unable to install a package. The Linux vendor may have to be engaged for issues related to the Linux image itself. For this Microsoft has joint support and engineering agreements with Linux vendors such as Red Hat, SUSE, and Canonical.

Always get your Linux administrator involved while working with Microsoft Support. In most troubleshooting scenarios, you might need superuser (often referred to as **sudo**) permissions, which only the admins will have.

Linux offers more room for customization than any other operating system available. Some organizations use custom Linux kernels or modules that cannot be supported by Microsoft Support. Although kernel-related issues are resolved by collaborating with the Linux vendor, in this scenario, even the vendor may not be able to help as they can typically only support the official kernel versions published by themselves.

Azure Advisor and Azure Security Center provide different security-, cost-, high availability-, and performance-related recommendations for our workloads. Following these recommendations is one of the best practices to run your workloads effectively on Azure. However, for performance tuning and optimization, customers may need to contact the vendor for resolution.

As mentioned earlier, Microsoft Support helps you to troubleshoot issues. This applies to the free Azure support, which is officially called "Basic" and is included for all Azure customers. If you need help to design, create architecture, or deploy applications on Azure, you have the option to purchase additional support, which ranges from development support to business-critical enterprise support plans. The paid plans include various levels of design and architecture support, and you can read more about them here: https://azure.microsoft.com/support/plans/.

Another option to get help with Azure design, architecture, and other technical questions is to engage with Microsoft's sales and partner teams, namely the **Customer Success Unit (CSU)** and **One Commercial Partner (OCP)**. These teams are able to assist named commercial customers and partners. It is good to remember that these organizations are not replacements for Microsoft Support but are part of Microsoft's Global Sales and Marketing organization. To get in touch with the technical staff of the CSU and OCP teams, you should contact your named Microsoft account manager.

A third and very popular option is to talk with the large network of Microsoft partners. They are able to provide a broad range of advisory, consulting, implementation, and operational assistance for Azure in general as well as Linux on Azure. Many of these partners are also partnered with some of the Linux vendors mentioned in this chapter. The easiest way to locate Microsoft partners is to use the Microsoft solution provider search tool: https://www.microsoft.com/solution-providers/home.

> **Note**
>
> Along with the endorsed Linux distribution support, Microsoft also provides production support for certain OSS technologies such as PHP, Java, Python, Node.js, MySQL, Apache, Tomcat, and WordPress. This list is subject to change and the technical support available may be very limited.

Now that we are familiar with the scope of Azure Technical Support, let's look at how pricing works on Azure.

Licensing on Azure

In Azure, there are three licensing models: **pay-as-you-go** (**PAYG**), Azure Hybrid Benefit, and prepay. We will look at how these models vary and what the benefits are, starting with the PAYG model.

The pay-as-you-go model

As the name implies, in the PAYG model, customers are charged for the license as they use resources. For example, if you run a VM for 12 hours, you will see charges for:

- 12 hours of compute (which includes vCPU, RAM, and so on).

- 12 hours of Linux "license" or "subscription" use (if you are using distros such as RHEL or SLES that require a paid subscription).

- The cost of a public IP address (if needed).

- The cost of egress network traffic.

- The cost of storage.

Usually, in the Azure Pricing Calculator (https://azure.microsoft.com/pricing/calculator/), when you select a Linux VM that is running RHEL or SLES, you will be able to see the license cost. If you are using Ubuntu/CentOS, there will be no license cost. In *Figure* 2.3, you can see that for an RHEL VM there are compute and license costs under PAYG. The calculation is for 730 hours of consumption:

Figure 2.3: Licensing cost for RHEL from the Azure Pricing Calculator

On the other hand, if we pick Ubuntu/CentOS, the license cost will not be there, as shown in *Figure 2.4*:

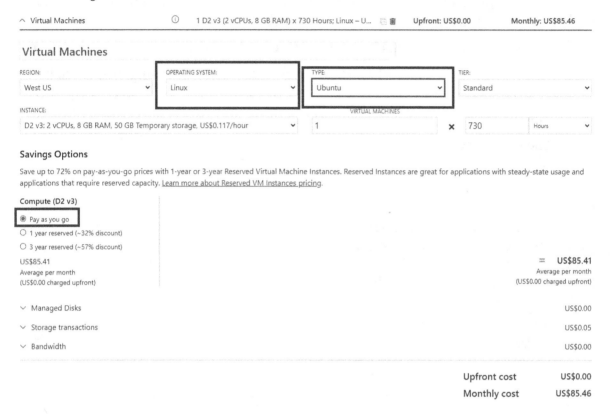

Figure 2.4: Licensing cost does not apply to Ubuntu

To summarize, in PAYG, customers pay based on how long a VM runs. When the VM is deallocated, the compute cores are not utilized, which means no charges are incurred for compute cores or the license. This model is ideal for VMs that are deployed for testing and will be running for a short period of time, but if you have VMs running 24/7/365, this might not be the ideal model, as the license cost will keep on accumulating based on hours used. In these cases, it is better to go with the Azure Hybrid Benefit or prepay plans for potential savings.

Azure Hybrid Benefit

If you revisit the screenshot of the pricing calculator in *Figure* 2.3, you can see another option under **Software (Red Hat Enterprise Linux)**, one that reads **Azure Hybrid Benefit**. Previously, Azure Hybrid Benefit was referred to as a licensing benefit available for Windows Server and SQL VMs by which customers can bring their own Windows Server and SQL licenses to Azure. Using this method, the licensing cost is nullified, and customers can utilize the licenses that they had already purchased from their software assurance or volume licensing. In November 2020, Azure Hybrid Benefit was made generally available for Linux.

Using Azure Hybrid Benefit, you can migrate your existing RHEL and SLES servers to Azure with **bring-your-own-subscription (BYOS)** billing. Normally, in the case of the PAYG model, you pay for both infrastructure (compute + storage + network) costs and software (license) costs. Since you are bringing your own subscription here, though, the software cost is nullified, and you pay only for the infrastructure, which drastically reduces the cost of hosting in Azure. You can convert your existing VMs under the PAYG model to BYOS billing without any downtime, which also means that the redeployment of these services is not required at all. When your BYOS expires, you can convert these VMs back to the PAYG model as required.

All RHEL and SLES PAYG images on Azure Marketplace are eligible for Azure Hybrid Benefit. However, if you are choosing a custom image or any RHEL/SLES BYOS images from Azure Marketplace, those are not eligible for the benefit.

Red Hat customers can follow the instructions below to get started with Azure Hybrid Benefit. Before we start, there are some prerequisites:

- You should have active or unused RHEL subscriptions that are eligible for Azure usage.

- You should have enabled one or more active or unused subscriptions for Azure usage with the Red Hat Cloud Access program. Red Hat Cloud Access is a program offered by Red Hat. Using this, you can run eligible Red Hat product subscriptions on Red Hat certified cloud providers such as Microsoft Azure, Amazon Web Services, and Google Cloud.

If you meet the prerequisites, the next step is to start using Azure Hybrid Benefit. Here are the steps you need to follow:

1. Choose one of the active or unused RHEL subscriptions and enable it for use in Azure. This is done from the Red Hat Cloud Access customer interface. Red Hat customers will be able to access this by logging in to https://www.redhat.com/technologies/cloud-computing/cloud-access. Only the subscriptions we enroll here are eligible to use Azure Hybrid Benefit.

2. Linking the subscription was the primary step; we can specify that the VMs use the RHEL subscription during the creation stage, or we can convert existing VMs.

3. During the creation of the VM, you can opt to use the existing RHEL subscription as shown in *Figure* 2.5:

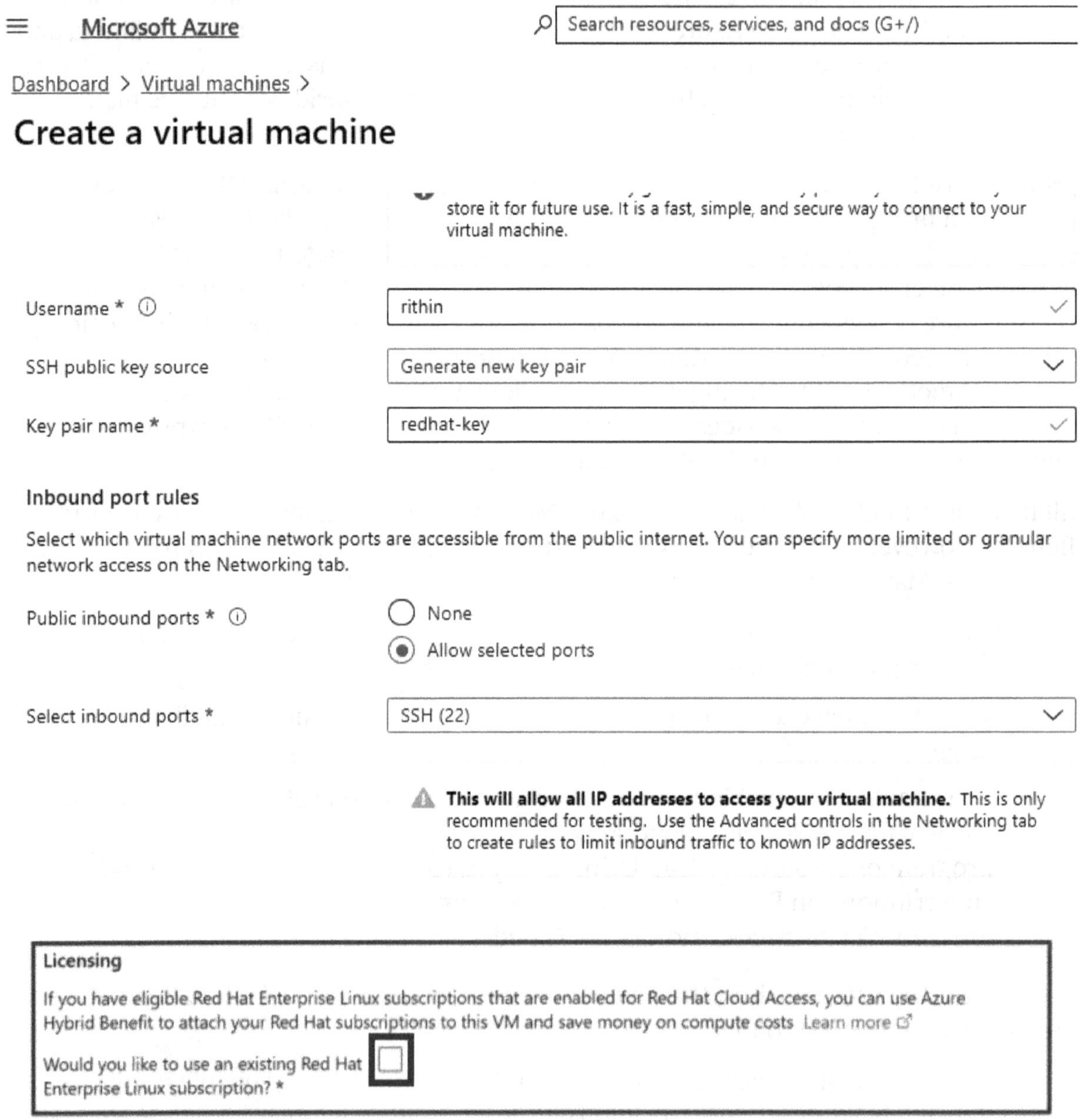

≡ **Microsoft Azure** | Search resources, services, and docs (G+/) |

Dashboard > Virtual machines >

Create a virtual machine

store it for future use. It is a fast, simple, and secure way to connect to your virtual machine.

Username * ⓘ	rithin	✓
SSH public key source	Generate new key pair	˅
Key pair name *	redhat-key	✓

Inbound port rules

Select which virtual machine network ports are accessible from the public internet. You can specify more limited or granular network access on the Networking tab.

Public inbound ports * ⓘ   ◯ None
                            ⦿ Allow selected ports

| Select inbound ports * | SSH (22) | ˅ |

⚠ **This will allow all IP addresses to access your virtual machine.** This is only recommended for testing. Use the Advanced controls in the Networking tab to create rules to limit inbound traffic to known IP addresses.

Licensing

If you have eligible Red Hat Enterprise Linux subscriptions that are enabled for Red Hat Cloud Access, you can use Azure Hybrid Benefit to attach your Red Hat subscriptions to this VM and save money on compute costs Learn more ☐

Would you like to use an existing Red Hat ☐
Enterprise Linux subscription? *

Figure 2.5: Enabling Azure Hybrid Benefit during VM creation

4. We can also convert existing VMs to Azure Hybrid Benefit without the need to redeploy. This can be achieved from the **Configuration** pane of the VM as shown in *Figure 2.6*:

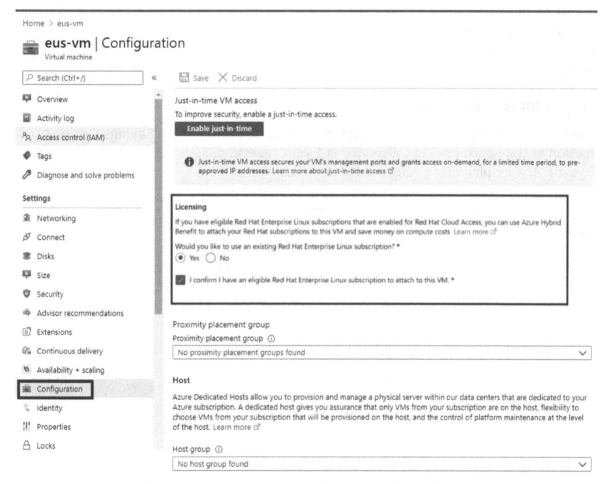

Figure 2.6: Converting existing VMs to Azure Hybrid Benefit

Once this process is complete, in your Azure usage, you will see that the cost for the VM has dropped significantly. The process of attaching the RHEL subscription to Azure VMs can be done from the CLI and ARM templates as well if you would like to do this programmatically.

As mentioned earlier, customers have the freedom to switch back to a PAYG model whenever their RHEL subscriptions expire. Conversion back to the PAYG model is also done via the **Configuration** pane of the VM.

For SUSE customers, the process of attaching is pretty much the same; however, registration for using SUSE subscriptions is done via the SUSE Public Cloud program.

This model is ideal for customers who have active or unused RHEL or SUSE subscriptions that they purchased from the respective vendors and who would like to utilize these in the cloud for potential savings over the PAYG model.

In this model, we were using the subscription that we purchased from Red Hat or SUSE and attaching it to use with our Azure subscription. However, in the prepay model, which we are going to cover next, we will be purchasing Red Hat or SUSE software plans directly from Microsoft.

Prepay for Azure software plans

The final option under **Software (Red Hat Enterprise Linux)** in the **Savings Options** section of the Azure Pricing Calculator is **1 year reserved**. *Figure* 2.7 demonstrates the 1-year software plan being selected for Red Hat:

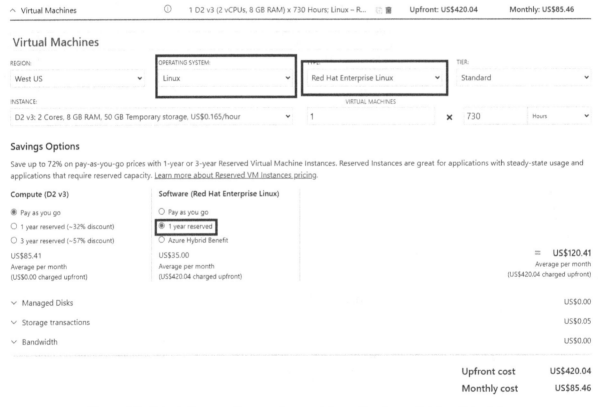

Figure 2.7: Calculating a software plan cost from the Azure Pricing Calculator

In this model, customers can buy software plans directly from Microsoft for a term of 1 year and they can also renew if required by term-end. One catch here is that the plan amount should be paid upfront. In *Figure 2.7*, you can see that this has been mentioned in the cost; the moment a customer purchases a software plan from Azure, that charge will be added to the next invoice as an upfront cost for the next year.

Another key point to keep in mind here is that cancellation or exchange of these plans is not allowed. This means you should be buying the right plan for your workload. For example, if your product is SLES Priority for 2-4 vCPUs, you should purchase SLES Priority for 2-4 vCPUs. If you were to purchase SLES for HPC 1-2 vCPUs instead of SLES Priority for 2-4 vCPUs by mistake, then you would not get the benefit and you would not be able to return or exchange this plan. A piece of advice here is to understand your workload and buy accordingly.

The software plan can be purchased from the **Reservations** pane in Azure, the very same place where we purchase reserved instances for Azure VMs, databases, and so on. The benefit will be applied automatically to the matching workload and no mapping is required.

For instance, if you have three SLES Priority instances, each with 4 vCPUs, then the right plan for you is SLES Priority for 2-4 vCPUs. Depending on the quantity you purchase, the discount is applied automatically to the instances. Assume that we purchased two SLES Priority for 2-4 vCPU plans; then, two out of three VMs will get the benefit and the remaining one will remain in the PAYG model. If you need the third one's cost also covered by the plan, then you need to buy another plan of the same kind. This new plan will automatically attach to the remaining VM.

Like Azure reserved instances, the software plans are a "use it or lose it" benefit. This means that if you deallocate all your VMs and the plan is not able to find a suitable VM to attach to, the benefit will be in vain. You cannot carry forward the unused hours.

> **Note**
>
> You can avoid losing the benefit in the case of a migration by opening a billing support case on the Azure portal.

You should always do proper planning for your workloads before buying software plans to ensure that the most cost-effective plan is selected. Reiterating some of the considerations that we should be keeping in mind:

1. The plan is ideal for 24/7/365 workloads; other servers need a billing support change request. If the plan is not able to discover the appropriate SKU, the utilization of the plan will be zero and you will lose a benefit.

2. No return or exchange is possible. Buy the right plan based on the product and vCores your VM has; buying the wrong plan or the wrong number of CPUs will result in a loss of money.

3. For SUSE plans, only certain SLES versions are supported. Make sure you check the version you are running using the `cat/etc/os-release` command and match with the documentation available here: https://docs.microsoft.com/azure/cost-management-billing/reservations/understand-suse-reservation-charges#discount-applies-to-different-vm-sizes-for-suse-plans.

4. The plan's costs are upfront and will appear on your next invoice.

In the next section, we will conclude the licensing part of the chapter with a helpful comparison of these licensing models and their benefits.

Savings comparison of licensing models

In the previous section, we saw the different types of licensing models that are available for your Linux workloads in Azure (refer to *Chapter 1, Linux: History and future in the cloud*). Here, we are going to make a comparison from the perspective of a customer and look at the savings percentage for each model.

For demonstration purposes, we will be using the cost of an RHEL D2v3 VM running in East US for 730 hours in US dollars. At the time of writing, the cost of the software is $43.80 and $35.00 per month for the PAYG and prepay software plan models respectively. We are not taking into account the Azure Hybrid Benefit monthly charge as this subscription is bought from the respective model. If you are already partnered with Red Hat or SUSE, you could get some discounts on these subscriptions. Now let's do the math; *Table 2.1* shows the cost per month for each model:

Model	Infrastructure Cost	Software Cost
PAYG	$70.08	$43.80
Software Plan	$70.08	$35.00
Azure Hybrid Benefit	$70.08	$0.00

Table 2.1: Azure licensing model comparison

If we plot these values on a graph and calculate the savings percentage for a year, we will get a graph like the one shown in *Figure 2.8*:

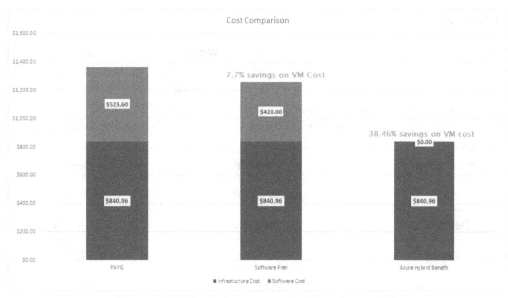

Figure 2.8: Calculating savings for licensing models

The value may look small, but this is only for a single VM; in an enterprise environment where there will be thousands of VMs, the potential savings are very high.

Each model has its own use case scenarios:

- PAYG is ideal for testing or development where you are not planning to keep the VM running 24/7.

- Azure Hybrid Benefit is appropriate if you have license subscriptions from Red Hat or SUSE and would like to use them in the cloud.

- Prepay software plans are perfect for customers who do not have RHEL or SUSE subscriptions and would like to get some discounts on the software cost. However, this is a long-term commitment with Microsoft.

Using Azure Reserved Instances, customers can also get a discount on the compute cost. In short, if you combine Azure Hybrid Benefit or a prepay software plan with Azure Reserved Instances, the overall savings percentage will be boosted to 50-70%. You can read more about Azure Reserved Instances for VMs here: https://docs. microsoft.com/azure/cost-management-billing/reservations/save-compute-costs-reservations. As this is not a licensing model, but more of a cost optimization technique, we will not cover this topic in this chapter. However, when we discuss assessment and migration in *Chapter 3, Assessment and migration planning*, we will discuss how to optimize cloud costs.

Now that we are familiar with the licensing models, let's see how we can use the Azure **command-line interface (CLI)** to find the versions of available distros.

Available distros

In the introduction of the *Linux on Azure* section, we saw that Microsoft Azure supports common Linux distros such as Red Hat, Ubuntu, SUSE, CentOS, Debian, Oracle Linux, and CoreOS. We also saw how we can make use of Azure Marketplace to find the appropriate image as per our organization's requirements. *Table 2.2* displays the endorsed distros and the vendors/publishers who are providing these images:

Distribution	Vendor	Version
CentOS	Rogue Wave Software	CentOS 6.x, 7.x, 8.x
Debian	Credativ	8.x, 9.x
Flatcar Container Linux	Kinvolk	Pro, Stable, Beta
Oracle Linux	Oracle	6.x, 7.x, 8.x
Red Hat Enterprise Linux	Red Hat	6.x, 7.x, 8.x
SUSE Linux Enterprise	SUSE	11.x, 12.x, 15.x
openSUSE	SUSE	openSUSE Leap 15.x
Ubuntu	Canonical	16.x, 18.x, 20.x

Table 2.2: Endorsed Linux distributions on Azure

Though generic version numbers are given in the preceding table, it is very easy to find the image name and version from a publisher using the **Azure CLI**. In order to use the Azure CLI, we need to install it on our workstation. The Azure CLI can be installed on Linux, Mac, or Windows systems. If you are using the Cloud Shell in the Azure portal, by default the Azure CLI is installed for you.

Assuming that we are using a local computer (an Ubuntu computer, for example), we need to install the Azure CLI. You can find the specific installation steps depending on your operating system here: https://docs.microsoft.com/cli/azure/install-azure-cli. For simplicity of demonstration, we will install the Azure CLI on an Ubuntu instance:

1. Microsoft has developed a script to run the installation in a single shot, which makes it convenient for beginners to ramp up quickly. If you prefer to perform this step by step, the Microsoft documentation has instructions for that as well. For Ubuntu, the installation can be done using the following command:

```
curl -sL https://aka.ms/InstallAzureCLIDeb | sudo bash
```

The output is shown in *Figure 2.9*:

```
rithin@azure-mgmt-vm:~$ curl -sL https://aka.ms/InstallAzureCLIDeb | sudo bash
Hit:1 http://azure.archive.ubuntu.com/ubuntu bionic InRelease
Get:2 http://azure.archive.ubuntu.com/ubuntu bionic-updates InRelease [88.7 kB]
Get:3 http://azure.archive.ubuntu.com/ubuntu bionic-backports InRelease [74.6 kB]
Get:4 http://azure.archive.ubuntu.com/ubuntu bionic/universe amd64 Packages [8570 kB]
Get:5 http://security.ubuntu.com/ubuntu bionic-security InRelease [88.7 kB]
Get:6 http://azure.archive.ubuntu.com/ubuntu bionic/universe Translation-en [4941 kB]
Get:7 http://security.ubuntu.com/ubuntu bionic-security/main amd64 Packages [1453 kB]
Get:8 http://azure.archive.ubuntu.com/ubuntu bionic/multiverse amd64 Packages [151 kB]
Get:9 http://azure.archive.ubuntu.com/ubuntu bionic/multiverse Translation-en [108 kB]
Get:10 http://azure.archive.ubuntu.com/ubuntu bionic-updates/main amd64 Packages [1790 kB]
Get:11 http://azure.archive.ubuntu.com/ubuntu bionic-updates/main Translation-en [376 kB]
Get:12 http://azure.archive.ubuntu.com/ubuntu bionic-updates/restricted amd64 Packages [206 kB]
Get:13 http://azure.archive.ubuntu.com/ubuntu bionic-updates/restricted Translation-en [27.9 kB]
Get:14 http://azure.archive.ubuntu.com/ubuntu bionic-updates/universe amd64 Packages [1697 kB]
Get:15 http://azure.archive.ubuntu.com/ubuntu bionic-updates/universe Translation-en [357 kB]
Get:16 http://azure.archive.ubuntu.com/ubuntu bionic-updates/multiverse amd64 Packages [35.6 kB]
Get:17 http://azure.archive.ubuntu.com/ubuntu bionic-updates/multiverse Translation-en [7180 B]
Get:18 http://azure.archive.ubuntu.com/ubuntu bionic-backports/main amd64 Packages [10.0 kB]
Get:19 http://azure.archive.ubuntu.com/ubuntu bionic-backports/main Translation-en [4764 B]
Get:20 http://azure.archive.ubuntu.com/ubuntu bionic-backports/universe amd64 Packages [10.3 kB]
Get:21 http://azure.archive.ubuntu.com/ubuntu bionic-backports/universe Translation-en [4588 B]
Get:22 http://security.ubuntu.com/ubuntu bionic-security/main Translation-en [284 kB]
Get:23 http://security.ubuntu.com/ubuntu bionic-security/restricted amd64 Packages [185 kB]
Get:24 http://security.ubuntu.com/ubuntu bionic-security/restricted Translation-en [24.3 kB]
Get:25 http://security.ubuntu.com/ubuntu bionic-security/universe amd64 Packages [1094 kB]
Get:26 http://security.ubuntu.com/ubuntu bionic-security/universe Translation-en [244 kB]
Get:27 http://security.ubuntu.com/ubuntu bionic-security/multiverse amd64 Packages [12.8 kB]
Get:28 http://security.ubuntu.com/ubuntu bionic-security/multiverse Translation-en [2872 B]
Fetched 21.8 MB in 5s (4490 kB/s)
Reading package lists... Done
Reading package lists... Done
Building dependency tree
Reading state information... Done
lsb-release is already the newest version (9.20170808ubuntu1).
lsb-release set to manually installed.
```

Figure 2.9: Azure CLI installation on Ubuntu

2. The next step is to log in to our account from the Azure CLI in order to connect our Azure account to the Azure CLI. This can be accomplished by running the az login command. The console will prompt you to open a browser window and provide a code to complete the authentication process, as shown in *Figure 2.10*:

```
rithin@azure-mgmt-vm:~$ az login
To sign in, use a web browser to open the page https://microsoft.com/devicelogin and enter the code HMW4GWXK5 to authenticate.
```

Figure 2.10: Logging in to Azure using the Azure CLI

3. In a browser window, you must enter the code shown in the terminal (as shown in *Figure* 2.10) and sign in using your credentials. Once signed in, the terminal will show all the subscriptions you have access to, as seen in *Figure* 2.11. If you do not want to authenticate using the code, you can log in using a service principal where you will be using the client ID and client secret as the username and password, respectively. Also, you can use Managed Identity if required:

```
[
  {
    "cloudName": "AzureCloud",
    "homeTenantId":
    "id":
    "isDefault": true,
    "managedByTenants": [],
    "name": "MSD-OSC",
    "state": "Enabled",
    "tenantId":
    "user": {
      "name": "rithin@rithin.net",
      "type": "user"
    }
  },
  {
    "cloudName": "AzureCloud",
    "homeTenantId":
    "id":
    "isDefault": false,
    "managedByTenants": [],
    "name": "MSD-Migration-Sub",
    "state": "Disabled",
    "tenantId":
    "user": {
      "name": "rithin@rithin.net",
      "type": "user"
    }
  }
]
```

Figure 2.11: Logged in to Azure

Now we will see how we can get information on the available VM images. The primary command used here is az vm image.

4. To list the images (offline) for the VMs/VMSSs that are available on Azure Marketplace, you can use `az vm image list`. The response will be in JSON and we can format it to a table by appending the `-o table` parameter to the command. This will list offline cached images as shown in *Figure 2.12*:

```
rithin@azure-mgmt-vm:~$ az vm image list -o table
You are viewing an offline list of images, use --all to retrieve an up-to-date list
Offer           Publisher              Sku               Urn                                                         UrnAlias
                Version
--------------  ---------------------  ----------------  ----------------------------------------------------------  -------------
--------------  ----------
CentOS          OpenLogic              7.5               OpenLogic:CentOS:7.5:latest                                 CentOS
                latest
CoreOS          CoreOS                 Stable            CoreOS:CoreOS:Stable:latest                                 CoreOS
                latest
debian-10       Debian                 10                Debian:debian-10:10:latest                                  Debian
                latest
openSUSE-Leap   SUSE                   42.3              SUSE:openSUSE-Leap:42.3:latest                              openSUSE-Lea
p               latest
RHEL            RedHat                 7-LVM             RedHat:RHEL:7-LVM:latest                                    RHEL
                latest
SLES            SUSE                   15                SUSE:SLES:15:latest                                         SLES
                latest
UbuntuServer    Canonical              18.04-LTS         Canonical:UbuntuServer:18.04-LTS:latest                     UbuntuLTS
                latest
WindowsServer   MicrosoftWindowsServer 2019-Datacenter   MicrosoftWindowsServer:WindowsServer:2019-Datacenter:latest Win2019Datac
enter           latest
WindowsServer   MicrosoftWindowsServer 2016-Datacenter   MicrosoftWindowsServer:WindowsServer:2016-Datacenter:latest Win2016Datac
enter           latest
WindowsServer   MicrosoftWindowsServer 2012-R2-Datacenter MicrosoftWindowsServer:WindowsServer:2012-R2-Datacenter:latest Win2012R2Dat
acenter         latest
WindowsServer   MicrosoftWindowsServer 2012-Datacenter   MicrosoftWindowsServer:WindowsServer:2012-Datacenter:latest Win2012Datac
enter           latest
WindowsServer   MicrosoftWindowsServer 2008-R2-SP1       MicrosoftWindowsServer:WindowsServer:2008-R2-SP1:latest     Win2008R2SP1
                latest
```

Figure 2.12: Listing the VM images available

To update the list and display all images, you can append the `-all` parameter to the command and call the command again.

The preceding command may take a minute or two to refresh the list of all available images. Usually, when we query the image list, it is recommended to use the publisher or SKU or offer parameters, so that the search is limited to a set of images and the results can be retrieved very easily.

In the next steps, we will be seeing how we can find the publisher, offer, or SKU for an image and use it in our `az vm image list` to narrow down the search.

5. In order to find the list of all publishers, we can use the `az vm image list-publishers` command. Location is a required parameter here, as some publishers publish only to a specific region, so it's recommended to check that the publisher has published to the region you are planning to deploy to. The following is the output:

```
rithin@azure-mgmt-vm:~$ az vm image list-publishers -l eastus -o table
Location        Name
----------      ----------------------------
eastus          128technology
eastus          1580863854728
eastus          1583465680865
eastus          1585118004523
eastus          1597644262255
eastus          1598955805825
eastus          1e
eastus          2021ai
eastus          3cx-pbx
eastus          42crunch1580391915541
eastus          4psa
eastus          5nine-software-inc
eastus          7isolutions
eastus          a10networks
eastus          a10networks1596136698788
eastus          abiquo
eastus          accedian
eastus          accelario1579101623356
eastus          accellion
eastus          accessdata-group
eastus          accops
```

Figure 2.13: Listing publishers in a region

6. For example, the publisher for Ubuntu is Canonical. If we want to list all the offers provided by this publisher, we can use the following command:

```
az vm image list-offers -p Canonical -l eastus -o table
```

Here the location is a required parameter, as offers may vary depending upon location. The output will be similar to the one shown in *Figure 2.14*:

```
rithin@azure-mgmt-vm:~$ az vm image list-offers -l eastus -p Canonical -o table
Location      Name
----------    --------------------------------------------
eastus        0001-com-ubuntu-minimal-focal-daily
eastus        0001-com-ubuntu-minimal-groovy-daily
eastus        0001-com-ubuntu-minimal-hirsute-daily
eastus        0001-com-ubuntu-pro-advanced-sla
eastus        0001-com-ubuntu-pro-advanced-sla-att
eastus        0001-com-ubuntu-pro-advanced-sla-nestle
eastus        0001-com-ubuntu-pro-advanced-sla-servicenow
eastus        0001-com-ubuntu-pro-advanced-sla-shell
eastus        0001-com-ubuntu-pro-bionic
eastus        0001-com-ubuntu-pro-bionic-fips
eastus        0001-com-ubuntu-pro-focal
eastus        0001-com-ubuntu-pro-hidden-msft-fips
eastus        0001-com-ubuntu-pro-trusty
eastus        0001-com-ubuntu-pro-xenial
eastus        0001-com-ubuntu-pro-xenial-fips
eastus        0001-com-ubuntu-server-eoan
eastus        0001-com-ubuntu-server-focal
eastus        0001-com-ubuntu-server-focal-daily
eastus        0001-com-ubuntu-server-groovy
eastus        0001-com-ubuntu-server-groovy-daily
eastus        0001-com-ubuntu-server-hirsute-daily
eastus        0002-com-ubuntu-minimal-bionic-daily
eastus        0002-com-ubuntu-minimal-disco-daily
eastus        0002-com-ubuntu-minimal-focal-daily
eastus        0002-com-ubuntu-minimal-xenial-daily
eastus        0003-com-ubuntu-minimal-eoan-daily
eastus        0003-com-ubuntu-server-trusted-vm
eastus        test-ubuntu-premium-offer-0002
eastus        Ubuntu15.04Snappy
eastus        Ubuntu15.04SnappyDocker
eastus        UbuntuServer
eastus        Ubuntu Core
```

Figure 2.14: Listing images from the Canonical publisher in East US

7. Let's pick an offer; for instance, `UbuntuServer`. Now we need to list the SKUs to find the available SKUs for the image. We need to pass the publisher, offer, and location to the `az vm image list-skus` command in order to list the SKUs. The aforementioned parameters are mandatory for this command, so the final command will be as follows:

    ```
    az vm image list-skus -l eastus -p Canonical -f UbuntuServer -o table
    ```

    The output is as shown in *Figure 2.15*:

```
rithin@azure-mgmt-vm:~$ az vm image list-skus -l eastus -p Canonical -f UbuntuServer -o table
Location    Name
----------  --------------------
eastus      12.04.3-LTS
eastus      12.04.4-LTS
eastus      12.04.5-LTS
eastus      14.04.0-LTS
eastus      14.04.1-LTS
eastus      14.04.2-LTS
eastus      14.04.3-LTS
eastus      14.04.4-LTS
eastus      14.04.5-DAILY-LTS
eastus      14.04.5-LTS
eastus      16.04-DAILY-LTS
eastus      16.04-LTS
eastus      16.04.0-LTS
eastus      16_04-daily-lts-gen2
eastus      16_04-lts-gen2
eastus      16_04_0-lts-gen2
eastus      18.04-DAILY-LTS
eastus      18.04-LTS
eastus      18.10
eastus      18.10-DAILY
eastus      18_04-daily-lts-gen2
eastus      18_04-lts-gen2
eastus      19.04
eastus      19.04-DAILY
eastus      19.10-DAILY
eastus      19_04-daily-gen2
eastus      19_04-gen2
eastus      19_10-daily-gen2
```

Figure 2.15: Listing SKUs available for the Canonical UbuntuServer offer in East US

8. Now we know the publisher, offer, and SKU. Let's use these values in the `az vm image list` command to see the available versions of an image. Here we will be using `Canonical` as the publisher (`-p`), `UbuntuServer` as the offer (`-f`), and `19_04-gen2` as the SKU (`-s`). Combine these and call the following command:

    ```
    az vm image list -p Canonical -f UbuntuServer -s 19_04-gen2 --all -o table
    ```

This will list the image version available for the specified publisher, offer, and SKU combination. The following is the sample output:

```
rithin@azure-mgmt-vm:~$ az vm image list -p Canonical -f UbuntuServer -s 19_04-gen2 --all -o table
Offer          Publisher    Sku         Urn                                                           Version
-----------    ---------    ----------  --------------------------------------------------------      --------------
UbuntuServer   Canonical    19_04-gen2  Canonical:UbuntuServer:19_04-gen2:19.04.201908230             19.04.201908230
UbuntuServer   Canonical    19_04-gen2  Canonical:UbuntuServer:19_04-gen2:19.04.201910030             19.04.201910030
UbuntuServer   Canonical    19_04-gen2  Canonical:UbuntuServer:19_04-gen2:19.04.201911080             19.04.201911080
UbuntuServer   Canonical    19_04-gen2  Canonical:UbuntuServer:19_04-gen2:19.04.201911131             19.04.201911131
UbuntuServer   Canonical    19_04-gen2  Canonical:UbuntuServer:19_04-gen2:19.04.202001220             19.04.202001220
```

Figure 2.16: Listing versions of an image for a specific publisher, offer, and SKU combination

9. We can use urn from the output in the az vm image show command to get the details of the VM image as shown in *Figure 2.17*:

```
rithin@azure-mgmt-vm:~$ az vm image show -l eastus --urn Canonical:UbuntuServer:19_04-gen2:19.04.201908230
{
  "automaticOsUpgradeProperties": {
    "automaticOsUpgradeSupported": false
  },
  "dataDiskImages": [],
  "disallowed": {
    "vmDiskType": "Unmanaged"
  },
  "hyperVGeneration": "V2",
  "id": "/Subscriptions/71766a1b-baf2-43e0-aa09-72ab0423b68f/Providers/Microsoft.Compute/Locations/eastus/Publishers/Canonical/Artifact
Types/VMImage/Offers/UbuntuServer/Skus/19_04-gen2/Versions/19.04.201908230",
  "location": "eastus",
  "name": "19.04.201908230",
  "osDiskImage": {
    "operatingSystem": "Linux",
    "sizeInBytes": 32213303808,
    "sizeInGb": 31
  },
  "plan": null,
  "tags": null
}
```

Figure 2.17: Finding VM image details

10. The same urn can be used in our az vm create command to create a VM with that particular image version. A quick illustration has been given in *Figure 2.18*:

```
rithin@azure-mgmt-vm:~$ az vm create -l eastus -n myUbuntuVM --image Canonical:UbuntuServer:19_04-gen2:19.04.201908230 --admin-username
rithin --generate-ssh-keys -g packt-demo
SSH key files '/home/rithin/.ssh/id_rsa' and '/home/rithin/.ssh/id_rsa.pub' have been generated under ~/.ssh to allow SSH access to the
VM. If using machines without permanent storage, back up your keys to a safe location.
{- Finished ..
  "fqdns": "",
  "id": "/subscriptions/71766a1b-baf2-43e0-aa09-72ab0423b68f/resourceGroups/packt-demo/providers/Microsoft.Compute/virtualMachines/myUb
untuVM",
  "location": "eastus",
  "macAddress": "00-0D-3A-13-B9-0D",
  "powerState": "VM running",
  "privateIpAddress": "10.0.0.4",
  "publicIpAddress": "52.188.151.219",
  "resourceGroup": "packt-demo",
  "zones": ""
}
```

Figure 2.18: Creating a VM using URN

Before we conclude, please check *Table* 2.3, which lists all the commands we used in the preceding steps for quick reference:

Command	Purpose	Required Parameters	Documentation
`az vm image list`	Lists VM/VMSS images (offline/cached).	NA	https://docs.microsoft.com/cli/azure/vm/image?view=azure-cli-latest
`az vm image list --all`	Lists all images from Azure Marketplace. This usually takes time due to the large dataset. It's recommended that you filter using publisher, offer, and SKU for a quicker response.	NA	
`az vm image list-publishers`	Lists publishers available.	Location (-1)	
`az vm image list-offers`	Lists VM image offers available.	Location (-1), publisher (-p)	
`az vm image list-skus`	Lists available SKUs for an offer from a publisher.	Location (-1), publisher (-p), offer (-f)	
`az vm image show`	Shows details for a given URN.	Location (-1), URN (-u)	
`az vm create`	Creates a VM.	Name (-n), resource group (-g)	https://docs.microsoft.com/cli/azure/vm?view=azure-cli-latest#az_vm_create

Table 2.3: Commands used for the hands-on exercise

In this hands-on exercise, we queried the image list to find the available images and created a VM using that. We learned how to narrow down the search using parameters such as publisher, offers, and SKU.

Although we used the Azure CLI to accomplish this task, if you are using PSCore or PowerShell, you can make use of the Azure Powershell module to perform the same operations. The documentation for this is available here: https://docs.microsoft.com/powershell/module/az.compute/get-azvmimage?view=azps-5.2.0.

With that, we have reached the end of this chapter, and we will now summarize the topics we have discussed so far.

Summary

In the first chapter, we learned that there are different distros or flavors of Linux available depending on the user requirements. This chapter was more of an overview of popular Linux distributions and how Linux on Azure works. We also talked about commercial and free open-source software.

There are several advantages to using commercial distributions of Linux. Since we are paying for these subscriptions, it is expected that they provide additional features that are not found out of the box in free distributions. These add-ons include support, extra modules, and extended customization options. This chapter threw light on these areas as well.

We looked closely at Linux on Azure. We started off with Azure Marketplace and the plethora of images it has. After that, we introduced the term "endorsed distributions"; this is where Microsoft works with different vendors such as Red Hat, Canonical, and SUSE to bring their Linux images to the cloud. Microsoft recommends using an endorsed image for your production deployment. We also discussed the technical support matrix and the scope of support given by Microsoft Support. We saw some scenarios where vendors need to be engaged for the resolution to a problem.

After covering the Linux distros on Azure, we talked about the licensing models available in Linux and which one is best for you depending on the type of deployment. We also plotted a graph to portray the potential savings in each of the models. The last part of the chapter was more hands-on, where we saw how we can use the Azure CLI to find the different VM images available on Azure. However, the range of choice does not stop here; if you are not able to find the image you are looking for, Azure allows you the freedom to bring your own image.

Linux on Azure is an extensive topic and there are many books that clearly discuss how Linux administration can be done on Azure. This book is geared more toward the migration and assessment of Linux workloads. The licensing models and distros were explained to help you understand how things are done in the Azure realm.

In the next chapter, we will start to talk about migration. Many organizations begin to move to the cloud without proper assessment or planning. Planning and assessment are the cornerstones of migration and they need to be done properly before moving to the cloud. The planning phase is more about getting to know the capacity and checking prerequisites, while assessment is done using assessment tools to verify whether your workloads are ready for Azure or if they need any sort of refactoring first. With that said, we will talk more about these strategies and steps in the next chapter. Keep on reading!

3

Assessment and migration planning

This chapter will focus on discussing useful methods for assessing your existing workloads in on-premises or hosted environments and provide some guidance on planning your migration project.

We will go into the technical details regarding a number of popular Linux workloads and explain why these specific workloads require extra careful planning prior to migration. Additionally, we will talk about various migration methodologies and tools, and will also show some practical examples of how to assess current workloads by using tools such as Azure Migrate.

Until now, we have been talking about the history of Linux and various Linux distributions that are available. We have not talked about migration or what happens prior to this. In this chapter, we are going to cover concepts related to pre-migration steps. You may be wondering why we need pre-migration steps and why cannot we move our workloads directly to the cloud. The answer is simply that migrating to the cloud requires a lot of planning and assessment. We need to make sure that our workloads are ready to be migrated to the cloud, otherwise the time and money spent investing in the migration will go to waste.

In this chapter, you will also learn that pre-migration mainly comprises assessment and capacity planning. Assessment is the process of creating an inventory of workloads we have in the current environment. Using this inventory, we will be able to understand the current infrastructure topology, which can be used to generate the expense for moving to the cloud and to verify whether the workloads are cloud-optimized.

We will also cover a service called **Azure Migrate**, which can handle both the assessment and migration of our Linux workloads. As we progress, we will walk you through the assessment process and its relevance to migration.

Some of the key takeaways from this chapter are as follows:

- Learning some of the popular workloads on Linux
- Preparing for a migration project
- Assessing the current environment
- An introduction to assessment tools

Additionally, we have created a hands-on lab exercise for you that you can use to learn to assess an environment by doing it yourself.

Let's now get started with some of the popular workloads that are running on Linux.

Popular workloads on Linux

In real-world scenarios, we only migrate servers with workloads running on them, as there is no point in migrating a VM with no services running to the cloud. Instead of doing that, you could deploy a new server in Azure directly and start developing on top of that. Let's have a quick recap of the popular workloads on Linux. Some of these were already explained in *Chapter 1, Linux: History and future in the cloud*. Let's recall the varieties of workloads, including application hosting (such as Java and LAMP), Search, and big data, and see how Azure supports these.

LAMP

The acronym LAMP stands for **Linux**, **Apache**, **MySQL**, **PHP/Perl/Python**. Typically, it is the first service stack that any Linux administrator would set up and is usually used to host dynamic and database-driven websites. In LAMP:

- **Linux** (**L**) refers to any Linux distribution; you can use Ubuntu or Fedora or CentOS or any other distribution.
- **Apache** (**A**) is the web server that presents the data or web page to the user. In short, this is the front end that users will be interacting with.
- **MySQL** (**M**) is the data store that will be used to save data.
- **PHP/Perl/Python** (**P**) is the programming language used to develop the dynamic websites.

Although we refer to it as a LAMP server installation, these are separate packages that you need to install individually, and it is not like installing CentOS on a computer. In certain cases, LAMP might not be the right choice; in other words, you may not require all the components of LAMP. Again, this entirely depends on what your application is. If you have a static website, which is created using HTML, CSS, and JS, then you do not need the MySQL or PHP functionality in your system. All you need is the Linux server and Apache web server running on top of that, which can deliver the static site to your clients.

Depending on what components of the LAMP server you are using, the migration needs to be planned accordingly. For the purpose of the hands-on lab in this chapter, we will be using a LAMP server for assessment and dependency analysis. *Figure 3.1* shows the architecture of the server. This architecture could be deployed on a hypervisor such as Hyper-V, VMWare ESXi, or on a physical server. In our lab, we are going to use Hyper-V as the virtualization platform:

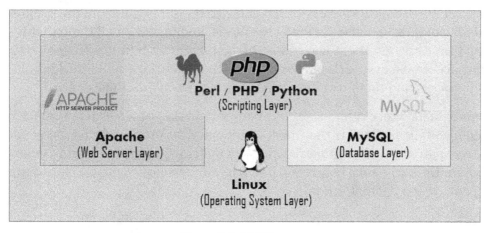

Figure 3.1: LAMP server

Figure 3.1 shows the architecture to be used in the hands-on lab.

Database servers

In LAMP, we saw how the Linux server hosts the MySQL database, which can act as a data store for the dynamic websites. MySQL is not the only database that can be deployed in Linux servers. There are a plethora of relational and non-relational databases that can be installed on Linux servers. Some of the open-source relational databases that can be deployed on Linux are listed below. Some of these are very popular and well known; others you may not have heard of before:

- MySQL
- MariaDB
- PostgreSQL
- SQLite
- LucidDB
- H2
- HSQLDB
- Firebird
- Derby
- CUBRID

There are many other relational database products that are not open source, such as Microsoft SQL Server, Oracle Database 18c, MaxDB, and IBM's DB2.

Apart from the relational databases, Linux is also a popular platform for NoSQL databases. MongoDB, Couchbase, CouchDB, RavenDB, and OrientDB are examples of NoSQL databases.

Azure has Database Migration Service available to migrate data from on-premises to managed **Platform-as-a-service (PaaS)** solutions. Regardless of all the benefits that are offered by PaaS services, there is a subset of customers who prefer to deploy these on **Infrastructure-as-a-service (IaaS)** servers and manage the administration fully. The migration process and technical details depend on the technologies chosen.

In addition to IaaS, Azure offers a set of open-source databases as PaaS solutions. The advantage of using PaaS is that most of the infrastructure-related tasks, such as updating and patching, will be taken care of by Microsoft Azure. These PaaS solutions include Azure Database for PostgreSQL, Azure Database for MySQL, Azure Database for MariaDB, and Azure Cache for Redis.

HPC, clustering, and SAP

In *Chapter 1, Linux: History and future in the cloud*, we looked at SAP, clustering, and HPC scenarios in Linux. To recap, **High Performance Computing (HPC)** is a collection of hundreds or even thousands of servers that are networked together. Each of the servers in the cluster is called a **node** and they work in parallel with one another to deliver higher processing speeds. The high combined processing speed contributes to higher performance.

Microsoft Azure offers a variety of VM series that are specifically designed with HPC in mind and can be used to carry out compute-intensive tasks. These include VM series, H series, HC series, HB series, and HBv2 series.

The main rationale behind customers migrating HPC to the cloud is the larger resource requirements. As these workloads are performing compute-intensive tasks, the amount of compute power needed is large and the infrastructure should be able to supply more servers if necessary. On-premises infrastructure will not be able to provide this liberty of scalability as the cloud does. The reality is that on-premises infrastructure is only capable of handling HPC clusters. Any scaling outside this safe zone is impossible to achieve. This is where Azure comes in. All you need to do is set up the scaling policy and Azure will take care of the rest.

The interesting thing is that you can also implement hybrid HPC clusters where the head nodes will be placed on-premises and compute nodes are placed in Azure. As the compute nodes are in Azure, scaling can be executed based on requirements.

Shared storage

By way of a recap from *Chapter 1, Linux: History and future in the cloud*, let's review the shared storage use case again. Linux is commonly used as a storage server and clients connect to the server via SMB or the NFS protocol. These servers can be used to store shared files and can be accessed by clients for several purposes. For example, you can have a shared file server to store all necessary installation packages of your internal applications. Your clients will be able to download these files from the shared storage and consume them.

Also, shared storage can be used to store files that require collaboration. Files uploaded to these drives can be used by collaborators depending on what level of permissions they have.

In Microsoft Azure, Azure Files can be used as shared storage and the advantage here is that this is a completely managed service. If you are planning to deploy a VM and host a shared storage on top of that, as a customer, you have to manage many things, starting with OS management, updates, patches, and so on. However, in the case of Azure Files, the service is managed by Microsoft and because of the various redundancy levels offered by Azure Storage, you do not have to worry about implementing high availability yourself.

Data from on-premises can be moved using command-line tools such as AzCopy and robocopy. AzCopy is optimized for best throughput for the copy job and can copy data directly between storage accounts. On the other hand, robocopy is useful if you would like to move from your on-premises storage to Azure File Storage, which is already mounted on the same server.

The aforementioned are the common scenarios; however, this does not mean that the use case scenarios or workload types are confined to these. Even for the same workload type, different customers will be using different components. For example, if we think about a database server, some customers will be using MySQL, while others will be using PostgreSQL.

Microsoft has a collection of documents, best practices, implementation guides, and tooling that are designed to accelerate your cloud adoption. This framework is called the Microsoft **Cloud Adoption Framework (CAF)** for Azure. Organizations are recommended to adopt this framework so that they can incorporate the best practices and tools from the very beginning of their cloud journey. The complete framework can be reviewed here: https://docs.microsoft.com/azure/cloud-adoption-framework/.

The action plan we are going to follow throughout this book is from the *Migrate* section of the CAF. In this book, we will focus on the main steps for migrating your Linux workloads to Azure. This roadmap consists of four main steps as shown in *Figure 3.2*:

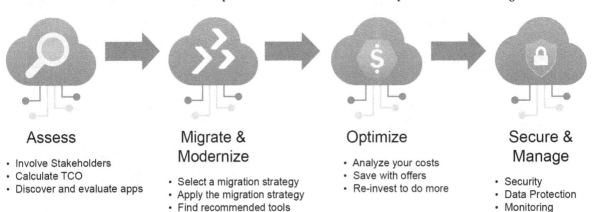

Assess

- Involve Stakeholders
- Calculate TCO
- Discover and evaluate apps

Migrate & Modernize

- Select a migration strategy
- Apply the migration strategy
- Find recommended tools

Optimize

- Analyze your costs
- Save with offers
- Re-invest to do more

Secure & Manage

- Security
- Data Protection
- Monitoring

Figure 3.2: Linux migration roadmap

As shown in the preceding diagram, we will start our migration journey with the first phase–*Assess*.

Pre-project preparations

All projects should start with proper planning, and the same applies to cloud migrations as well. At this point, we have already gathered all the necessary technical information, but how do we know what kind of project team we need? Let's take a closer look.

Identifying relevant roles and responsibilities

Quite often, the responsibilities of on-premises applications are distributed to many internal stakeholders within different teams, and sometimes even different departments or companies.

For example, a typical production environment for any business application requires several different roles in order to function:

- Hardware administrator
- Virtualization administrator
- Storage administrator
- Network administrator
- Linux administrator
- Database administrator
- Backup administrator

When you add the internal and external users, the list grows:

- Identity management administrator
- Connectivity administrator
- Application owners
- Business owners
- Application users

Now, let's imagine you plan to move this system to Azure: Which of these people will you need to talk to in order to ensure that the work undertaken by the business users of this application is not disrupted? Let's look at some of the key roles and why they are quite important in cloud migration projects.

Network administrator

Applications running only in one datacenter and serving users in a single country are quite easy to migrate to the cloud compared to distributed applications and users across the globe.

Let's take an example (refer to *Figure* 3.3) company that has four offices in two continents and four countries. The European teams in **Paris** and **London** are using a datacenter in **London**, and the teams in **Singapore** and **Bangkok** are using a datacenter in **Singapore**:

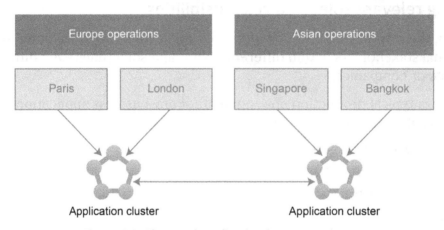

Figure 3.3: Clustered application in two continents

This scenario adds one obvious aspect of complexity to the total architecture: **global network connectivity**. From a project planning point of view, this means that you will need to add at least one international network provider company to the list of roles involved in the project.

Typically, this kind of network structure can be moved to the cloud without any dramatic changes, but there is one special category of applications that will require lots of planning: financial applications. Traditionally, the financial industry has relied on dedicated internet connections with private links in their systems. This, in itself, is not an issue as Azure has various options for VPN and other private connections. The tricky part here is the use of the `Multicast` protocol in many trading applications used by the financial sector. Another industry that often uses the `Multicast` protocol is healthcare, especially hospitals.

> **Note**
>
> If you would like to learn more about use cases of Multicast in enterprise environments, you could look at the book *Multicast Design Solutions*, published by *Cisco Press*: https://www.ciscopress.com/articles/article. asp?p=2928192&seqNum=5.

What makes multicast worth mentioning in this section is the fact that public clouds do not support multicast networking. This makes it very challenging to migrate applications relying on multicast routing directly to Azure. Luckily, there are ways to work around the problem, for example, by using Multicast-to-Unicast gateways, but this approach will require re-architecting your network design and possibly applications.

Another networking detail that requires careful planning is VPN and ExpressRoute connections. It is good to remember that it is not guaranteed that you may be able to move your connections from your current locations to public clouds easily. As those existing connections may be owned or operated by a third-party company, you need to make sure to involve them in your network planning sessions.

The point to understand here is that things such as networking may sound easy and straightforward, but it is one of the most difficult technological areas in public cloud migration, not only from the technology point of view, but also from a staffing and planning perspective, as there are so many stakeholders involved.

If you could add just one networking person to your migration team, pick someone with experience of working with telecom providers and legacy networking technologies. This person is going to be more valuable than any cloud networking specialist.

Let's now move on to the next key role.

Linux administrator

In earlier chapters, we talked about the business aspects of Linux subscription management. It also has some technical details that need to be considered when planning to migrate to the public cloud. One of these details is update management: where will you get security patches and package updates when using Linux on Azure?

Your Linux administrator is a key person here as they already know how the various package managers and subscription systems work in the current system. With some training, it is quite easy for them to understand what kind of changes need to be implemented when moving your systems to Azure.

Does having a Linux administrator in your migration project team sound obvious? In real life, we have seen migration projects where the project manager did not think this was necessary and had a Windows administrator trying to figure out how to migrate Linux to Azure. You can probably make a guess as to whether those projects were successful.

By Linux administrator, in this context, we mean someone who understands things such as filesystems, disk performance, SELinux, and subscription management if you are using a commercial Linux distribution.

With a bit of luck, the system you are planning to migrate is well maintained, all security patches and updates are applied, and everything is well documented. In real life however, this is rarely the case. It really helps to have someone in the team who has extensive experience of working with various Linux services and application stacks as they often can find the information that is missing from your documentation.

Let's take an example of having an RHEL server with SELinux turned off. Your application documentation does not mention anything about SELinux, and your security team says that in the public cloud, you will need to have SELinux enabled or they will not approve the migration. What could possibly go wrong? Everything, especially if the security team turns on **Enforcing Mode** in SELinux without first checking how the application behaves.

We recommend that you familiarize yourself with all the relevant roles and personas related to the system you are planning to migrate to Azure and to investigate very carefully, following the pattern introduced here, to find out who you need to involve in your project team.

Cloud governance and operations

Microsoft has developed a CAF, a set of documentation, implementation guidance, best practices, and tools to help customers to start using Azure in the best way possible.

> **Note**
>
> CAF is available for free to everyone at https://docs.microsoft.com/azure/cloud-adoption-framework/.

Several sections from CAF are very important when learning about cloud migrations. For example, *Landing Zone* is a term you should be very familiar with going forward. In Azure, a landing zone means a set of pre-designed architecture or services where you can deploy your new or migrated resources, for example, VMs. An analogy in the software development world would be **Minimum Viable Product** (**MVP**).

> **Note**
>
> Read more about Azure landing zones here: https://docs.microsoft.com/azure/cloud-adoption-framework/ready/landing-zone/.

Another very important topic worth mentioning at this point is cloud operations, or **CloudOps**. In most cases, the team who develops a software solution will not be the same team that operates the cloud infrastructure – or landing zone – after the solution is deployed. Typically, cloud operations are managed by the company's IT department, or this work is outsourced to a specialized cloud management service provider.

The worst thing you can do is to have no one take care of the application or the infrastructure it is using after it is deployed. Someone needs to monitor the application and infrastructure performance, react to system alerts, ensure that security patches are applied, and, most likely, also run cost optimization processes every now and then.

The Microsoft CAF also covers these cloud management aspects, not only from a technology point of view, but also from the organization and business alignment angles. Read more about cloud management in the CAF here: https://docs.microsoft.com/azure/cloud-adoption-framework/manage/.

To apply all the theory that we have learned so far in relation to discovery and assessment, let's go through a hands-on assessment lab. In this lab, you will see how Hyper-V VMs are discovered and assessed in Azure.

Migration assessment

The migration journey continues by getting to know your current infrastructure. Assess is the first step in migration and, in this phase, we will be creating an inventory of our source. When we say *source*, this is not necessarily always on-premises. It could be other cloud vendors or platforms as well. The assessment tools available in Azure can be used to assess infrastructure in AWS, GCP, virtualized platform, and on-premises physical servers. The reason we need to perform the assessment is because we need to make sure what the migration of our workloads will look like post-migration.

The assessment consists of four steps along with a set of tools. Let's proceed and learn about these steps.

Preparing a cloud migration plan

As Benjamin Franklin said, "By failing to prepare, you are preparing to fail." At first glance, migration may seem uncomplicated; however, if we start without planning and in the absence of a proper strategy, then migration will fail. A failed migration would be an utter waste of time, energy, and productivity. You should begin your planning by setting objectives and priorities. Not every migration happens in one go; it will be done in phases. Usually, servers that are part of the same solution are migrated together rather than migrating random servers. Assume that you have a registration application, payroll application, ticketing application, and so on in your environment. In this case, you need to set some priorities and project deadlines, as in the payroll application is the priority and should be handled before the end of Q1. This approach ensures that you are taking one step at a time and following a discipline, thereby ensuring a successful migration.

The general rule of thumb is to prioritize applications with fewer dependencies; this will act as a catalyst for the migration. Once these are done, you can focus on the applications with a large number of dependencies. Moving those will give you more time to focus as the other applications were migrated earlier. This will also ensure more optimal use of your time. If you start with applications having a large number of dependencies, you may take longer to optimize and plan them. This will mean that the deadlines for other workloads will be extended further. Hence, it is better to complete the simple ones prior to handling the complex ones.

The next step is *Discovery and evaluation* this is where the full assessment takes place.

Discovery and evaluation

Now that we have a plan in mind, we need to begin a full assessment of the environment. The outcome of these steps is to identify servers, applications, and services that are within the scope of migration.

Next, we will be producing a full inventory and dependency map of servers and services that are within the scope of migration. The inventory and map help us to understand how these dependency services talk to one another. It is strongly recommended that you thoroughly investigate each application and its dependencies. A failure to assess or account for one of the dependencies will result in major problems post-migration.

Some of your applications may not be suitable for lift and shift migration, so you need to consider other options as well. For each application, you need to evaluate the following migration options:

- **Rehost**: This is what we normally call "lift and shift." Basically, you are recreating your infrastructure in Azure. This requires minimal changes to your applications and so will have the least impact. An example of this is the replication of VMs to the cloud and then recreating them in Azure with the replicated disk.
- **Refactor**: This is done when you are moving an IaaS server to a PaaS solution, for instance, from the VM to a PaaS solution such as Azure App Service. As we already know, moving to PaaS solutions reduces management tasks and, at the same time, helps to keep your costs low.
- **Rearchitect**: In certain scenarios, you may need to re-architect some systems so that they can be successfully migrated. This architecture is mainly implemented to make the system cloud-native or to take advantage of newer paths such as containerization and microservices.
- **Rebuild**: If the cost, time, and manpower required to rearchitect the application is more than starting from scratch, then you may rebuild the application. This approach helps the software development team to develop applications that can get the most out of the cloud.

- **Replace**: Sometimes, when you review the overall expenditure for rebuilding or rearchitecting the solution, it could be higher than buying third-party software. Assuming that you have your own CRM solution, the cost of rearchitecting or rebuilding is higher than buying a license for a similar SaaS product such as Dynamics 365.

Once we have discovered the entire infrastructure, the next step in the pipeline is to involve the key stakeholders.

Involving key stakeholders

In the discovery stage, we will have a complete picture of the infrastructure; however, the owners and superusers of the applications will also have a complete picture of the architecture of the application. These owners and other key stakeholders we mentioned earlier in this chapter will be able to share valuable suggestions and information regarding the architecture of the application, and incorporating these suggestions at this early stage of migration will enhance the probability of a successful migration.

It is better to involve the IT and business owners when it comes to filling any knowledge gaps. Also, these individuals will be useful in providing any guidance regarding the application architecture.

When it comes to migration, the CxO stakeholders, such as the CEO, CTO, and CIO, will always be interested in knowing the numbers, as in what the potential savings could be were we to move from on-premises to Azure. Let's see how we can estimate the cost.

Estimating the savings

Many organizations adopt the migration path to save infrastructure costs. The agility and scalability of the cloud are major driving factors here. For example, if you buy a new server and this server is not utilized as expected, then this constitutes a loss for the company. In the cloud, however, things are different; if you do not need it, you can deallocate the server in seconds. Once deallocated, you do not have to worry about the server, and you are no longer paying for it.

Before moving to the cloud, all organizations do the math and verify whether they are deriving any profit or savings as a result of this migration. Once you are done with the initial scoping, you can use the Azure **Total Cost of Ownership (TCO)** calculator to estimate the cost of running workloads in on-premises versus Azure.

Starting with the assessment to savings calculation, there are different tools involved in the process. Let's identify the tools available at the assessment stage.

Identifying tools

Tools play a vital role in the migration assessment. Without tools, it will be a cumbersome task to go to each of the servers that you have on-premises and create an inventory. Hence, tools increase productivity and accelerate migration. *Table 3.1* shows the list of tools that can be leveraged at the Assess stage:

Service or Tool	Purpose
Azure Migrate	Used for assessment and migration of VMware VMs, Hyper-V VMs, cloud VMs (AWS, GCP, and other cloud vendors), and physical servers, as well as databases and web applications to Azure
Service Map	Used to identify dependencies and map communication between application components on Linux and Windows servers
Azure TCO calculator	Creates a comparison between the cost of running infrastructure on-premises versus Azure

Table 3.1: Assessing tooling

The aforementioned are the tools used at the Assess stage. Likewise, there are other tools leveraged at each stage (**Migrate**, **Optimize**, and **Secure & Manage**) in the adoption plan. Once we get to these stages, you will be acquainted with the tools used at each respective stage.

There are other third-party tools that can be used to perform an assessment. These are available in Azure Migrate and can be selected during project creation.

Now that we are familiar with the steps that are part of the Assess stage, let's try to understand more about each of these tools and their usage.

Assessing tooling

As explained in the preceding *Identifying tools* section, the inevitable roles played by these tools make the assessment, mapping, and savings calculation easier. Now we will evaluate each of these tools and see how they are used and what the use case scenarios are. We will start with Azure Migrate.

Azure Migrate

The purpose of Azure Migrate is already evident from *Table* 3.1. With the help of Azure Migrate, we can run environment discovery without installing any agents on the servers. If we install agents, we can also perform dependency analysis, which can be used to generate service maps. The best part of the assessment is that all of this is natively integrated into the Azure portal and you do not have to be dependent on any other portals.

Following the assessment, Azure Migrate generates an assessment report with the estimated cost, recommendations, and size of the VM that you will need to provision to match your on-premises configuration. Azure Migrate can discover and assess VMs deployed on Hyper-V and VMWare virtualization environments, as well as physical machines, while extending the list to other cloud vendors, too.

To use Azure Migrate, we need to create an Azure Migrate project in the Azure portal. This project will be used to store the assessments that we perform. Also, the same project can be used when we are migrating our workload to Azure. Since we are in the assessment phase of the migration plan, this chapter will focus on the assessment tools available in the project. Once we reach the migration stage in *Chapter 4, Performing migration to Azure*, we will discuss the migration tools in the Azure Migrate project.

Let's now familiarize ourselves with the next tool, *Service Map*.

Service Map

Service Map is another great tool that is part of Azure Monitor for server assessment that performs the dependency analysis for us. There are several advantages to leveraging dependency analysis and this boosts the overall migration confidence and success rate. Some of the advantages are as follows:

If you have a large number of servers to migrate, you can group them based on solutions as we know which server hosts which dependency:

- It helps in identifying the right machines in a solution and migrating them together.
- It helps in understanding the topology of the environment.

Makes sure that you migrate everything and that no server is excluded from migration due to human errors or negligence. There are two types of dependency analysis:

- Agentless analysis
- Agent-based analysis

Let's take a closer look at each of these.

Agentless analysis

As the name implies, no agents are installed on the VMs to perform the dependency analysis. The discovery or analysis is done by using the TCP connection data capture from machines. However, one thing to note here is that agentless analysis is in preview at the time of writing this book and is available for VMWare VMs only. Data polling and collection is accomplished with the help of vSphere APIs.

If we run a `netstat` command on our Linux or Windows computer, we will be able to see the connections, state of connections, source, destination, and ports of all the network connections made from our computer. As mentioned earlier, these TCP metrics are used for the logical grouping of servers.

Once they are grouped, you can visualize the service map to understand the dependencies or you can export this as a CSV for your reference. The assessment tools include an Azure Migrate appliance, which is a VM that you need to deploy in your environment for discovery. This appliance will constantly gather data and push it to Azure for assessment.

Agent-based analysis

As the name suggests, we need an agent to perform the dependency analysis in the case of agent-based analysis. This method of analysis utilizes the Service Map feature of Azure Monitor. We need to install the **Microsoft Monitoring Agent** (**MMA**), which is essentially for Windows machines, or OMS Agent (in the case of Linux machines), as well as the dependency agent. The data sent by these agents will be used to create the service map.

We need a Log Analytics workspace to ingest the logs and data pushed by these agents. One thing to note here is that the workspace should be deployed in a region where Service Map is supported.

Unlike agentless analysis, since we have the data ingested to the workspace, we can use **Kusto Query Language** (**KQL**) to analyze this data.

When we move on to the hands-on exercise toward the end of this chapter, we will see how these agents are installed and are used for the dependency analysis. Dependency analysis can be very useful in the case of applications that have complex architectures. Next, we will talk about the Azure TCO calculator.

Azure TCO calculator

Total Cost of Ownership (**TCO**) is something every organization wishing to start their cloud adoption should consider. The **Return on Investment** (**ROI**) is evaluated using the TCO and the Azure TCO calculator helps in calculating the estimated cost of migration to Azure and forecasting your potential savings compared to your current costs.

It is recommended that you perform a TCO calculation before migrating to the cloud, and there are some charges that you should consider while estimating the total cost of ownership. These costs include:

- **Migration costs**: Migration is expensive and requires the utmost attention. Failures in migration can lead to potential loss. Hence, you should account for the costs incurred in terms of resources, technicians, and the other hardware procured for migration in your TCO.

- **Infrastructure costs**: You need to keep your on-premises infrastructure up and running until the migration is complete. At a certain stage during migration, you will be paying for the resources in the cloud as well as the on-premises datacenter. The changeover only happens once the migration is complete.

- **Risk factor**: Migration is not a simple task and there is always risk involved in this. If your application is not optimized for the cloud, or if you have not properly assessed your application prior to migration to the cloud, this could lead to potential failures. Examples include functionality and performance issues compared to the on-premises application. Once the resources are deployed in the cloud, you will be charged; if something goes wrong, you should have the budget to roll back the changes and perform a failover back to your on-premises application. As this is a calculated risk, we should include this in our TCO.

The Azure TCO calculator can be accessed from any browser by navigating to the following link: https://azure.microsoft.com/pricing/tco/calculator/.

The TCO calculation involves a three-step process, starting with defining your workloads. In this first step, you will be inputting the details of your on-premises workloads and this will be plotted against the cloud cost to understand the savings. These workloads are categorized into servers, databases, storage, and networking components. For each category, there will be a set of information that you need to pass to the TCO calculator. As an example, if we take **Servers**, we will be asked to input the OS type, OS, license, processors, cores, and RAM, as shown in *Figure 3.4*:

Define your workloads

Enter the details of your on-premises workloads. This information will be used to understand your current TCO and recommended services in Azure.

Servers

Enter the details of your on-premises server infrastructure. After adding a workload, select the workload type and enter the remaining details.

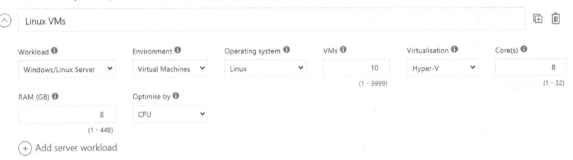

Figure 3.4: Defining server workloads

After defining your workloads, you will reach the **Adjust assumptions** step. Here, we are going to share details about whether you already have licenses for these machines, followed by storage costs, IT labor costs, electricity costs, and so on. You need to tune these assumptions as per your on-premises data.

Once you have stated the assumptions, the TCO calculator will give the potential savings based on the data you have shared. Here, for example, based on the workloads and assumptions, we are getting estimated cost savings of $18,472 over 1 year. *Figure 3.5* shows a sample output from the TCO calculator:

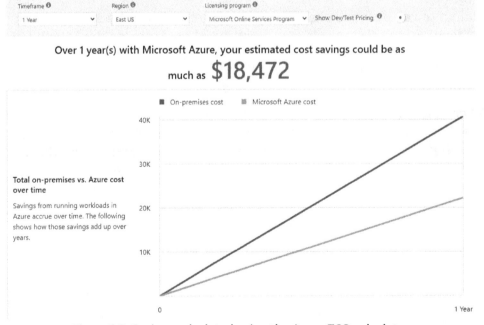

Figure 3.5: Savings calculated using the Azure TCO calculator

There are other graphs (category-wise breakdown) that are available in the TCO calculator and the best part is that you can download this report and it can be shared with stakeholders for review.

With that, we have covered the main tools that are used during the **Assess** phase shown in *Table 3.1*). As mentioned earlier, there are other tools that are used in other phases in the adoption plan. We will cover the **Migrate & Modernize** stage in *Chapter 4, Performing migration to Azure*, and the **Optimize** and **Secure & Manage** stages in *Chapter 5, Operating Linux on Azure*.

Now that we have gathered all the necessary details of our application and infrastructure, we are ready to create the migration project plan.

Hands-on assess lab

So far, we have discussed different planning strategies and assessment methodologies. In this hands-on lab, we are going to assess servers that are running in a Hyper-V environment. Here is the architecture of the environment that we are going to assess:

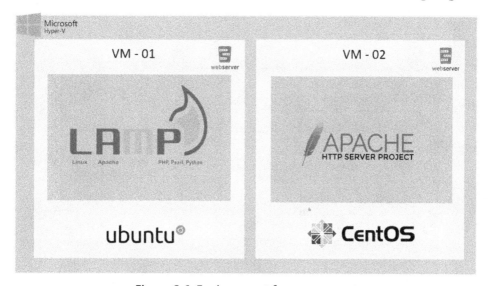

Figure 3.6: Environment for assessment

In *Figure* 3.6, we can have a Hyper-V host, and two VMs are deployed on it. One VM (**VM - 01**) runs Ubuntu and has a LAMP server set up on it. The second VM (**VM - 02**) is a CentOS VM that is running a static website using Apache Webserver.

Our goal is to assess this environment and create an assessment report along with a dependency analysis.

As mentioned earlier in *Assessing tooling* section, we need to create an Azure Migrate project to kick off the assessment process.

Prerequisites

Some of the prerequisites for this hands-on lab are as follows:

- You should have at least contributor permission on your Azure subscription.
- Users should have permissions to register Azure AD apps or else should have an application developer role in Azure AD.

Setting up the Azure Migrate project

The first step in using Azure Migrate starts with the creation of the Azure Migrate project. This service is used to store the metadata that is captured during the assessment and migration phases. The Azure Migrate project provides a centralized platform to keep a tab of all your assessments and migrations to Azure. Let's navigate to the Azure portal and create an Azure Migrate project:

1. To create an Azure Migrate project, navigate to **All services** in the Azure portal and search for **Azure Migrate**, as shown in *Figure 3.7*:

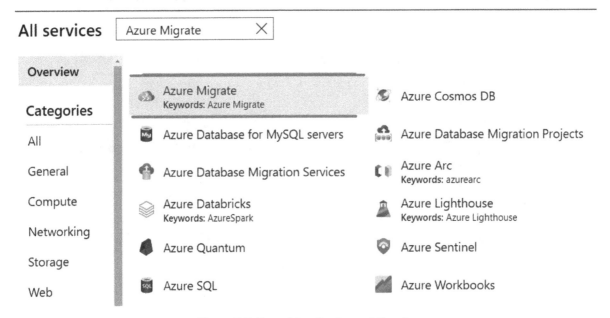

Figure 3.7: Searching for Azure Migrate

Once you are in the **Azure Migrate** blade, you will see different migration options for servers, databases, and so on.

2. Since we are assessing servers, you need to choose **Assess and migrate servers** or you can click on **Servers** from the **Azure Migrate** blade, as shown in *Figure 3.8*:

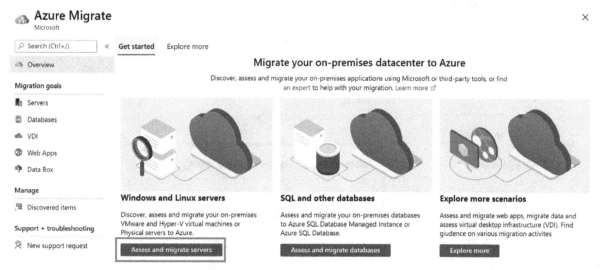

Figure 3.8: Starting the Azure Migrate project

3. In the next window, you will get the **Create project** option and, once selected, you need to input basic details such as **Subscription**, **Resource group**, **Migrate project**, and **Geography**, as shown in *Figure 3.9*:

Figure 3.9: Creating an Azure Migrate project

4. Once the project is created, we will be presented with the **Assessment tools** and **Migration tools** options for servers. Since we are currently in the Assess phase, we will explore **Assessment tools**, as shown in *Figure 3.10*:

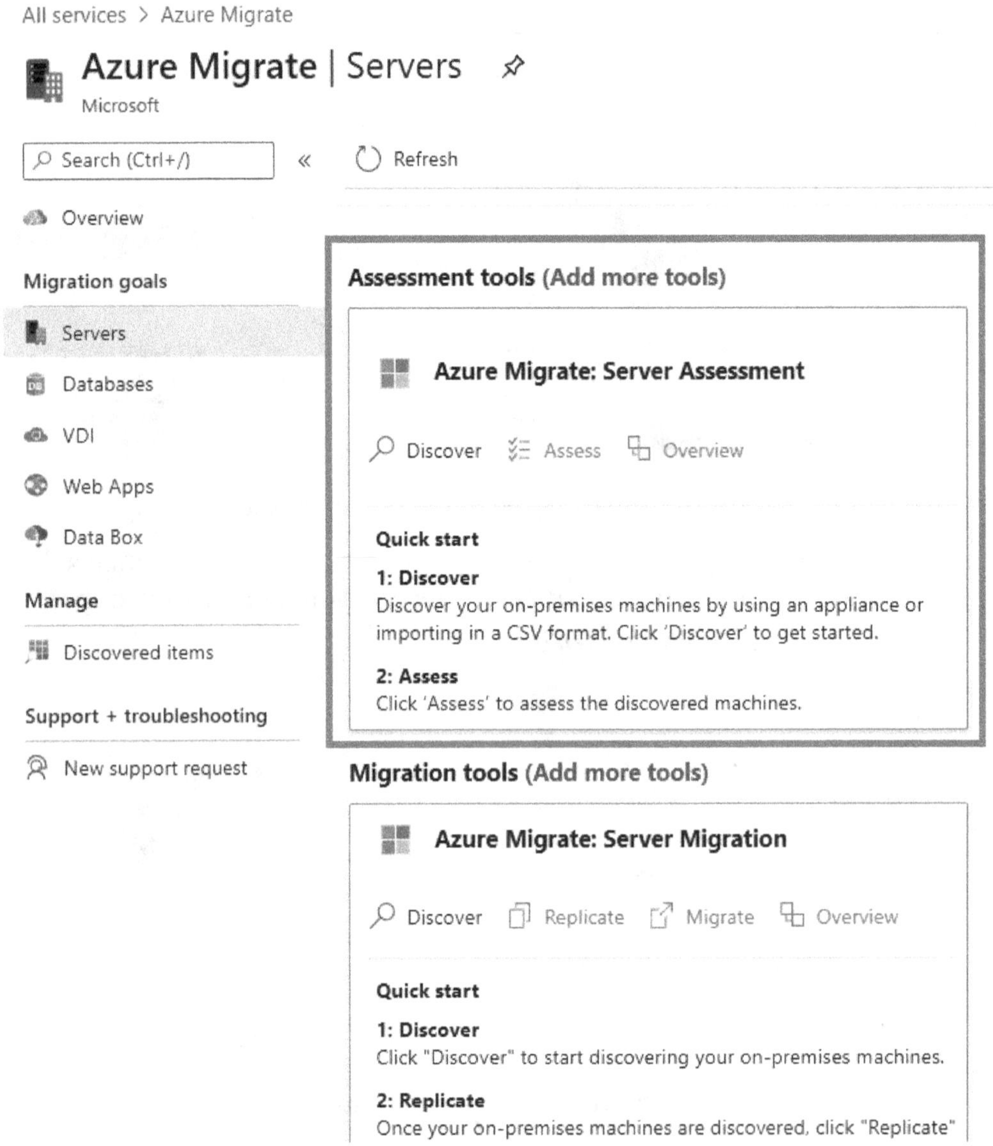

All services > Azure Migrate

Azure Migrate | Servers 📌
Microsoft

🔍 Search (Ctrl+/)   «   🔄 Refresh

🌥 Overview

Migration goals

📇 Servers

📇 Databases

🖥 VDI

🌐 Web Apps

📦 Data Box

Manage

📑 Discovered items

Support + troubleshooting

🧑 New support request

Assessment tools (Add more tools)

🔳 **Azure Migrate: Server Assessment**

🔍 Discover   📋 Assess   🔲 Overview

Quick start

1: Discover
Discover your on-premises machines by using an appliance or importing in a CSV format. Click 'Discover' to get started.

2: Assess
Click 'Assess' to assess the discovered machines.

Migration tools (Add more tools)

🔳 **Azure Migrate: Server Migration**

🔍 Discover   📄 Replicate   📤 Migrate   🔲 Overview

Quick start

1: Discover
Click "Discover" to start discovering your on-premises machines.

2: Replicate
Once your on-premises machines are discovered, click "Replicate"

Figure 3.10: Server Assessment tools

5. The next step is to initiate the discovery of servers in our Hyper-V environment so that we can create the assessment. We will be using the **Discover** option shown in *Figure 3.10* to start the discovery process.

   Now, we must select the platform where our servers are currently deployed. You will get an option to choose from VMWare vSphere Hypervisor, Hyper-V, and Physical or others (AWS, GCP, and so on). Since our VMs are deployed on Hyper-V, let's select this option, as shown in *Figure 3.11*.

   To run the discovery against our on-premises infrastructure, we need to deploy a new VM to our on-premises environment. This VM is called the **Azure Migrate appliance**, which will discover servers and send that information to Azure Migrate.

6. We need to give a name to the migrate appliance and generate a key, as shown in *Figure 3.11*. This key is later used to set up the migrate appliance on our Hyper-V host. You need to copy this key and keep this handy:

Figure 3.11: Generating the Azure Migrate project key

After creating the key, we need to download the Azure Migrate appliance. Basically, there are two ways in which to deploy the appliance, as shown in *Figure 3.11*.

You can download the VHD file and deploy it as a new VM in your Hyper-V environment or you can download a zip file that will contain the PowerShell scripts that can convert an existing VM to an Azure Migrate appliance. If you prefer to use an existing server as Migrate Appliance, Microsoft recommends using Windows Server 2016 with at least 8vCPUs and 16 GB of RAM.

In this hands-on lab, we will be downloading the VHD directly to our Hyper-V Host and creating a new VM. Using the VHD file, we need to create a new VM in our Hyper-V server using the following steps:

1. Open **Hyper-V Manager**, on the right-hand side. From **Actions**, select **Import Virtual Machine**.

2. You will get the **Before you begin** page with the set of instructions. Click **Next**.

3. Using the **Locate** folder, browse the folder where you have extracted the VHD and hit **Next**.

4. Select **Virtual Machine** and then click on **Next**.

5. Select **Copy the virtual machine (create a new unique ID)** as **Import type** and then hit **Next**.

6. Leave **Destination** and **Storage** as their default settings and then click **Next**.

7. Select the appropriate virtual switch that the VM will be using to connect to the network and click **Next**.

8. Finally, in the **Summary** page, review the configuration we selected and click **Finish** to initiate the VM import.

9. After a period of time, you'll be able to see the new VM in your **Hyper-V Manager**.

We now have our VM deployed in our environment. Now, it is time to start the discovery and send the information to the Azure Migrate project. Let's set up the appliance to push the data to Azure.

Setting up and registering the Azure Migrate appliance

The VM is deployed to the Hyper-V environment and now must configure it and connect to our Azure Migration project. We need to provide the password for the Windows Server and after that, we need to log in just like we do for any Windows server.

You can connect to the Migrate appliance by going to `https://appliance name` or IP `address:44368`. If you open the Edge browser on the desktop, you will be redirected to the **Appliance Configuration Manager** page. The next step is to register the appliance with the project, as outlined in the following steps:

1. We must agree to the terms and conditions to start using the Azure Migrate appliance.

2. The prerequisite check will be done automatically and if there is any new update, the system will install it automatically, as shown in *Figure 3.12*:

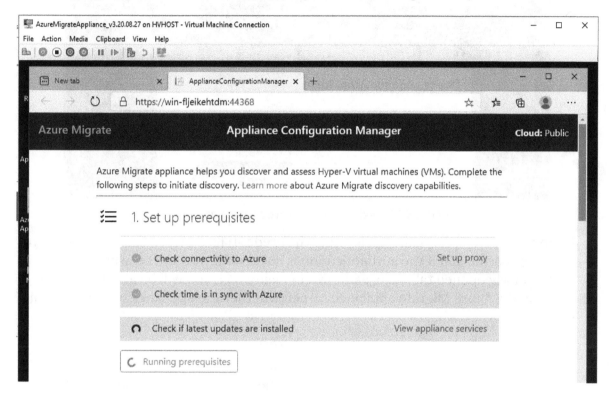

Figure 3.12: Prerequisite check in the Migrate appliance

3. The next step is to input the Migrate appliance key, which we generated from the Azure portal when we initiated the **Discover** process (*Figure 3.11*).

   The key needs to the entered into the textbox in order for the system to validate the key and register the appliance. Once the validation is done, you will be prompted with a device code to log in to Azure. We need to use **Copy code & Login** to authenticate with Azure, as shown in *Figure 3.13*:

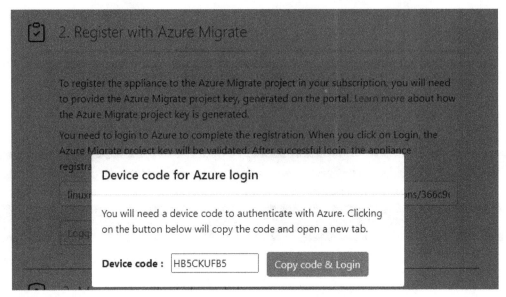

Figure 3.13: Registering an Azure Migrate appliance

4. In the new tab, you can sign in using the credentials that you use to sign into the Azure portal, and if the authentication is successful, you will be asked to close the newly opened tab. Also, as shown in *Figure 3.14*, you will be able to confirm from the Azure Migrate appliance screen whether the appliance was successful:

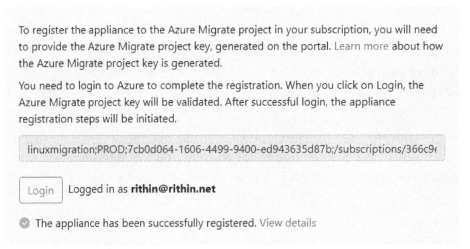

Figure 3.14: Successful registration

5. The next step is to provide the credentials for the Hyper-V cluster to the Azure Migrate appliance so that it can run **Discovery**. You can use **Add credentials** and enter the credentials for your Hyper-V host as shown in *Figure 3.15* and save it:

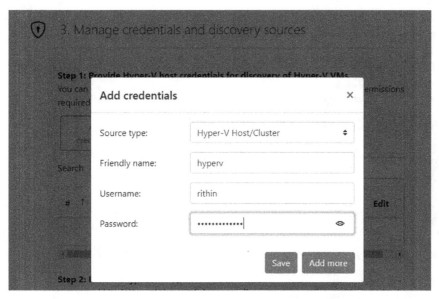

Figure 3.15: Adding Hyper-V credentials

6. Since we have stored the credentials, we will be using the credentials to connect to our Hyper-V host. You can add multiple Hyper-V clusters in a single shot, or you can import the list as a CSV. In our case, we have a single server, and we need to provide the IP address for the server and select the credentials created in *Step* 5, as shown in *Figure 3.16*:

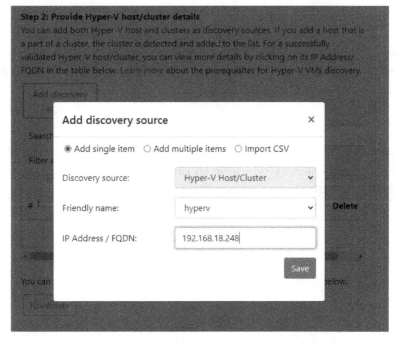

Figure 3.16: Adding Hyper-V cluster details

7. The Migrate appliance will use the credentials against the IP address we have entered to perform validation. If the credentials are correct, you will be able to see the successful message, as shown in *Figure 3.17*:

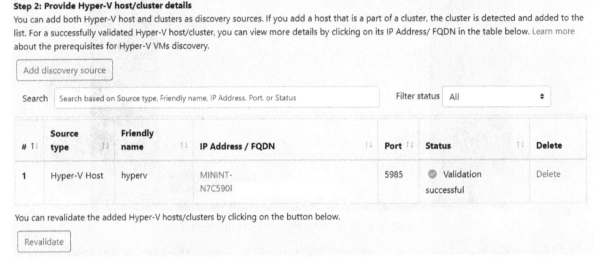

Step 2: Provide Hyper-V host/cluster details

You can add both Hyper-V host and clusters as discovery sources. If you add a host that is a part of a cluster, the cluster is detected and added to the list. For a successfully validated Hyper-V host/cluster, you can view more details by clicking on its IP Address/ FQDN in the table below. Learn more about the prerequisites for Hyper-V VMs discovery.

Add discovery source

Search	Search based on Source type, Friendly name, IP Address, Port, or Status			Filter status	All	

# ⇅	Source type ⇅	Friendly name ⇅	IP Address / FQDN ⇅	Port ⇅	Status ⇅	Delete
1	Hyper-V Host	hyperv	MININT-N7C590I	5985	● Validation successful	Delete

You can revalidate the added Hyper-V hosts/clusters by clicking on the button below.

Revalidate

Figure 3.17: Successful connection to the host

8. Now that we have completed the configuration of the appliance, we can start the discovery using the **Start Discovery** option. The discovery process may take some time and the discovered number will be reflected on the Azure portal.

> **Note**
>
> Since the appliance uses the FQDN for connection, if the name of the host cannot be resolved by DNS, you will not be able to discover any VMs and the revalidation would fail. The workaround is to modify the host file and add the FQDN and IP address.

The next step in our process is to verify from the Azure portal whether the discovery was successful and the appliance was able to discover all the VMs. In the following section, we will see how the discovery can be verified from the portal.

Verifying discovered VMs in the portal

Once the discovery process is complete, you will be able to see the confirmation from the Migrate appliance. Now, it is time to check in the portal to see whether the appliance was able to push the information to our Azure Migrate project. You can verify this using the steps mentioned here:

1. Open the **Azure Migrate** dashboard.

2. In **Azure Migrate | Servers | Azure Migrate: Server Assessment** page, click the icon that displays the count for **Discovered servers**.

In *Figure 3.18*, you can see that discovery was successful and the Azure portal indicates that three VMs have been discovered:

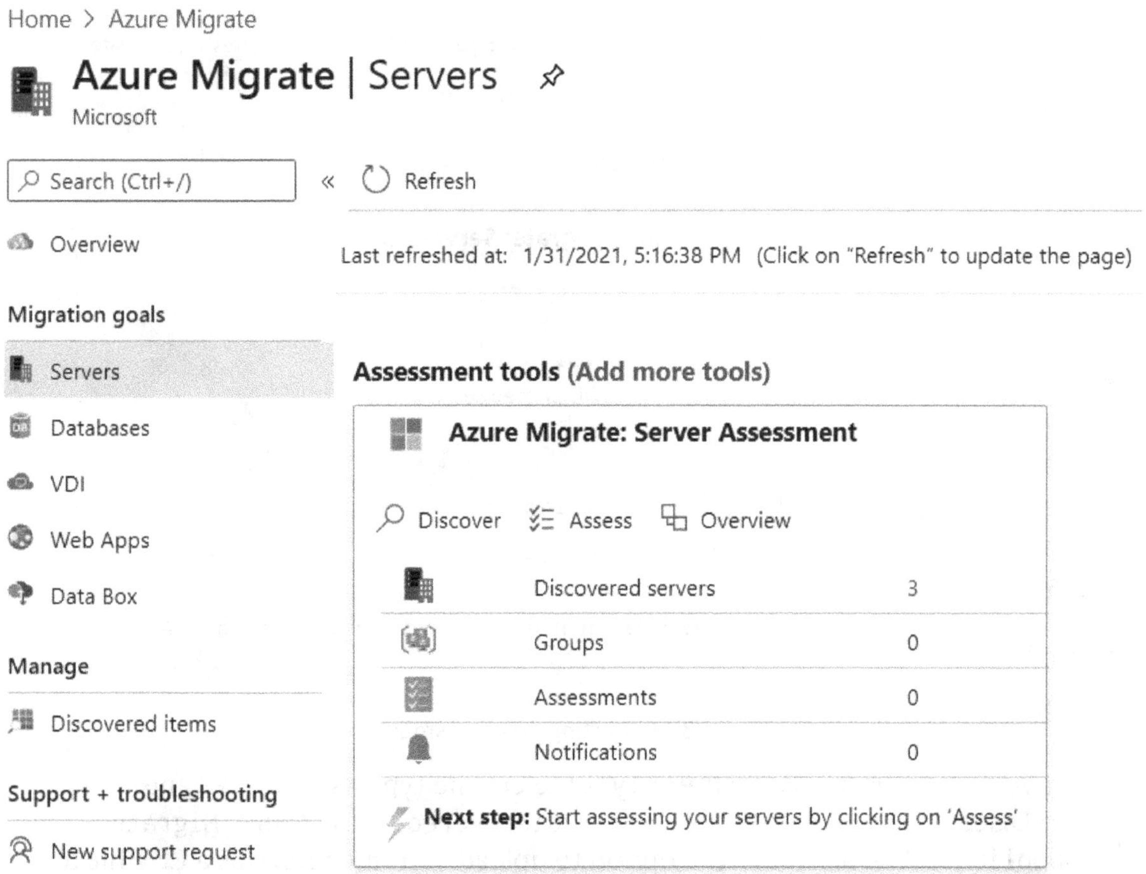

Home > Azure Migrate

Azure Migrate | Servers 📌
Microsoft

🔍 Search (Ctrl+/)	«	🔄 Refresh

☁ Overview

Last refreshed at: 1/31/2021, 5:16:38 PM (Click on "Refresh" to update the page)

Migration goals

🏢 Servers

🗄 Databases

💻 VDI

🌐 Web Apps

📦 Data Box

Manage

▤ Discovered items

Support + troubleshooting

☒ New support request

Assessment tools (Add more tools)

Azure Migrate: Server Assessment

🔍 Discover ⌯≡ Assess   ⊞ Overview

🏢	Discovered servers	3
(▦)	Groups	0
✓	Assessments	0
🔔	Notifications	0

Next step: Start assessing your servers by clicking on 'Assess'

Figure 3.18: Verifying discovered servers

Here, we see three VMs because the discovery process included the Migrate appliance as well. The next process is to run the assessment on the discovered servers, and this can be done by clicking on the **Assess** option next to **Discover**.

Running an assessment

As mentioned in the *Migration Assessment* section, the assessment creates the inventory of your on-premises servers. Run an assessment as follows:

1. Select the **Assess** option from **Azure Migrate: Server Assessment**, as shown in *Figure 3.19*:

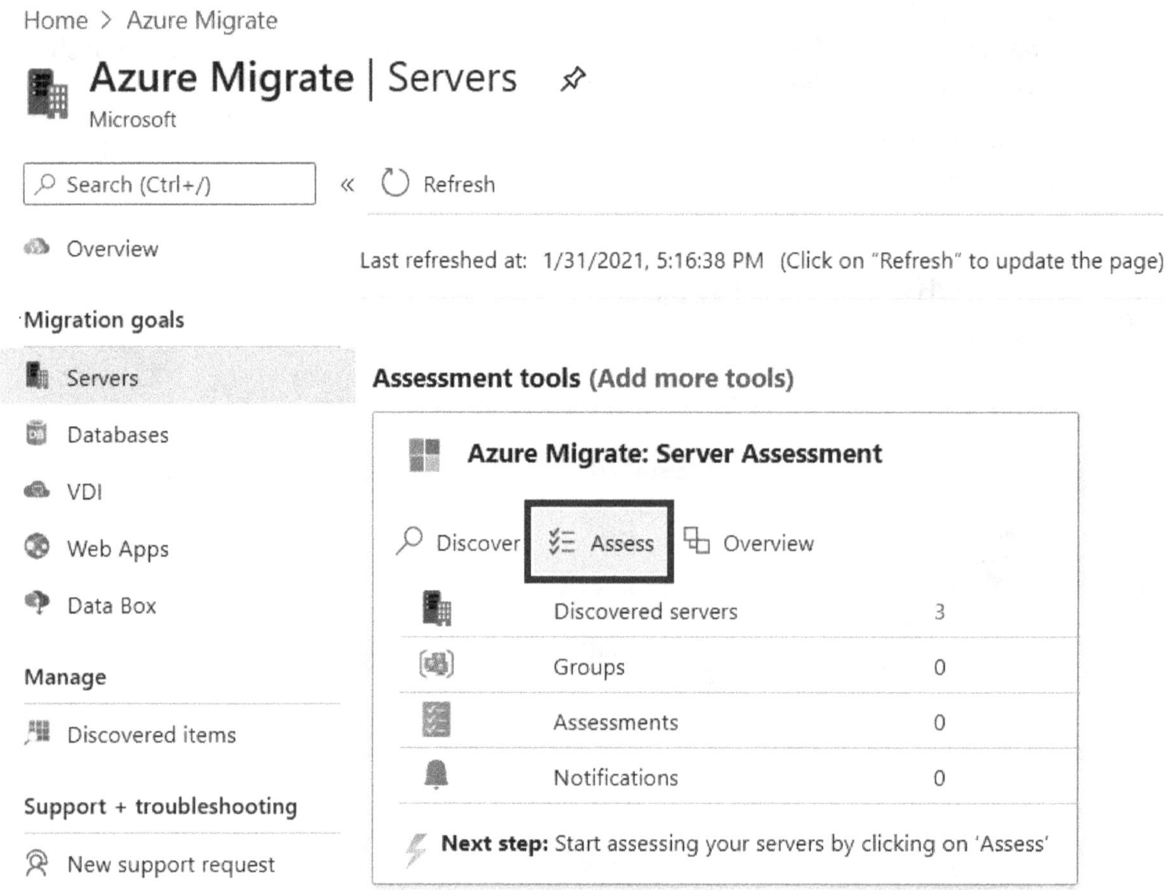

Home > Azure Migrate

Azure Migrate | Servers 📌
Microsoft

🔍 Search (Ctrl+/)   «   ○ Refresh

☁ Overview   Last refreshed at: 1/31/2021, 5:16:38 PM (Click on "Refresh" to update the page)

Migration goals

📇	Servers

🗄	Databases

☁	VDI

🌐	Web Apps

📦	Data Box

Manage

🗄 Discovered items

Support + troubleshooting

🙋 New support request

Assessment tools (Add more tools)

▮▮ **Azure Migrate: Server Assessment**

🔍 Discover   ▤ Assess   ⊞ Overview

📇	Discovered servers	3
📇	Groups	0
☑	Assessments	0
🔔	Notifications	0

⚡ **Next step:** Start assessing your servers by clicking on 'Assess'

Figure 3.19: Starting an assessment

2. In **Assess servers | Assessment Type**, select the type as Azure VM and, in **Discovery source**, select Machines discovered from Azure Migrate appliance. You also have the option to upload your inventory as a CSV file and perform an assessment on that. The **Assessment properties** section will be populated automatically, and you can edit them using the **Edit** button if required, as shown in *Figure 3.20*:

Home > Azure Migrate >

Assess servers

Basics   Select machines to assess   Review + create assessment

An assessment is created on a group of machines that you migrate together. Assessment helps you determine Azure readiness of your physical Migrate appliance as well as the machines imported into Azure Migrate. Learn more.

Assessment details

Assessment type * ⓘ

| Azure VM | ∨ |

 ⓦ Help me choose

Discovery source * ⓘ

| Machines discovered from Azure Migrate appliance | ∨ |

Assessment properties   (Showing 4 of 14)   [Edit]

Sizing criterion   Performance-based
Target location   West US 2
Reserved instances   3 years reserved
Azure Hybrid Benefit   Yes

[< Previous]   [Next >]

Figure 3.20: Setting up the basics

3.   In the **Assessment properties** edit window, you will have the option to customize **TARGET PROPERTIES, VM SIZE,** and **PRICING**. These factors are used to run the assessment and generate the report. Also, you can include the Azure Hybrid Benefit in your calculation to exclude the license cost if you already have licenses purchased. You can update each of these factors as per your requirements. A sample configuration has been shown in *Figure 3.21*:

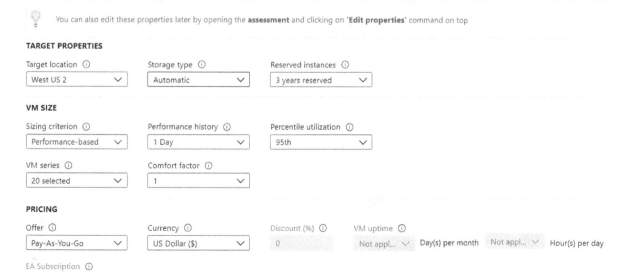

Home > Azure Migrate > Assess servers >

Assessment properties

ⓦ You can also edit these properties later by opening the **assessment** and clicking on '**Edit properties**' command on top

TARGET PROPERTIES

Target location ⓘ

| West US 2 | ∨ |

Storage type ⓘ

| Automatic | ∨ |

Reserved instances ⓘ

| 3 years reserved | ∨ |

VM SIZE

Sizing criterion ⓘ

| Performance-based | ∨ |

Performance history ⓘ

| 1 Day | ∨ |

Percentile utilization ⓘ

| 95th | ∨ |

VM series ⓘ

| 20 selected | ∨ |

Comfort factor ⓘ

| 1 | ∨ |

PRICING

Offer ⓘ

| Pay-As-You-Go | ∨ |

Currency ⓘ

| US Dollar ($) | ∨ |

Discount (%) ⓘ

| 0 |

VM uptime ⓘ

| Not appl... ∨ | Day(s) per month | Not appl... ∨ | Hour(s) per day

EA Subscription ⓘ

Figure 3.21: Assessment properties

4. Next, you can provide a name for your assessment and a name for the group of servers. Grouping helps you to assess a set of servers together. Finally, we will select the servers that need to be assigned and add them to the group, as shown in *Figure 3.22*:

Figure 3.22: Selecting servers to assess

5. The final step is to create the assessment, which will create the group and run the assessment on the grouped servers.

If you refresh **Assessment tools**, you can see that **Groups** and **Assessments** have the value of **1**, as visible in *Figure 3.23*:

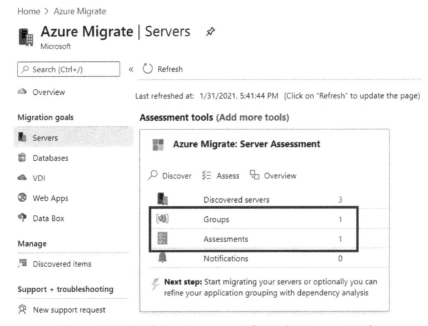

Figure 3.23: Verifying assessment from the Azure portal

> **Note**
>
> If the data is not visible, try using the **Refresh** button and wait for the system to refresh.

Now we have the assessment, and it is time to review it.

Reviewing the assessment

An assessment primarily talks about three main factors:

- **Azure readiness**: Whether the discovered machines are suitable to run on Azure – in other words, are they ready for Azure?
- **Monthly cost estimate**: Provides the estimated cost required to run these VMs on Azure once they are migrated. The cost breakdown is also provided in terms of what the cost for compute and the cost for storage would be.
- **Storage – Monthly cost estimate**: Estimated disk storage costs following migration.

These are the steps involved in viewing an assessment:

1. In **Servers | Azure Migrate: Server Assessment**, click the number next to **Assessments** visible in *Figure 3.23*.

2. In **Assessments**, select an assessment to open it. You will be able to see the assessment report as shown in *Figure 3.24*:

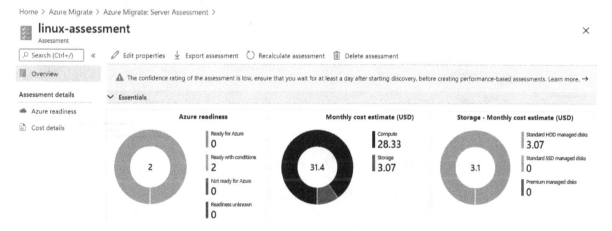

Figure 3.24: Reviewing an assessment

3. If you would like to recalculate based on another target region or any other properties, you can edit the properties (using the **Edit properties** option as shown in *Figure 3.24*) and re-run the assessment.

Here, we have only discovered the VMs; however, we have not performed a dependency analysis. This assessment report can be exported to an Excel sheet and you can share it with the stakeholders.

In the next section, we will see how to use the agents to set up the dependency analysis in Azure Migrate.

Dependency analysis

Dependency analysis is only supported for VMWare VMs and Hyper V VMs. VMs discovered from other platforms such as Xen, or even from other cloud providers such as AWS and GCP, do not support dependency analysis.

As mentioned in the *Service Map* section, we can only run the agent-based dependency analysis on the Hyper V environment. In the case of VMWare VMs, it supports both agentless and agent-based dependency analysis.

To start with the analysis, we need to associate a Log Analytics workspace with our Azure Migrate project. The following steps can be performed to associate the workspace with **Azure Migrate: Server Assessment**:

1. Once you have discovered the machines for assessment, in **Servers | Azure Migrate: Server Assessment**, click **Overview**.

2. In **Azure Migrate: Server Assessment**, click **Essentials**.

3. In **OMS Workspace**, click **Requires configuration**, as shown in *Figure 3.25*:

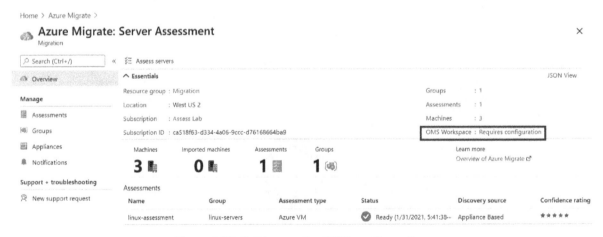

Figure 3.25: Setting up the OMS configuration

4. Once you select **Requires configuration**, as shown in *Figure 3.25*, you will be prompted to create a new Log Analytics workspace or associate an existing one in your Azure subscription.

5. If you do not have an existing workspace, create a new one as shown in *Figure 3.26*:

Figure 3.26: Creating a Log Analytics workspace

6. The next step is to download and install the agents for dependency visualization. For this, we need to navigate to **Discovered servers** and check the **Dependencies (Agent-based)** column. Sometimes, this column will be hidden, and you can enable it using the **Columns** option.

7. We will select **Requires agent installation** against our discovered VM, as shown in *Figure 3.27*, to install the agents. For ease of demonstration, let's install the agents on the LAMP server:

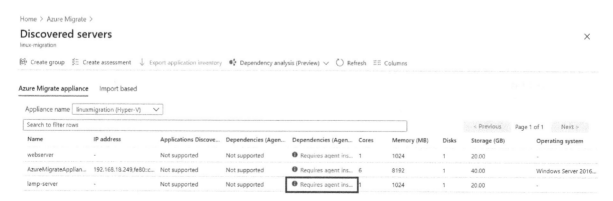

Figure 3.27: Selecting agent installation

8. The portal will give you the steps to install the agents on both Windows and Linux servers. We are interested in the Linux servers, and so will follow that process. Also, we need to make a note of **Workspace ID** and **Workspace key**, shown in *Figure 3.28*. This is required in order to configure the agent:

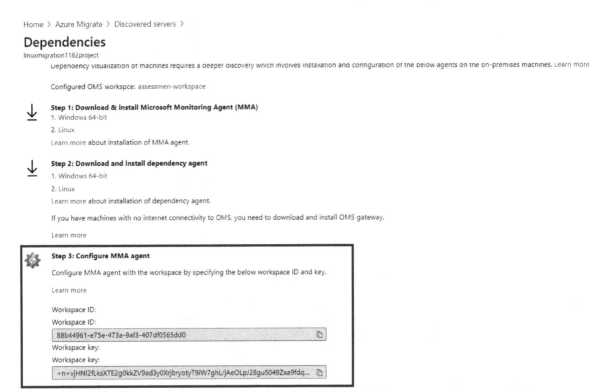

Figure 3.28: Workspace information

9. You can either download it in Linux using the wget command, or download it to your computer and transfer it to a Linux machine using SFTP/SCP. Let's download it using wget and configure the agents on the Linux server.

10. You can copy the link for the agents from the portal and pass that to wget to download the file, as shown in *Figure 3.29*:

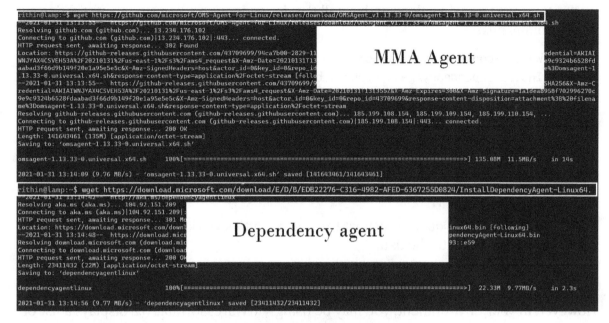

Figure 3.29: Downloading agents

11. The MMA agent can be installed using the following command:

```
sudo wget https://raw.githubusercontent.com/Microsoft/OMS-Agent-for-Linux/
master/installer/scripts/onboard_agent.sh && sh onboard_agent.sh -w <YOUR
WORKSPACE ID> -s <YOUR WORKSPACE PRIMARY KEY>
```

workspace id and workspace key can be obtained from the Azure portal, as shown in *Figure 3.28*. At the time of writing this book, the latest version for the MMA agent is 1.13.33-0 and we install this as shown in *Figure 3.30*:

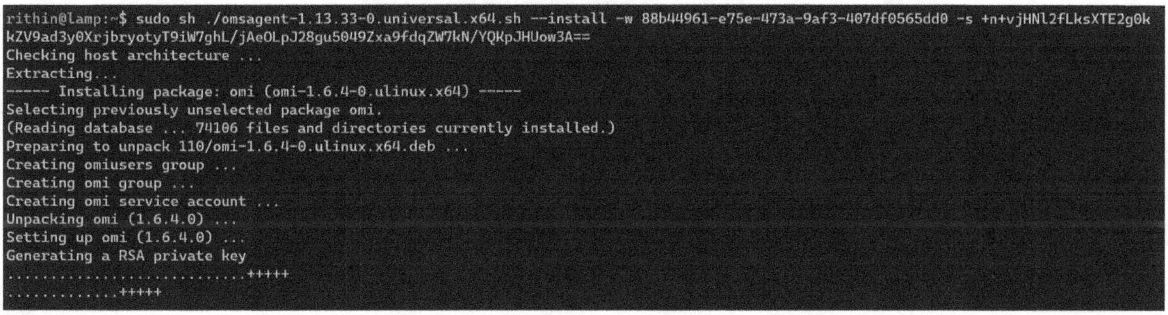

Figure 3.30: Installing the MMA agent

12. Now, we must download and install the dependency agent using the following commands:

```
wget --content-disposition https://aka.ms/dependencyagentlinux -O
InstallDependencyAgent-Linux64.bin

sh InstallDependencyAgent-Linux64.bin
```

13. Once the dependency agent is installed, we will be able to see the dependencies from **Azure Migrate: Server Assessment**. Click **Discovered servers**. In the **Dependencies** column, click **View dependencies** to view the dependencies for the server. It's expected to take some time to load the dependencies.

You can also run Kusto queries against the Log Analytics workspace to review the connections and validate the data.

With that, we have successfully assessed the workloads that are deployed in the Hyper-V host and set up dependency analysis. We have used Hyper-V for a demo. However, in your environment, you may be using VMWare, so *Table 3.2* displays a list of links that can be used to assess other environments, along with the documentation for Hyper-V:

Platform	Discover	Assess
Hyper-V	https://docs.microsoft.com/azure/migrate/tutorial-discover-hyper-v	https://docs.microsoft.com/azure/migrate/tutorial-assess-hyper-v
VMWare	https://docs.microsoft.com/azure/migrate/tutorial-discover-vmware	https://docs.microsoft.com/azure/migrate/tutorial-assess-vmware-azure-vm
Physical Servers	https://docs.microsoft.com/azure/migrate/tutorial-discover-physical	https://docs.microsoft.com/azure/migrate/tutorial-assess-physical
AWS	https://docs.microsoft.com/azure/migrate/tutorial-discover-aws	https://docs.microsoft.com/azure/migrate/tutorial-assess-aws
GCP	https://docs.microsoft.com/azure/migrate/tutorial-discover-gcp	https://docs.microsoft.com/azure/migrate/tutorial-assess-gcp
Import CSV	N/A	https://docs.microsoft.com/azure/migrate/tutorial-discover-import

Table 3.2: Assessment documentation for other platforms

The rationale behind this hands-on lab was to give you an idea of the steps and familiarize you with the process. Before we conclude this chapter, let's quickly go through a quick summary of the topics we have discussed so far.

Summary

Assessing the current architecture and workloads is a very important part of a migration project, as we learned in this chapter. For this, we used Azure Migrate to create a solid assessment report. We also discussed tools for calculating cost savings on Azure and went through a hands-on lab for a migration assessment.

In this chapter, we also discussed some of the popular workloads on Linux, including the LAMP stack and database servers. We also covered some of the more technically difficult scenarios regarding high-performance computing, clustering, shared storage, and SAP applications.

In the *Pre-project preparations* section, the importance of involving the right project team members was also covered as this ensures that you have all the necessary skills, including networking and Linux administration, for your migration project.

The next chapter will focus on practical migration, and you will have the opportunity to use everything learned so far in a hands-on lab.

4

Performing migration to Azure

This chapter outlines how to execute a real migration project based on the workload assessment done in the previous chapter. We have created two hands-on labs to show you how real-life migrations can be implemented.

The first hands-on lab gives you practical examples of how to migrate Linux servers from a Hyper-V host to Azure using Azure Migrate. The second lab guides you through migrating a MySQL server to Azure using Azure **Database Migration Service (DMS)**.

Executing migrations in real life is not always as easy as it sounds. Most problems we have seen are fortunately not actually technology-related, but more about planning and project management. If you apply the lessons of this book to your projects, you will be able to avoid the same pitfalls.

For example, one specific migration project we know of was originally planned to take a couple of months and it had about 500 virtual servers to migrate to Azure. The project turned out to be a bit more complex than originally planned. Some problems on the project started right after the project kickoff. The team in charge of the migration had severely underestimated the resources and skills required in the project. Eventually, the project scope was shrunk, and external cloud specialists were invited to advise on some of the most difficult parts of the project. It is no surprise that some of those parts were related to Linux patch management, subscription management, and security. Do you remember that we talked about these topics earlier in this book? Now you know why.

The project schedule got quite a few extensions and the project took much longer than originally planned. During the project, the customer also decided not to migrate some of the older applications, and instead decided to start to develop new cloud-native versions of those applications. From the migration project's point of view, this caused some major challenges in project scheduling. In the previous chapter, we talked about the importance of assessments and quality project planning for a good reason.

Why was the project unsuccessful? The project team didn't use any migration assessment tooling and they also lacked a proper migration execution tool. Additionally, they had little experience managing projects like this, and they also lacked expertise in cloud migrations and some of the workloads to be migrated.

Even after successful migration to Azure, there can be unexpected issues due to the wrong configuration or human error. You can reach out to Microsoft Azure support in the event of issues like virtual machine booting problems, remote SSH access not working, and so on. In *Chapter 6, Troubleshooting and problem solving*, we will talk more about possible problems and troubleshooting scenarios and also about how they can be resolved.

We have mentioned it already a couple of times in this book, but since it is such important advice, let's say it again: a key element to a successful migration project is ensuring that your customer—be they internal or external—is committed to the project. The second piece of advice we want to repeat is to use the right tools to help you with migration. In the previous chapter, we covered Azure Migrate for running successful assessments, so we can be quite sure the project team has the correct facts about the workloads to be migrated.

In this chapter, we will cover the following topics:

- Hands-on migration lab
  - Migrating servers to Azure
  - Migrating databases

By the end of the chapter, you will have learned how to use the right tools the right way.

Hands-on migration lab

In the *Hands-on assess lab* section of *Chapter 3, Assessment and migration planning*, we saw how the assessment of workloads and dependency analysis are done. These are vital steps in the migration framework and we're currently in the *Migrate* phase. We have two sections in this lab. The first part deals with the migration of servers, where we're going to migrate one of our LAMP servers to the cloud and verify that the site is working as expected. In the second scenario, we are migrating a MySQL database on Linux to an Azure MySQL managed database. In the first, we are migrating from IaaS to IaaS, whereas in the second, we're migrating from IaaS to a PaaS solution. Let's get started with the migration of the servers.

Migrating servers to Azure

As explained earlier, the Azure Migrate service is tooling for both the *Assess* phase and the *Migrate* phase. In the *Assess* phase, we rely on the Server Assessment tools, and in the *Migrate* phase, we focus on the server migration tools. If you're following along, you can use the same migration project from the assessment hands-on lab from *Chapter 3, Assessment and migration planning*. Otherwise, you can create a new one.

In this phase, your **virtual machine (VM)** will get replicated to the cloud, and later this replicated disk is used to spin up a VM. It is pretty much similar to how we set up cross-region failover in Azure Site Recovery. Azure Migrate uses Site Recovery in the back end to accomplish the migration process, where your servers are constantly replicated to the Site Recovery vault.

Figure 4.1 shows the servers we're going to migrate to Azure:

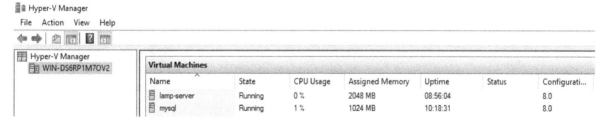

Figure 4.1: VMs in Hyper-V

The LAMP server will be used to demonstrate server migration using Azure Migrate and the MySQL VM will be migrated using DMS. You could deploy a LAMP application from GitHub—there are many repos that have files for a simple LAMP server. The one used in the demo is cloned from https://github.com/Anirban2404/phpMySQLapp. The LAMP installation is covered in the GitHub repo.

We'll break down the process into various stages, starting with the installation of providers, all the way to cutover.

Installing the providers

In the case of assessment, we deployed an Azure Migrate appliance on our on-premises Hyper-V server for sending the discovered data to the cloud. Similarly, in the *Migrate* phase, we'll be installing some software providers on our Hyper-V server, namely a Site Recovery provider and a Microsoft Azure Recovery Services agent. The Migrate appliance that we deployed during the assessment stage has no role in server migration—the purpose of that server was to discover the on-premises VMs and create an inventory. The following steps can be used to install the providers:

1. Navigate to the **Azure Migrate** project | **Servers**, and under **Azure Migrate: Server Migration** click on **Discover**, as shown in *Figure 4.2*:

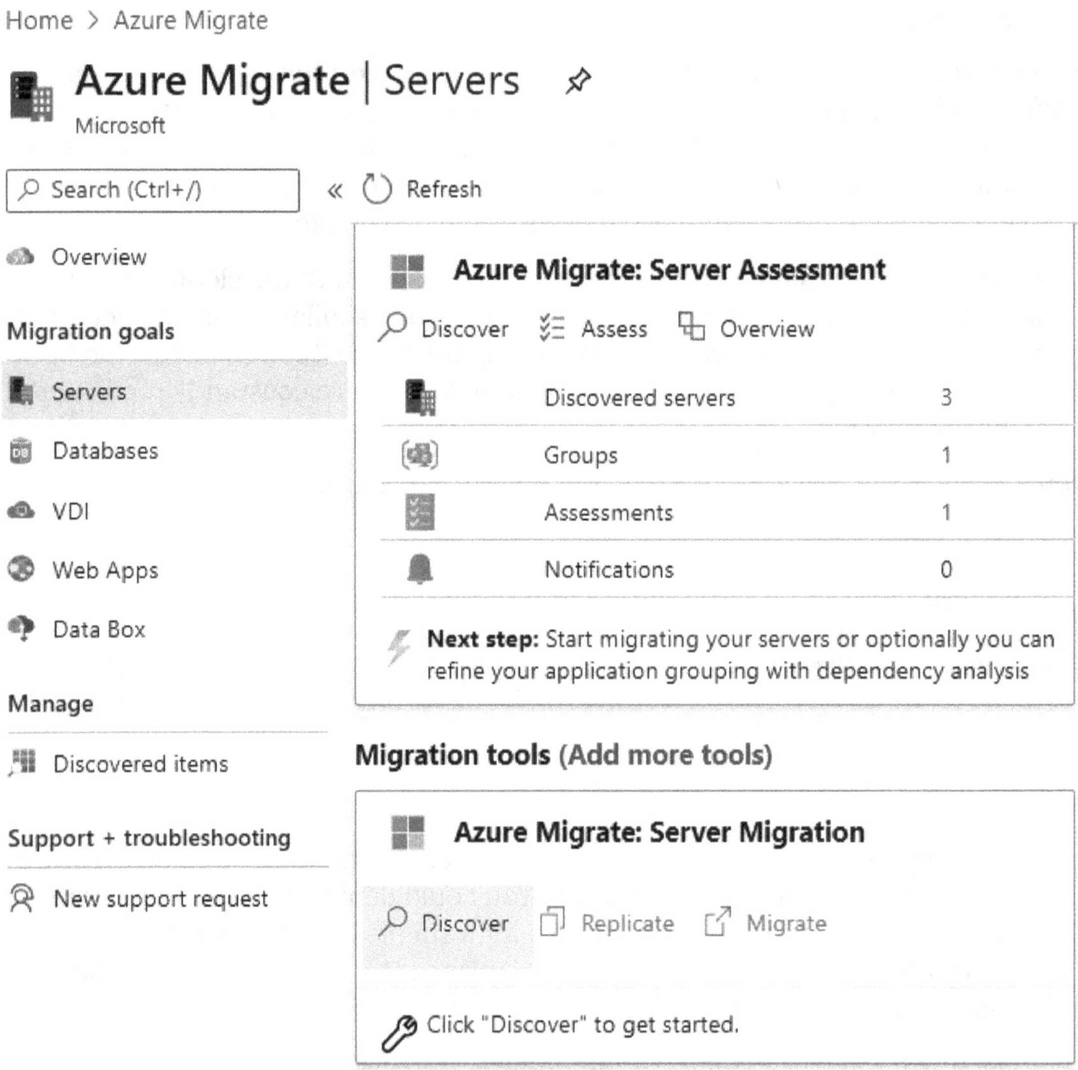

Home > Azure Migrate

Azure Migrate | Servers 📌
Microsoft

| 🔍 Search (Ctrl+/) | « ⟳ Refresh |

| **Overview** | |

Migration goals

📋 Servers	
🗄 Databases	
☁ VDI	
🌐 Web Apps	
📦 Data Box	

Azure Migrate: Server Assessment

🔍 Discover ☰ Assess ⧉ Overview

Discovered servers	3
Groups	1
Assessments	1
Notifications	0

⚡ **Next step:** Start migrating your servers or optionally you can refine your application grouping with dependency analysis

Manage

| 📑 Discovered items | |

Support + troubleshooting

| 👤 New support request | |

Migration tools (Add more tools)

Azure Migrate: Server Migration

🔍 Discover ☐ Replicate ↗ Migrate

🔧 Click "Discover" to get started.

Figure 4.2: Navigating to Migration tools

In *Figure 4.2*, you can see the server assessment tools, the results from the previous lab, and the migration tools that we're going to use in this lab.

2. Once we click on **Discover**, we'll be asked to confirm the platform where our servers are deployed. We will select **Yes, with Hyper-V** as shown in *Figure 4.3*. Along with that, we'll set **Target region**. This is the region where your server will be deployed post-migration. One thing to keep in mind here is that once **Target region** is confirmed, it cannot be changed for the project. Azure will show a banner with the same content and you have to agree to this condition by checking the checkbox. After that, we can click on **Create resources** and the Site Recovery vault gets created behind the scenes:

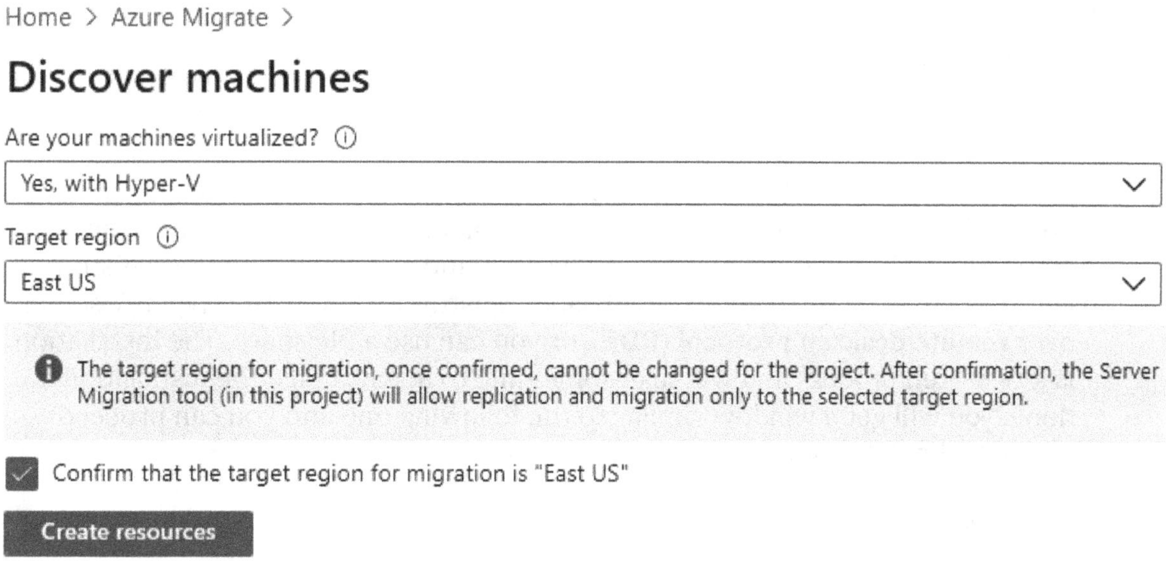

Home > Azure Migrate >

Discover machines

Are your machines virtualized? ⓘ

| Yes, with Hyper-V   ⌄ |

Target region ⓘ

| East US   ⌄ |

ⓘ The target region for migration, once confirmed, cannot be changed for the project. After confirmation, the Server Migration tool (in this project) will allow replication and migration only to the selected target region.

☑ Confirm that the target region for migration is "East US"

Create resources

Figure 4.3: Confirming the target region and creating resources

3. Azure provides very intuitive steps to complete the replication, starting with the installation of the replication provider software on our Hyper-V server. Steps will be prompted to you as shown in *Figure 4.4*:

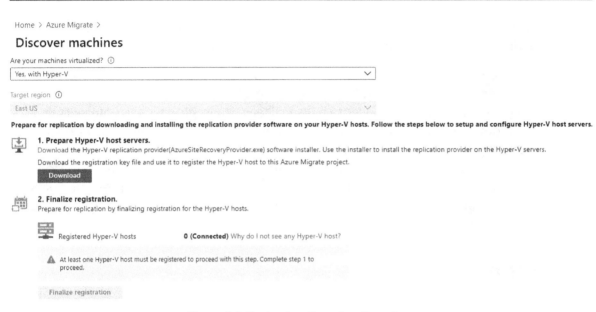

Figure 4.4: Reviewing the migration steps

4. We'll follow the steps in *Figure 4.4*. Let's download the Site Recovery provider software and install it on our Hyper-V server, and also download the registration key. You can copy the installation file and registration key to the Hyper-V server over **remote desktop protocol** (**RDP**), or you can use a file share. The installation is a two-step process and will take some time to install. Once the installation is done, you will get a window similar to the following one and you can proceed using the **Register** button, not the **Finish** button:

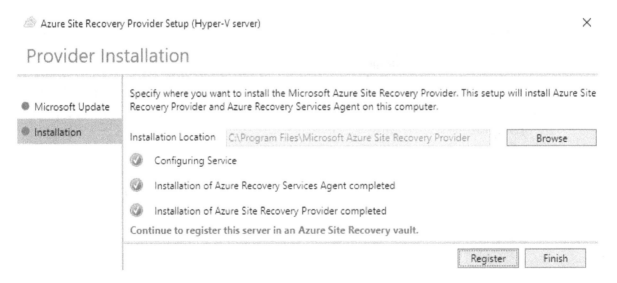

Figure 4.5: Installing the Site Recovery provider

5. It's time to use the registration key that we copied earlier. Click on the **Register** button shown in *Figure 4.5*. On the next screen, you will be asked to choose the registration key and the rest of the details are auto-filled, as shown in *Figure 4.6*. Proceed by clicking on the **Next** button:

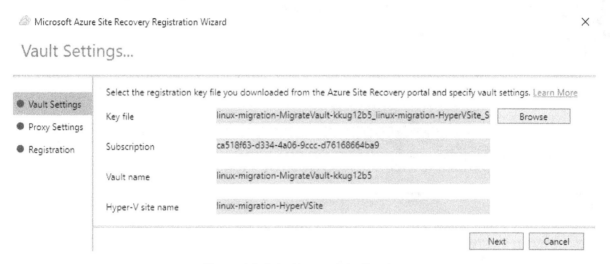

Figure 4.6: Selecting registration key

6. You don't have to configure to connect using a proxy—let the server directly connect to Site Recovery without a proxy server. Hit **Next** and continue with the registration process.

7. The last stage is **Registration**, which will take some time. Once the registration is done, the window will prompt as shown in *Figure 4.7*:

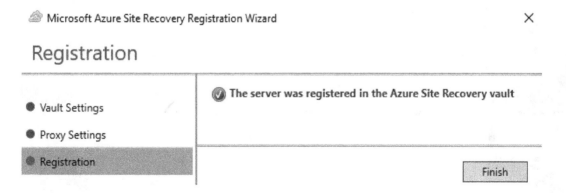

Figure 4.7: Completing registration

8. Now we need to go back to the Azure portal and reopen the project to finalize the registration. If the connection was successful, you will see the registered Hyper-V host under **2. Finalize registration**. Click on the **Finalize registration** button as shown in *Figure 4.8*. If you are not able to see the host as registered, follow the troubleshooting guide provided by Azure on the same page:

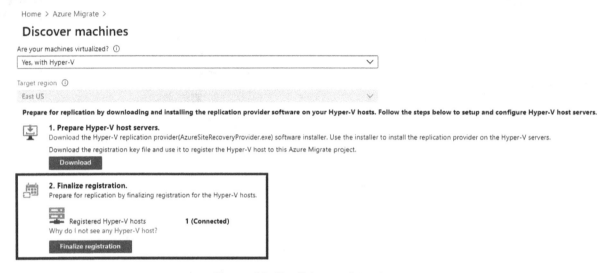

Figure 4.8: Finalizing registration

9. You will get a message on the screen to say that the registration may take around 15 minutes to complete. We need to wait for this process to complete before we replicate our machines to Azure. Once the process is complete, you will get a **Registration finalized** message, as shown in *Figure 4.9*:

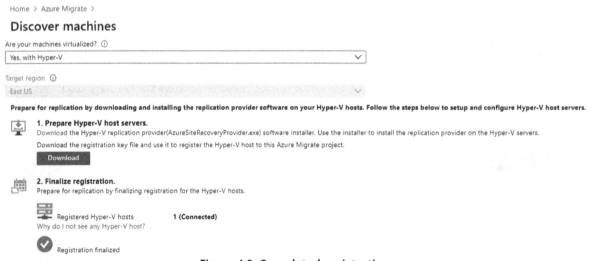

Figure 4.9: Completed registration

Let's take a look at how to discover the servers that are available to be migrated.

Discovering servers

Our Hyper-V server is configured with the providers, and we need to make sure that our Azure Migrate project discovered the VMs. Let's head back to the Azure Migrate landing page and refresh the toolset. As shown in *Figure 4.10*, you will be able to see that the migration tool discovered two VMs:

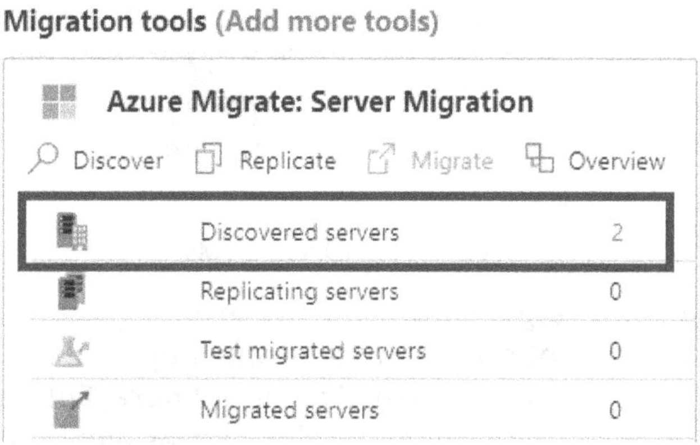

Migration tools (Add more tools)

Figure 4.10: Discovered servers

We can see that our VMs were discovered by the Azure Migrate project and we're ready to replicate these discovered servers.

Replicating servers

As *Figure 4.10* displays, the next step is to replicate our servers to Azure. For that, you need to click on the **Replicate** option next to **Discover**. As a side note, you need to have certain resources created before we replicate, else you may need to restart the replication process. So, it's better to have your resource group, virtual network, and replication storage account created before starting the replication:

1. Replication is a five-step process, and we'll start with **Source settings**. Here you'll select the virtualization platform or your source as **Hyper-V**.

2. In the second step, you have to select the VMs that you are migrating to the cloud. You could use the results of an assessment and migrate, or you can specify the migration settings manually. For demonstration purposes and to explain the steps, let's go with the manual option. Select the VMs and hit **Next** as shown in *Figure 4.11*:

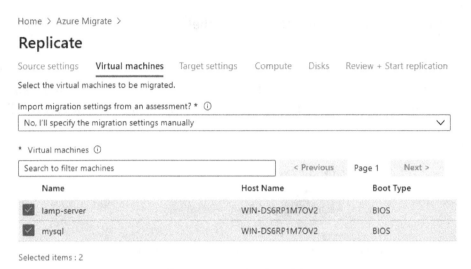

Figure 4.11: Selecting VMs

3. It's time to configure **Target settings** as in the configuration on the Azure side. You have to set **Subscription**, **Resource group**, **Replication Storage Account** (this is where the data will be replicated), **Virtual Network**, **Subnet**, and **Availability options**. The target location cannot be changed. As mentioned earlier, if you don't have these resources created, feel free to create these resources in your selected target region and start from *Step 2* again. Here is how the configuration will look if you already have the target resources in place:

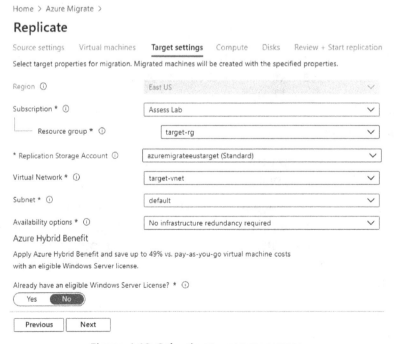

Figure 4.12: Selecting target resources

4.   Hitting **Next** in the **Target settings** tab will take you to the **Compute** tab, where you can set **Azure VM Size**, **OS Type**, and the **OS Disk** name you are going to migrate. You could set **Azure VM Size** as **Automatically select matching configuration**, as shown in *Figure 4.13*, and Azure will select a size matching your on-premises configuration:

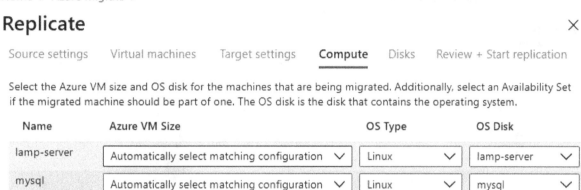

Figure 4.13: Selecting compute size

5.   After selecting the **Compute** configuration, you can click on **Next** and the wizard will take you to the **Disks** tab. Here you will get a chance to select the disks that you want to replicate from on-premises. You can also replicate the data disks if required; however, in our case, we only have the OS disks. The configuration will look like *Figure 4.14*:

Home > Azure Migrate >

Replicate

| Source settings | Virtual machines | Target settings | Compute | **Disks** | Review + Start replication |

Select the managed disk type to use for the disks of the migrated machine. Optionally, you may also choose to exclude certain disks from replication by unselecting those disks from the list of disks to replicate.

Name	Disks To Replicate		Disk Size(GB)
lamp-server	All selected	∨	20
	lamp-server		20
mysql	All selected	∨	20
	mysql		20

Previous   Next

Figure 4.14: Selecting disks to replicate

6. Once you have selected the disks, you can click on **Next** and you will reach the last step. In this step, we will review the target configuration and click on **Replicate** to replicate the server to Azure.

7. We can confirm from the landing page whether the replication has started or not. As shown in *Figure 4.15*, the **Replicating servers** section should show two as we selected two servers for replication:

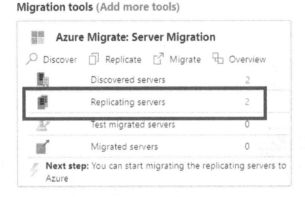

Figure 4.15: Verifying replication

8. We could also click on **2**, which has a hyperlink to show the status of the replication. This is a lengthy process, and you can track it as shown in *Figure 4.16*:

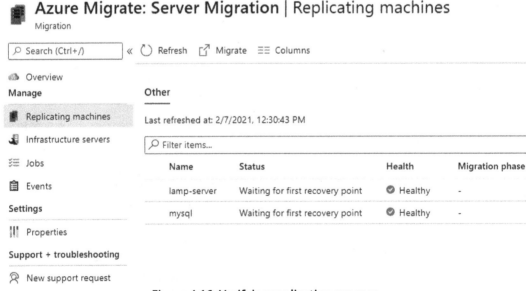

Figure 4.16: Verifying replication process

9. Once the replication is done, you will be able to see the status of both the servers change to **Protected** as demonstrated in *Figure 4.17*:

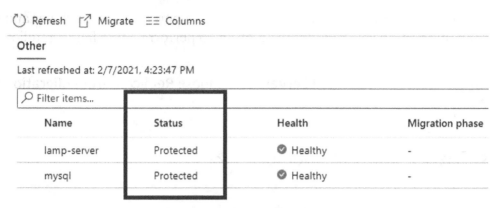

Figure 4.17: Replication completed

Our servers are successfully replicated to Azure. Before we migrate to production, we can perform a test failover. Test failovers are helpful for understanding whether an application is working properly before we make the production cutover. Let's perform the test failover and finish off the migration process.

Migrating to Azure

Since the servers are replicated, we can perform the test failover anytime we want. Performing a test failover will not interrupt any of the services—this stage is to confirm whether an application is functioning as expected. If not, we can take measures to remediate this and reattempt the migration without any production downtime.

Let's see how the application looks in our on-premises LAMP application, which is a demo LAMP application created from https://github.com/Anirban2404/phpMySQLapp:

Figure 4.18: On-premises application index page

As mentioned at the beginning of this section, we can perform a test failover and see whether our application is working fine. In order to perform a test failover, follow these steps:

1. Navigate to **Azure Migrate | Servers** and choose **Replicate** from **Migration tools** as shown in *Figure 4.19*:

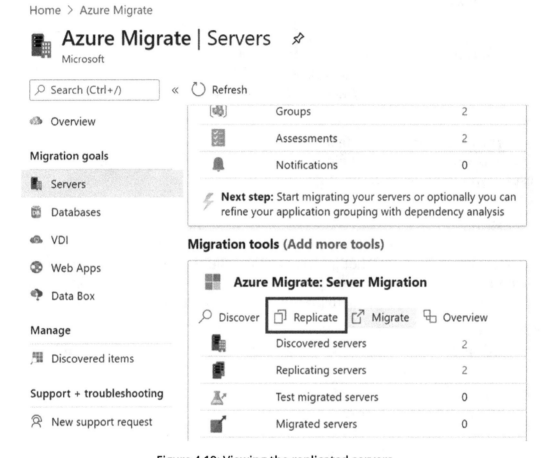

Figure 4.19: Viewing the replicated servers

2. From the next screen, select the VM that you want to test failover for and click on the three dots on the far-right side. You'll see a **Test migration** option as shown in *Figure 4.20*:

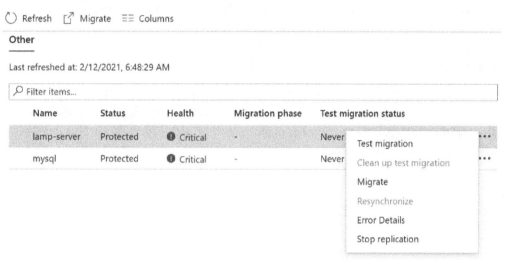

Figure 4.20 Selecting Test migration

3. Select the virtual network where you want to deploy the resources and select **Test migration** as shown in *Figure 4.21*:

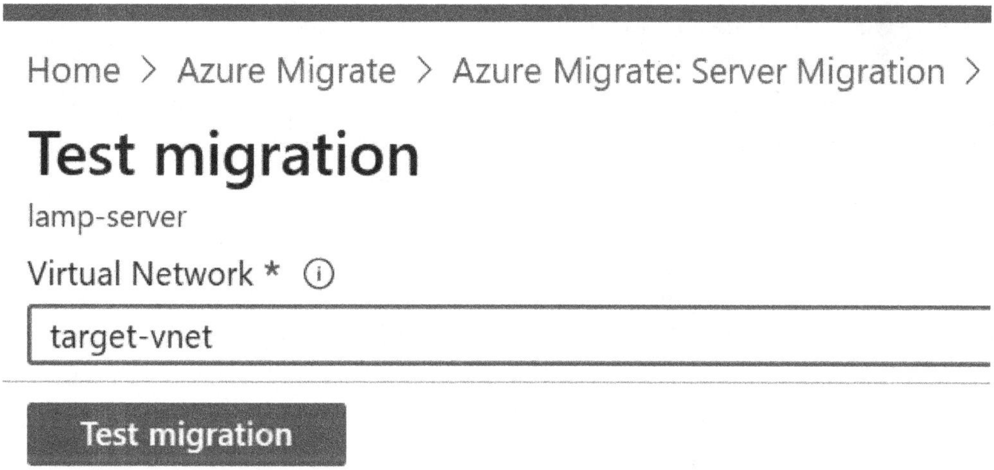

Home > Azure Migrate > Azure Migrate: Server Migration >

Test migration

lamp-server

Virtual Network * ⓘ

target-vnet

Test migration

Figure 4.21: Starting test migration

4. After some time, you will see that the resources have been created. One thing to note here is that there won't be a public IP or NSG attached to the resources that are created during the test migration. For us to check them using the internet, we need a public IP and NSG with SSH and HTTP rules added. If you are not sure how to make this change, refer to https://docs.microsoft.com/azure/virtual-network/manage-network-security-group and https://docs.microsoft.com/azure/virtual-network/associate-public-ip-address-vm.

5. Once the test migration status shows as completed, you can navigate to the target resource group that you selected in the Azure Migrate project during the initial configuration. The resources will be deployed, with the **test** keyword added as a suffix to the resource name, as visible in *Figure 4.22*:

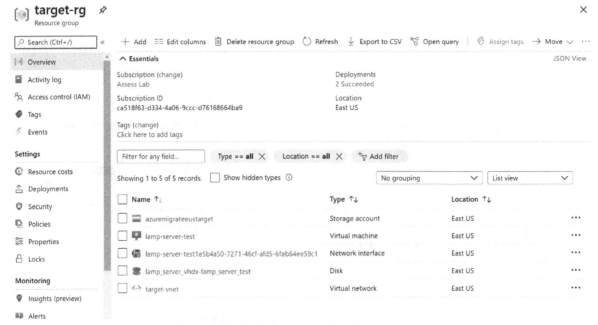

Figure 4.22: Exploring test migration resources

6. You can attach an NSG and public IP address as mentioned in the aforementioned documentation, and then you can test the migration by opening the displayed IP address in your browser as shown in *Figure 4.23*:

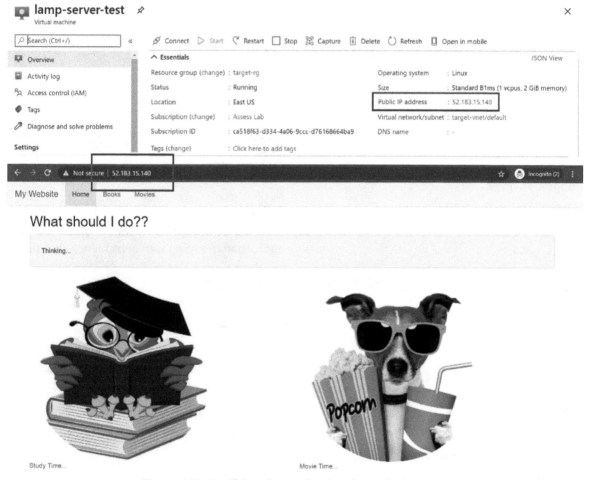

Figure 4.23: Verifying the application from the browser

7. Once the test migration is done, you need to clean up the test migration before we perform the actual migration. This can be done using the **Clean up test migration** option, which is shown in *Figure 4.20*. You will be asked to add your notes and confirm the deletion of the test resources.

8. After cleaning up the test resources, we can perform the actual migration of resources. To start the migration, navigate to **Azure Migrate | Servers** and choose **Migrate** from **Migration tools** as shown in *Figure 4.24*:

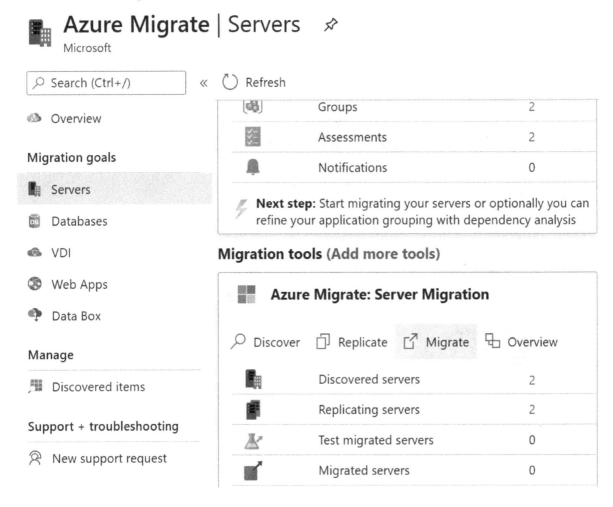

Figure 4.24: Migrating servers

9. You will be asked whether you want to shut down the machines to minimize data loss. Select **Yes** to shut down the machines and perform a planned migration with zero data loss. If you choose not to shut down the VMs, a final sync will be performed before the migration, but any changes that happen on the machine after the final sync is started will not be replicated. Let's go with **No** and select the machines we want to migrate, as shown in *Figure 4.25*:

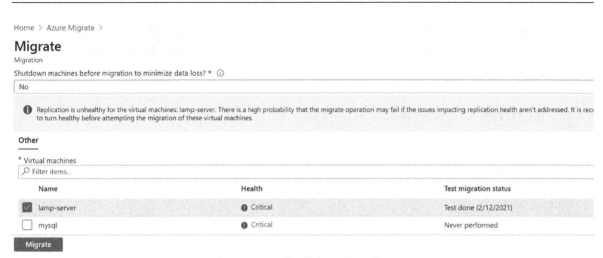

Figure 4.25: Finalizing migration

10. As we saw in the case of the test migration, this process will take some time and the resources will be created in the target resource group. The servers will have no public IP or NSG attached to them. You need to follow the process outlined in the documentation we followed in the test migration to attach the NSG and public IP. You can reuse the NSG and public IP from the test migration if you haven't deleted them.

11. Voilà, we have our resources in our target resource group:

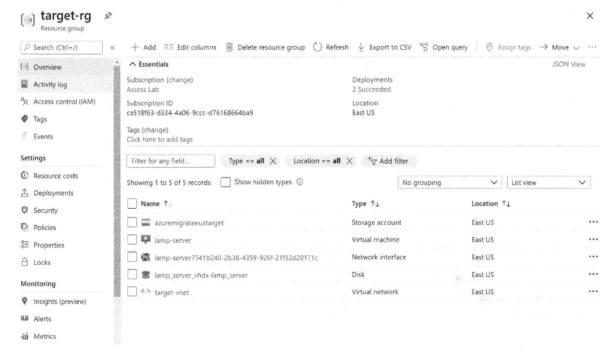

Figure 4.26: Reviewing migrated resources

12. If we navigate back to **Azure Migrate | Servers** and refresh the project, we will get the summary of the migration we have done as shown in *Figure 4.27*:

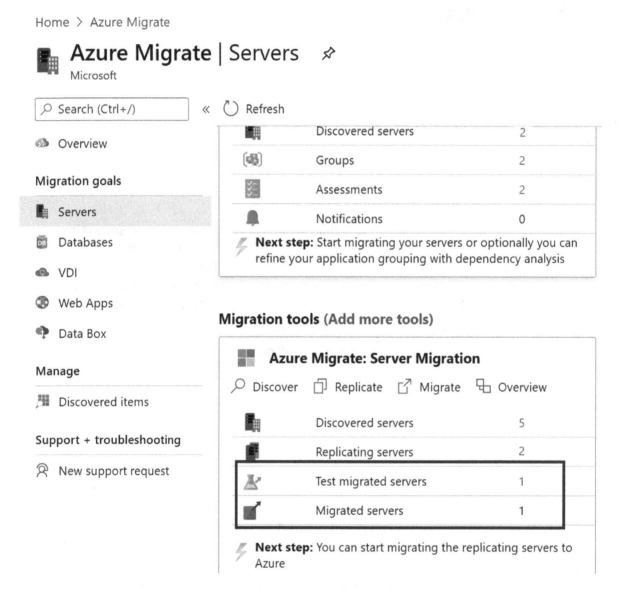

Figure 4.27: Summary of the project

With that, we've seen the end-to-end process of migrating servers from an on-premises Hyper-V host to Azure using Azure Migrate. As mentioned in the introduction of this section, we are going to see how we can migrate databases to PaaS solutions in the next hands-on lab.

Migrating databases

In the *Migrating servers to Azure* section, we saw how servers can be migrated to Azure with the help of Azure Migrate. We can directly migrate databases from IaaS to IaaS as we did in the case of the LAMP server. However, in this section, we will be migrating the database to a PaaS solution. You can use any on-premises MySQL server that can be accessed publicly. If you don't have one, for demonstration purposes, you can create a VM in Azure and install MySQL. In order to work with the hands-on data, you need to run the following SQL script in your MySQL server:

```
CREATE DATABASE MOVIES;
USE MOVIES;
CREATE TABLE horror_tbl (movie_id int NOT NULL PRIMARY KEY auto_increment,
movie_title varchar(100) NOT NULL, movie_year int NOT NULL);
INSERT INTO horror_tbl(movie_title, movie_year) VALUES ('Exorcist',1973),
('Hereditary',2018), ('The Conjuring',2013), ('The Shining',1980),
('Texas Chainsaw Massacre',1980), ('The Ring',2002), ('Halloween',1978),
('Sinister',2012), ('Insidious',2010), ('IT',2017);
```

Though IaaS offers a lot of flexibility in terms of control and administration, PaaS helps developers or administrators to deploy at ease and be more productive, as most of the management tasks are performed by Microsoft. PaaS offers a lot of time savings as the underlying hardware, OS patches and updates, and maintenance tasks are taken care of by Azure.

To migrate databases to PaaS, we will be using a service called Azure DMS. DMS empowers customers to perform online and offline migration from a plethora of database sources to Azure data platforms, with minimal service interruption or downtime.

DMS offer two different methods to migrate databases: offline migration or online migration. Offline migration requires the server to be shut down at the start of the migration, so there is downtime involved in this method. On the other hand, online migration follows a continuous replication of the live data, also allowing a cutover to Azure at any time with minimal downtime.

Azure DMS offers two pricing tiers:

- **Standard**: Only offline migrations are supported. This tier has no charge.
- **Premium**: Offline and online migrations are supported. There is no charge for the first six months–after that, this tier will incur charges.

Now that we have some idea about DMS, let's go ahead and create an instance.

Creating a Database Migration Service instance

This process consists of multiple steps:

1. Find **Azure Database Migration Services** in the **All Services** pane, or simply search for it. You can kick off the creation process by clicking **New** or **Create azure database migration service** as shown in *Figure 4.28*:

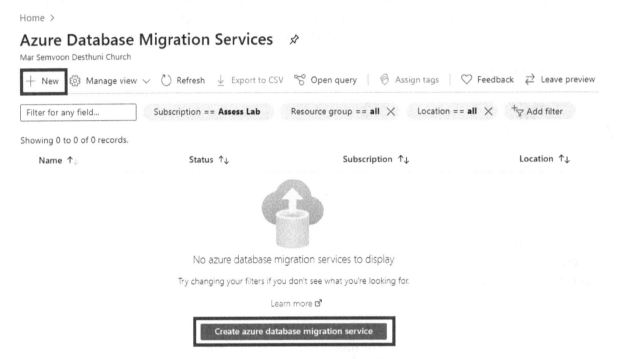

Figure 4.28: Creating a Database Migration Service instance

2. The creation process is very straightforward—you need to input values for **Subscription**, **Resource group**, **Migration service name**, and **Location**. Additionally, there is an option to choose **Pricing tier** and **Service mode**. As mentioned previously, there are two pricing tiers for this service: **Standard** (supports only offline migration) and **Premium** (supports both offline and online migration). Also, there are two service modes: **Azure**, where we'll be choosing one of the aforementioned pricing tiers, and **Hybrid**, where the worker is hosted on-premises. At the time of writing this book, **Hybrid** mode is in preview. The creation process is shown in *Figure 4.29*:

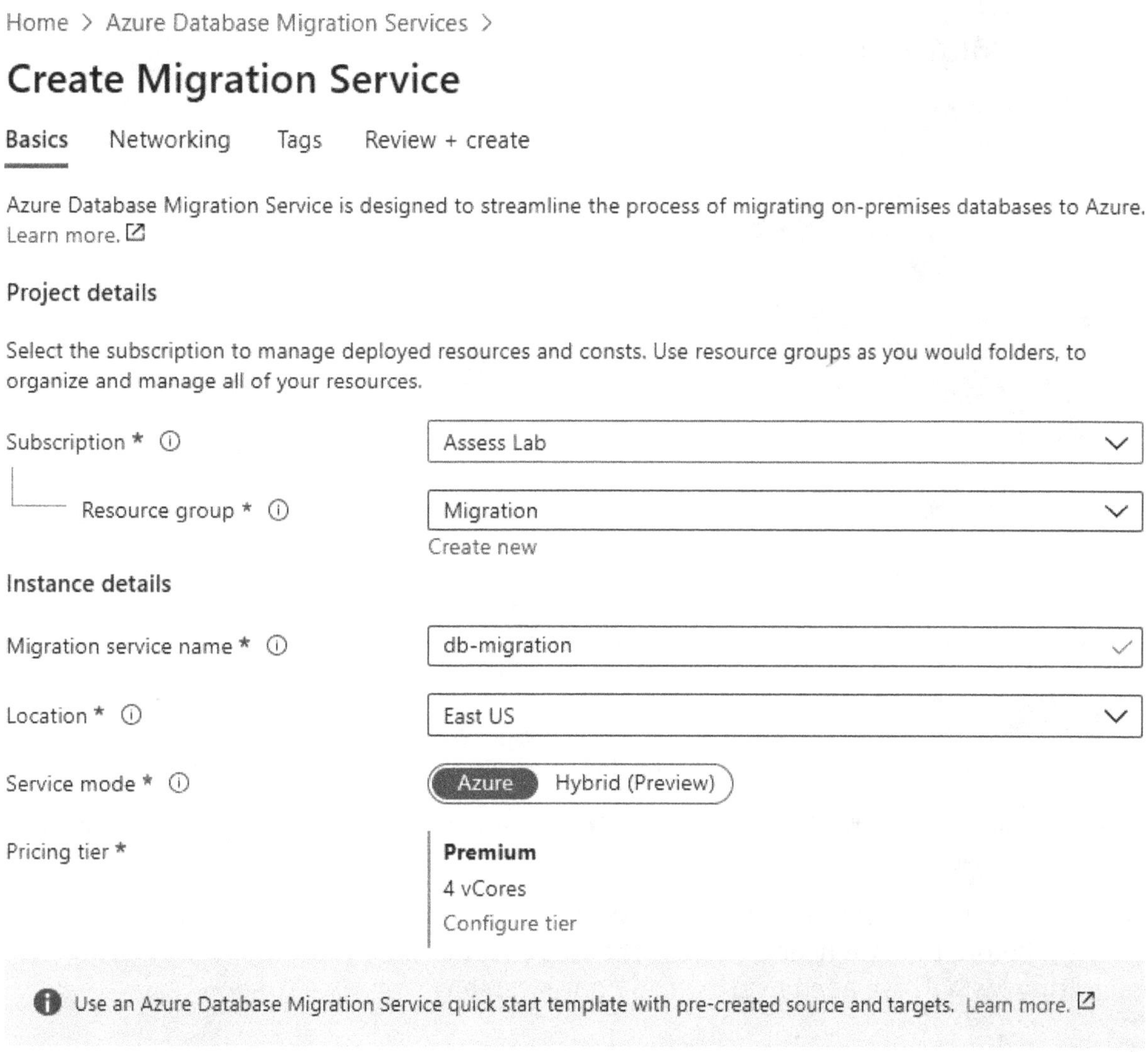

Home > Azure Database Migration Services >

Create Migration Service

Basics   Networking   Tags   Review + create

Azure Database Migration Service is designed to streamline the process of migrating on-premises databases to Azure. Learn more. ☑

Project details

Select the subscription to manage deployed resources and consts. Use resource groups as you would folders, to organize and manage all of your resources.

Subscription * ⓘ	Assess Lab ∨
└── Resource group * ⓘ	Migration ∨
	Create new

Instance details

Migration service name * ⓘ	db-migration ✓
Location * ⓘ	East US ∨
Service mode * ⓘ	(**Azure**) Hybrid (Preview)
Pricing tier *	**Premium**
	4 vCores
	Configure tier

ⓘ Use an Azure Database Migration Service quick start template with pre-created source and targets. Learn more. ☑

Figure 4.29: Configuring Basics

3. The next configuration we need is the **Networking** configuration, where will be creating a virtual network. You could choose an existing virtual network or create a new one. This virtual network will be used by the service to communicate with the source databases over the internet. The configuration is as shown in *Figure 4.30*:

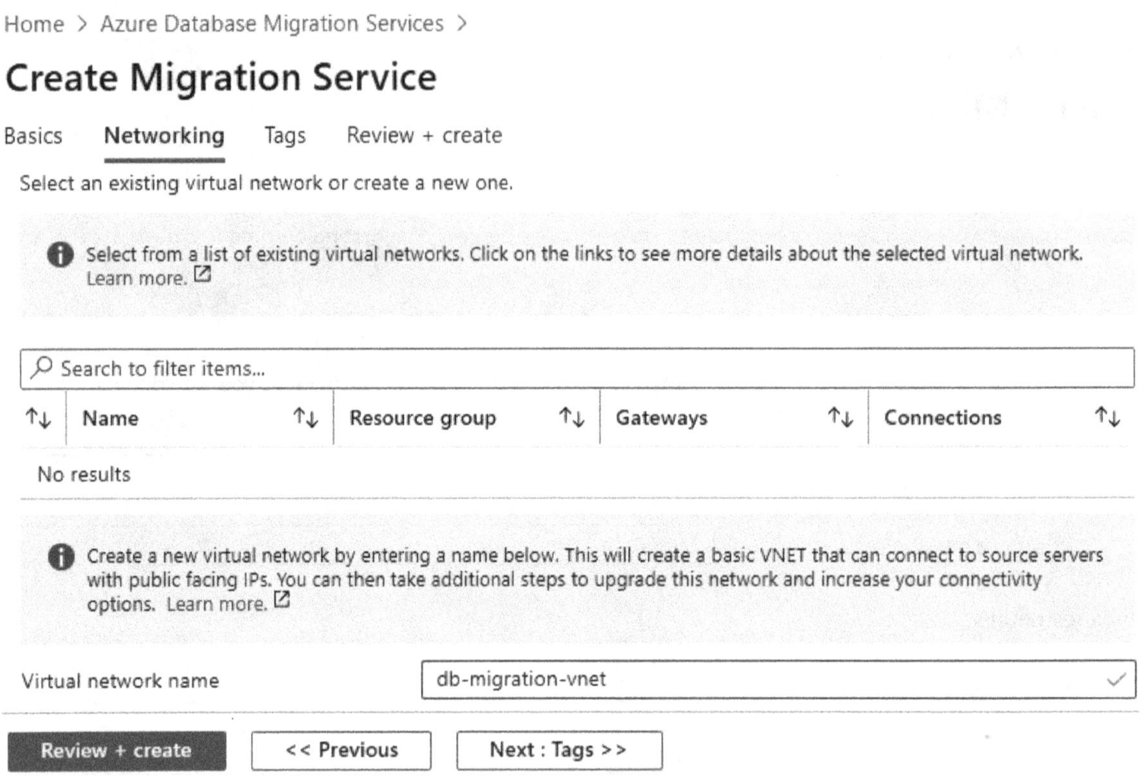

Home > Azure Database Migration Services >

Create Migration Service

Basics   **Networking**   Tags   Review + create

Select an existing virtual network or create a new one.

> ⓘ Select from a list of existing virtual networks. Click on the links to see more details about the selected virtual network. Learn more. ☑

🔍 Search to filter items...

↑↓	Name	↑↓	Resource group	↑↓	Gateways	↑↓	Connections	↑↓
	No results							

> ⓘ Create a new virtual network by entering a name below. This will create a basic VNET that can connect to source servers with public facing IPs. You can then take additional steps to upgrade this network and increase your connectivity options. Learn more. ☑

Virtual network name | db-migration-vnet | ✓

[Review + create]   [<< Previous]   [Next : Tags >>]

Figure 4.30: Creating a new virtual network

4. Clicking **Review + create** will initiate the validation process and the service will be created.

Now that we have created a DMS instance, the next step is to configure the migration project. Before this, we need to create the target database in Azure. Since we are migrating MySQL, we need to create an Azure Database for MySQL server.

Creating and configuring the target resource

As mentioned earlier, the service we're going to create is an Azure Database for MySQL server. This is a managed offering by Microsoft Azure that utilizes MySQL Community Edition version 5.6, 5.7, and 8.0. Let's create the target resource to migrate the data:

1. Search for **MySQL** in the search bar and you will be able to see Azure Database for MySQL in the Azure portal. Start creating a new database by clicking on the **New** button.

2. We will go with the single-server model as it is production-ready, cost-optimized, and has built-in high availability. You do get an option to choose **Flexible server**, which offers advanced customization and is in preview at the time of writing this book.

3. The wizard will take you through the creation process. You need to fill in the details and configure the compute, storage, and pricing tier for the server as per your requirements. Since we're dealing with a very small database, a **Basic** server with 1 vCPU and 8 GB of storage will suffice. In real-world scenarios, you should match the compute and storage of the Azure server with the on-premises configuration to avoid performance issues. The configuration is as shown in *Figure 4.31*:

Home > Select Azure Database for MySQL deployment option >

Create MySQL server

Microsoft

⚠ Changing Basic options may reset selections you have made. Review all options prior to creating the resource.

Subscription * ⓘ	Assess Lab ∨
Resource group * ⓘ	Migration ∨
	Create new

Server details

Enter required settings for this server, including picking a location and configuring the compute and storage resources.

Server name * ⓘ	mysql-rithin ✓
Data source * ⓘ	(None) Backup
Location * ⓘ	(US) East US ∨
Version * ⓘ	5.7 ∨
Compute + storage ⓘ	**Basic** 1 vCores, 8 GB storage Configure server

Administrator account

Admin username * ⓘ	rithin ✓
Password * ⓘ	•••••••••••• ✓
Confirm password *	•••••••••••• ✓

Review + create   Next : Additional settings >

Figure 4.31: Creating an Azure Database for MySQL server

4. With that, we can select the **Review + create** option, then the **Create** option, and the database will be provisioned.

5. After provisioning the database, we need to create a target table where the data from the on-premises database table should be migrated. We will create an empty table and map this to our on-premises database when we create a migration project.

6. The server admin login name can be obtained from the **Overview** pane of the database that we created in *Step 3*.

7. You can use any Linux or Windows computer with MySQL tools installed or Azure Cloud Shell to work with the server we deployed in Azure. Here, let's connect from the Bash shell as shown in *Figure 4.32*:

```
rithin@mysql:~$ mysql -h mysql-rithin.mysql.database.azure.com -u rithin@mysql-rithin -p
Enter password:
ERROR 9000 (HY000): Client with IP address '13.66.244.116' is not allowed to connect to this MySQL server.
rithin@mysql:~$
```

Figure 4.32: Connecting to Azure MySQL using Bash

Here the connection will fail, as the IP address of the machine from which we are connecting is not in the allowed list of IP addresses and the firewall will stop us from connecting.

8. To add your IP address to the allowed list of IP addresses, you can navigate to the server we created and click on **Connection security**. If you are using Azure Cloud Shell, you have to enable **Allow access to Azure services**. Since we are using a local machine, we will add our IP address as shown in *Figure 4.33* and save the configuration:

Figure 4.33: Configuring firewall

9. Now that we've added our IP address to the firewall, let's try to reconnect from Bash and see if the connection succeeds. You can see in *Figure 4.34* that the login was successful:

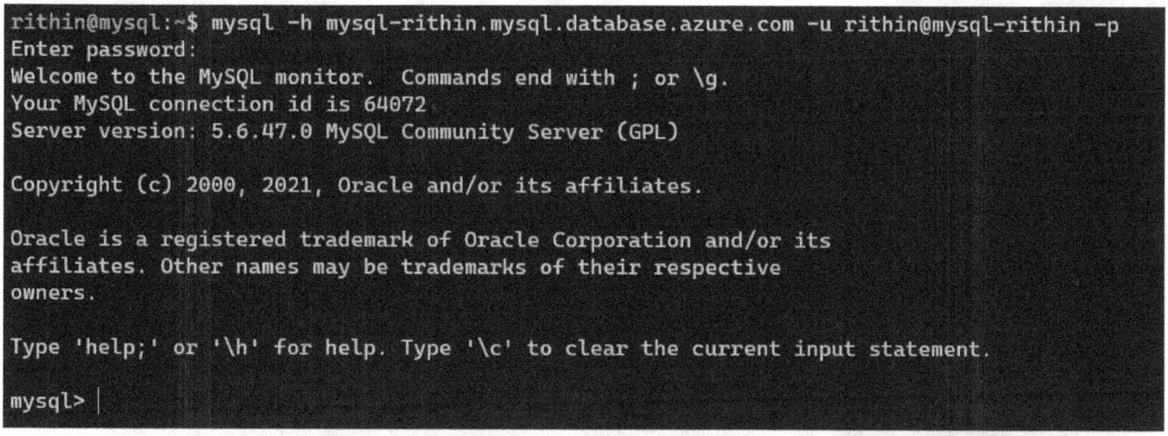

```
rithin@mysql:~$ mysql -h mysql-rithin.mysql.database.azure.com -u rithin@mysql-rithin -p
Enter password:
Welcome to the MySQL monitor.  Commands end with ; or \g.
Your MySQL connection id is 64072
Server version: 5.6.47.0 MySQL Community Server (GPL)

Copyright (c) 2000, 2021, Oracle and/or its affiliates.

Oracle is a registered trademark of Oracle Corporation and/or its
affiliates. Other names may be trademarks of their respective
owners.

Type 'help;' or '\h' for help. Type '\c' to clear the current input statement.

mysql>
```

Figure 4.34: Logging in to MySQL

10. Our on-premises server consists of a database and has a table named horror_tbl. Basically, this table stores the names of horror movies and the years they were released. We need to create a similar table in the MySQL server as we created in Azure so that the data can be migrated. Let's create a new database and table using the following commands:

```
CREATE DATABASE movies;

USE movies;

CREATE TABLE horror_tbl(
        movie_id INT NOT NULL AUTO_INCREMENT,
        movie_title varchar(150) NOT NULL,
        movie_year int NOT NULL,
        PRIMARY KEY ( movie_id ) );
```

11. Here is how the databases look in on-premises infrastructure and in Azure:

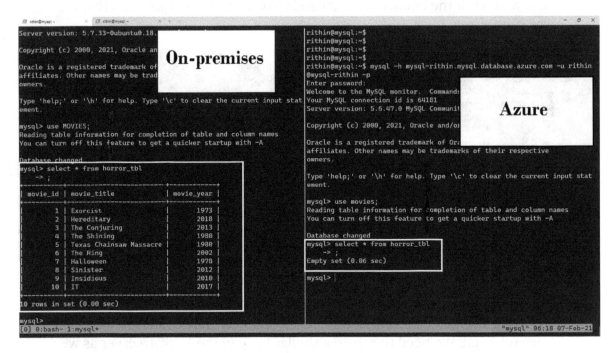

Figure 4.35: Comparing dataset in on-premises and Azure

It's evident from the preceding figure that the on-premises database contains data, and the Azure database is empty. Now we need to extract the schema from the source database and apply it to the destination.

Migrating the sample schema

In order to extract the schema, you can use the `mysqldump` command with the `--no-data` parameter. The syntax is as follows:

```
mysqldump -h {servername} -u {username} -p --databases {database name} \
    --nodata > /path/to/file
```

In our scenario, we need to extract the schema of the MOVIES database. Since we are executing the command from the MySQL server itself, we don't need to use the `-h` parameter. However, if you're doing this on a remote server, consider using the `-h` parameter. The following command will suffice in our scenario:

```
mysqldump  -u root -p --databases MOVIES --no-data > schema.sql
```

You can also use the `--all-databases` parameter if you have multiple databases and would like to extract the schema of all of them in a single shot. If you look at the schema file, it will be similar to the following SQL script:

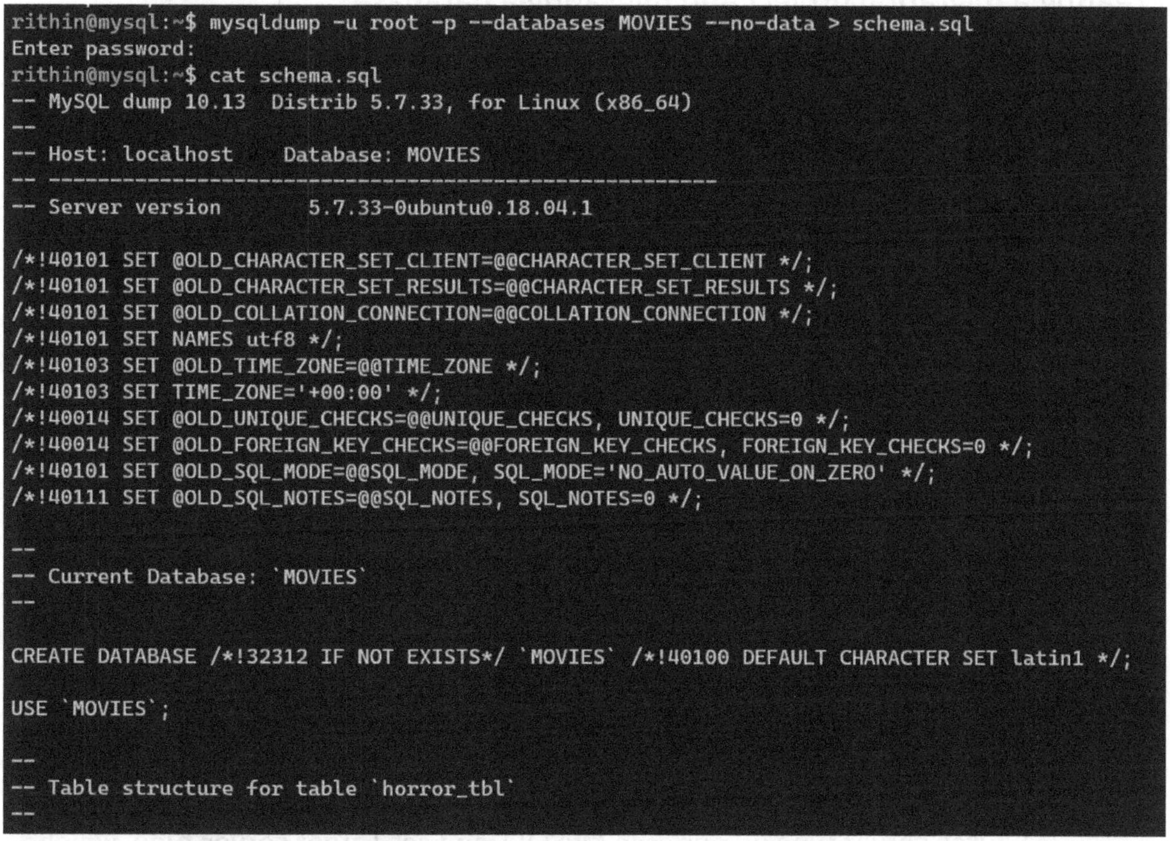

```
rithin@mysql:~$ mysqldump -u root -p --databases MOVIES --no-data > schema.sql
Enter password:
rithin@mysql:~$ cat schema.sql
-- MySQL dump 10.13  Distrib 5.7.33, for Linux (x86_64)
--
-- Host: localhost    Database: MOVIES
-- ------------------------------------------------------
-- Server version       5.7.33-0ubuntu0.18.04.1

/*!40101 SET @OLD_CHARACTER_SET_CLIENT=@@CHARACTER_SET_CLIENT */;
/*!40101 SET @OLD_CHARACTER_SET_RESULTS=@@CHARACTER_SET_RESULTS */;
/*!40101 SET @OLD_COLLATION_CONNECTION=@@COLLATION_CONNECTION */;
/*!40101 SET NAMES utf8 */;
/*!40103 SET @OLD_TIME_ZONE=@@TIME_ZONE */;
/*!40103 SET TIME_ZONE='+00:00' */;
/*!40014 SET @OLD_UNIQUE_CHECKS=@@UNIQUE_CHECKS, UNIQUE_CHECKS=0 */;
/*!40014 SET @OLD_FOREIGN_KEY_CHECKS=@@FOREIGN_KEY_CHECKS, FOREIGN_KEY_CHECKS=0 */;
/*!40101 SET @OLD_SQL_MODE=@@SQL_MODE, SQL_MODE='NO_AUTO_VALUE_ON_ZERO' */;
/*!40111 SET @OLD_SQL_NOTES=@@SQL_NOTES, SQL_NOTES=0 */;


--
-- Current Database: `MOVIES`
--

CREATE DATABASE /*!32312 IF NOT EXISTS*/ `MOVIES` /*!40100 DEFAULT CHARACTER SET latin1 */;

USE `MOVIES`;


--
-- Table structure for table `horror_tbl`
--
```

Figure 4.36: Checking the schema file

Now we need to import this data to Azure Database for MySQL using the following syntax. This can be run directly from the VM hosting the on-premises database if the networking allows the connection. Otherwise, the schema needs to be imported on a machine that has the option to connect to the Azure database or into Cloud Shell directly:

```
mysql -h {servername} -u {username} -p {database name} < /path/to/schema
```

In our scenario, you need to replace the server name and login name with your Azure Database for MySQL credentials:

```
mysql -h mysql-rithin.mysql.database.azure.com -u rithin@mysql-rithin \
-p movies < schema.sql
```

After the import process, we need to switch back to DMS and create a migration project.

Creating a migration project and migrating a database

To create a migration project for databases, we need to head back to DMS. The project can be created using the following steps:

1. Navigate to **Azure Database Migration Service** and select **New Migration Project** as shown in *Figure 4.37*:

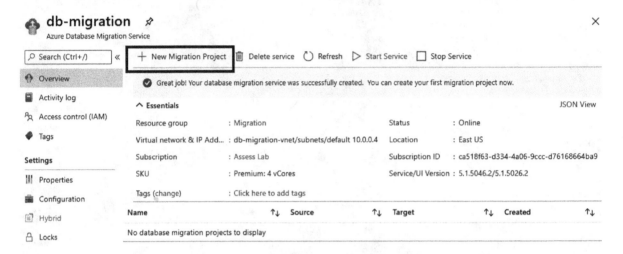

Figure 4.37: Creating a migration project

2. The creation is a very simple process. We need to input a name for the project, set **Source server type** (in our case MySQL), and set **Target server type**, which is **Azure Database for MySQL**. Finally, set the type of activity as **Online data migration**, as we are planning to migrate without any downtime. The offline option is not currently available for MySQL. The configuration is as shown in *Figure 4.38*:

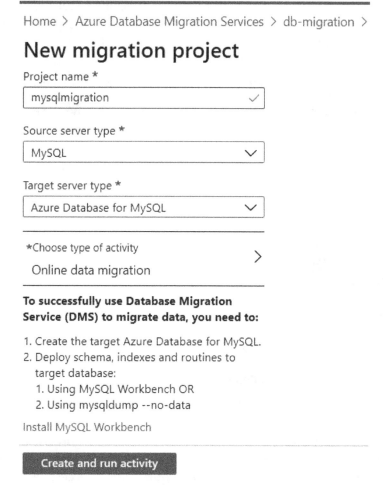

Figure 4.38: Configuring the project

3. Once the project is configured, click on **Create and run activity**. This will take you to **MySQL to Azure Database for MySQL Online Migration Wizard.**

4. The first step in the wizard is to configure the source. Here we need to set **Source server name**, **Server port**, **User Name**, and **Password** for our publicly available on-premises server as shown in *Figure 4.39*:

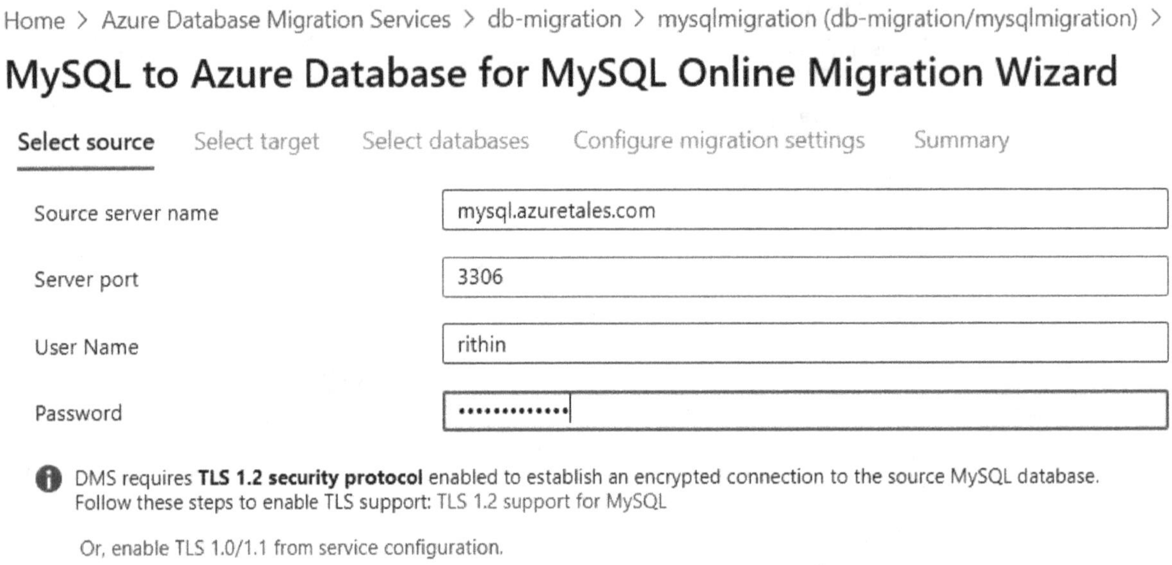

Home > Azure Database Migration Services > db-migration > mysqlmigration (db-migration/mysqlmigration) >

MySQL to Azure Database for MySQL Online Migration Wizard

Select source   Select target   Select databases   Configure migration settings   Summary

Source server name	mysql.azuretales.com
Server port	3306
User Name	rithin
Password	••••••••••••

🛈 DMS requires **TLS 1.2 security protocol** enabled to establish an encrypted connection to the source MySQL database. Follow these steps to enable TLS support: TLS 1.2 support for MySQL

Or, enable TLS 1.0/1.1 from service configuration.

Figure 4.39: Connecting to the source database

> **Note**
>
> You might encounter errors if the MySQL server is not configured properly. Configuration of the bind-address, bin-logs in `mysqld.cnf`, and the creation of a new user with admin privileges might be required for a successful connection. Refer to https://docs.microsoft.com/azure/dms/tutorial-mysql-azure-mysql-online#prerequisites.

5. Now we need to configure the target, which includes setting **Target server name**, **User Name**, and **Password**. **Target server name** and **User Name** can be found from the **Overview** pane of our MySQL server in Azure. The password is the one you entered during the service creation—if forgotten, you can use the **Reset Password** option. The target server details should be configured as follows:

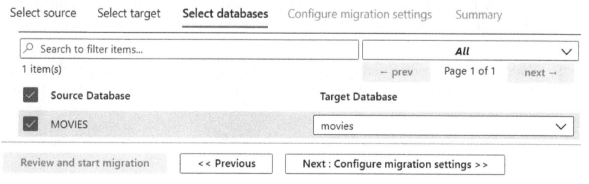

Home > Azure Database Migration Services > db-migration > mysqlmigration (db-migration/mysqlmigration) >

MySQL to Azure Database for MySQL Online Migration Wizard

Select source   **Select target**   Select databases   Configure migration settings   Summary

Target server name ⓘ   mysql-rithin.mysql.database.azure.com

User Name   rithin@mysql-rithin

Password   •••••••••••••

Review and start migration   [<< Previous]   [Next : Select databases >>]

Figure 4.40: Configuring the target server

> **Note**
>
> You may get an error message stating that the IP address is not allowed to connect to the MySQL server. From the error message, you can get the public IP of DMS and add this IP to the **Connection Security** pane of MySQL for successful connection, or enable **Allow access to Azure Services**. However, this would give all Azure services in your subscription access to the database.

6. The next step is to select the source databases that need to be migrated to the cloud. The tool will show you the databases that are available on the on-premises server. Select the source database and corresponding database as the target. In our case, we will map the MOVIES database, which is on-premises, to the movies database that we created earlier. *Figure 4.41* shows how the mapping is done from source to target:

Home > Azure Database Migration Services > db-migration > mysqlmigration (db-migration/mysqlmigration) >

MySQL to Azure Database for MySQL Online Migration Wizard

Select source   Select target   **Select databases**   Configure migration settings   Summary

🔍 Search to filter items...   All   ⌄

1 item(s)   ← prev   Page 1 of 1   next →

☑ **Source Database**   **Target Database**

☑ MOVIES   movies   ⌄

Review and start migration   [<< Previous]   [Next : Configure migration settings >>]

Figure 4.41: Mapping databases

7. We're approaching the last step, where we can configure the migration settings. At this stage, you can specify which tables need to be migrated and settings for **large objects** (**LOB**) data. Since our dataset is small, we don't need to configure LOB settings. From *Figure 4.42*, we can see that the `horror_tbl` table has been selected:

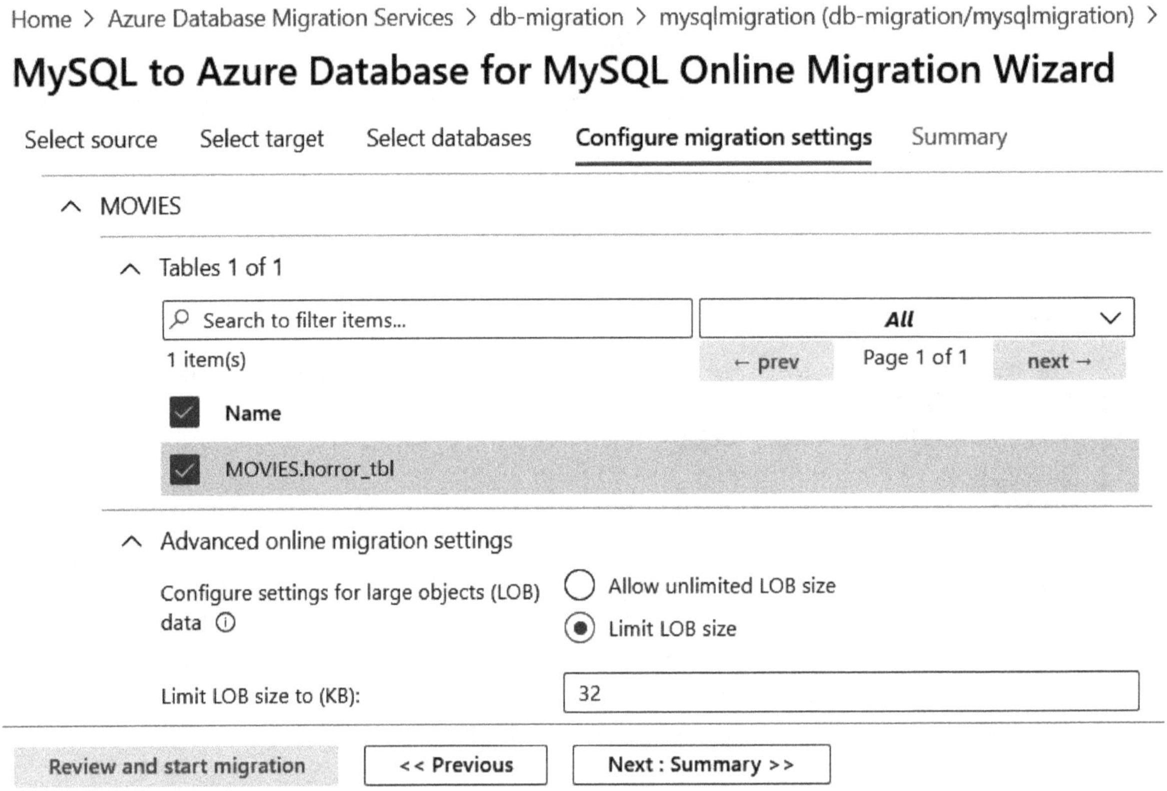

Home > Azure Database Migration Services > db-migration > mysqlmigration (db-migration/mysqlmigration) >

MySQL to Azure Database for MySQL Online Migration Wizard

Select source   Select target   Select databases   **Configure migration settings**   Summary

∧ MOVIES

    ∧ Tables 1 of 1

🔍 Search to filter items...	*All* ∨
1 item(s)	← prev Page 1 of 1 next →

☑ **Name**

☑ MOVIES.horror_tbl

    ∧ Advanced online migration settings

Configure settings for large objects (LOB) data ⓘ
    ◯ Allow unlimited LOB size
    ◉ Limit LOB size

Limit LOB size to (KB):
32

Review and start migration	<< Previous	Next : Summary >>

Figure 4.42: Configuring database migration settings

8. With that, we proceed to the **Summary** tab, where we need to add a name for this activity and review the configuration we have done so far. Clicking on **Start Migration** will initiate the migration from the on-premises server to the Azure server.

9. Soon we will be redirected to a page with the migration status and details of the source and destination servers, as shown in *Figure 4.43*:

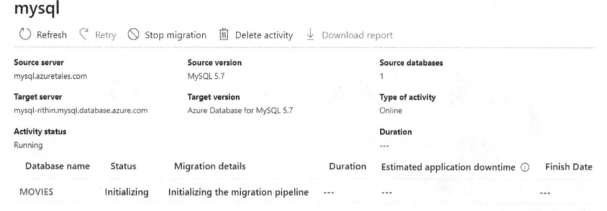

Figure 4.43: Checking migration status

10. Since our dataset was 10 rows, it took less than 5 seconds to complete the migration and notify us that we are ready to cut over. If you choose **Start Cutover**, Azure will provide the steps to commit any pending transactions, as shown in *Figure 4.44*, and after that you are ready to point your applications to this database:

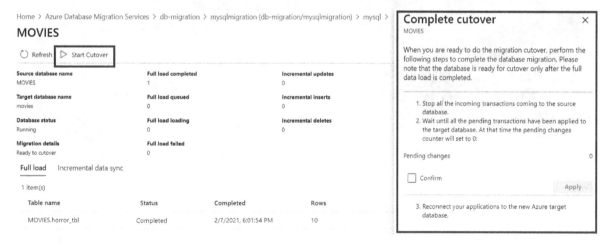

Figure 4.44: Starting cutover

11. Even without initiating the cutover, you can check the Azure MySQL instance and verify that our records are there. The following shows verification done with Bash by connecting to the instance:

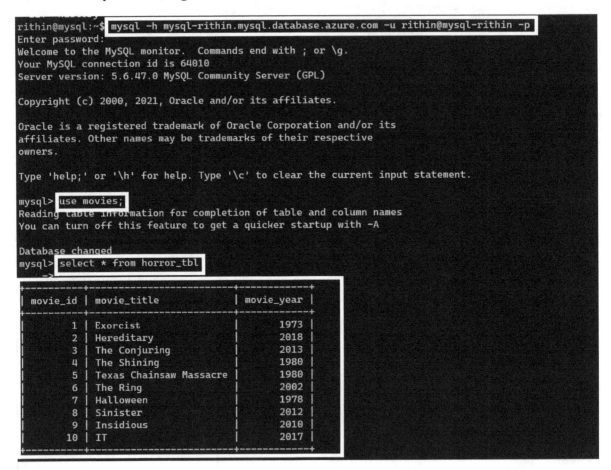

Figure 4.45: Verifying data in the Azure Database for MySQL server after migration

From *Figure* 4.45, it's evident that we are indeed connecting to the Azure MySQL instance.

Though we performed the migration from Hyper-V for demonstration, Azure Migrate supports other platforms and DMS supports other database types as well. *Table 4.1* shows links to the official Microsoft content for other platforms including Hyper-V:

Platform	Link
VMware	https://docs.microsoft.com/azure/migrate/server-migrate-overview
Physical servers	https://docs.microsoft.com/azure/migrate/tutorial-migrate-physical-virtual-machines
AWS instances	https://docs.microsoft.com/azure/migrate/tutorial-migrate-aws-virtual-machines
GCP instances	https://docs.microsoft.com/azure/migrate/tutorial-migrate-gcp-virtual-machines
Hyper-V	https://docs.microsoft.com/azure/migrate/tutorial-migrate-hyper-v
Database Migration	https://datamigration.microsoft.com/

Table 4.1: Migration documentation for other platforms

With that, we have reached the end of the hands-on lab. To conclude, this hands-on was divided into sections where you were migrating servers using Azure Migrate and migrating databases using DMS.

Summary

This chapter focused on practical learning via hands-on labs. First, we went through how to install providers in VMs, then we ran discovery and replication procedures. The first hands-on lab concluded with the migration of a VM to Azure using Azure Migrate.

Our second hands-on lab focused on MySQL database migration to the Azure Database for MySQL service using DMS. In this lab, we first created the migration service and configured it with our target resources. Then we migrated a sample schema. Finally, we created a migration project and migrated the database to Azure.

Migrating operating systems and databases to Azure is just one step on our cloud journey. Naturally, the next step is to operate the migrated Linux workloads on Azure. *Chapter 5, Operating Linux on Azure*, will give you some practical guidance on this topic.

5

Operating Linux on Azure

If you recall the migration roadmap we shared earlier, it was a four-stage process. In the last two chapters, we covered the *Assess* and *Migrate* milestones. In *Chapter 3, Assessment and migration planning*, we discussed the need for proper assessment and thorough planning of the migration, as they are an inevitable part of the process. We also discussed the tooling used to complete these milestones in our migration journey in *Chapter 4, Performing migration to Azure*, and we migrated two Linux servers from Hyper-V into Azure. The first server was an Ubuntu LTS, and the second was a MySQL server, which was converted into an Azure Database for MySQL service.

One thing to keep in mind is that the journey doesn't stop there. In this chapter, we will focus primarily on the remaining stages: *Optimize* and *Manage & Secure*. We need to make sure that workloads are optimized, and that security is top-notch. In an on-premises environment, security is typically entirely handled by you. However, in the case of the cloud, you are deploying the workloads to the cloud provider's datacenter. Here, security will be a major concern, but you need not worry. Azure provides a lot of services that can change the security landscape of your cloud deployments.

The *Optimize* stage mainly focuses on analyzing your costs, improving the infrastructure using recommendations, and reinvesting to achieve more. On the other hand, the *Manage & Secure* phase talks more about security, data protection, and finally monitoring.

Some of the key takeaways from this chapter include:

- Optimizing costs on Azure
- Working with Azure Linux agents and extensions
- Linux patching on Azure
- Infrastructure monitoring

Let's continue our migration journey by moving on to the next milestone, *Optimize*, where we are going to learn about a number of cost optimization techniques in Azure.

Optimize

At this stage, you may have successfully migrated your services to the Azure cloud. As mentioned in the introduction to this chapter, however, the journey doesn't end here. If you remember, during our migration, we had an option to choose the size of the virtual machines that need to be created in Azure. For demonstration purposes, we let Azure decide the size of the target virtual machines. A couple of questions will surface at this point, for example: *Is the sizing decision correct? Are the migrated workloads running efficiently?*

The answer to these questions is delivered in the *Optimize* phase. In this phase, we ensure that the migrated workloads are running efficiently from a cost standpoint as well as a performance standpoint. Let's go ahead and cover some of the tools that are used to optimize the workloads, mainly from a cost perspective.

In the previous chapters, we discussed the relevant tools that are used in the respective phases. Likewise, the *Optimize* phase also has a set of tools that can be leveraged by customers to optimize workloads. Let's take a look at these tools.

Azure Cost Management

Azure Cost Management (ACM) is an amazing tool that can be used to analyze running costs at different management scopes, like billing accounts, management groups, subscriptions, resource groups, and even at the resource level. For instance, you can choose any subscriptions from the Azure portal, and clicking on the **Cost analysis** blade will give you a complete breakdown of the costs associated with all the resources in your subscription. *Figure 5.1* shows how the cost is visualized using different graphs in ACM:

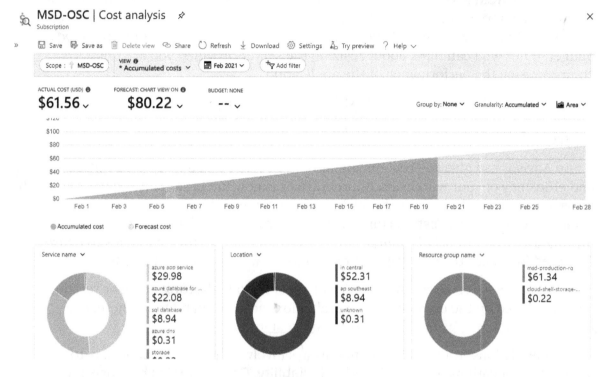

Figure 5.1: ACM view

If you look closely at *Figure 5.1*, right next to **ACTUAL COST (USD)**, you can see the forecasted cost under **FORECAST: CHART VIEW ON**. The forecast is done using resources that are currently deployed. Alongside this, ACM provides budgeting and alerting features so that you will be notified whenever you cross the threshold of your budget. Furthermore, you can integrate budgets with action groups and invoke Azure Functions or Azure Logic Apps to automatically shut down workloads when you are crossing the threshold.

In addition to the aforementioned features, ACM also offers the following advantages:

- You can monitor your AWS costs from ACM using the AWS connector.
- ACM offers richer APIs that can be utilized to build dashboards in your favorite visualization tool.

ACM also has a Power BI connector that you can leverage to bring the data from Cost Management to Power BI. At the time of writing this book, the Power BI connector is only supported for **Enterprise Agreement (EA)** and **Microsoft Customer Agreement (MCA)** customers. **Pay-As-You-Go (PAYG)** customers have to use the APIs to create dashboards in Power BI.

To conclude, ACM is very powerful in terms of the features it offers and the visibility it provides in terms of cloud spending. You can analyze the costs of the services or servers that you have migrated and verify whether they are within your projected budget. If not, you can think about resizing the server provided you are not compromising the performance of the application.

With that, we will move on to the next tool used in the *Optimize* phase–Azure Advisor.

Azure Advisor

Azure Advisor can give you recommendations to review and improve the optimization and efficiency of your workloads. Azure Advisor is now integrated into the ACM blade to provide recommendations on cost reduction. Recommendations from a cost reduction standpoint include suggestions for resizing underutilized Azure virtual machines, making use of additional discounts, and converting PAYG virtual machines to Azure Reserved Instances to get significant discounts on workloads that run 24x7.

For underutilized resources, Azure Advisor recommends shutting down or resizing the instance based on the evaluation. The evaluation metrics can be found here: https://docs.microsoft.com/azure/advisor/advisor-cost-recommendations.

Recommendations from Advisor do not always involve costs–you will be able to see recommendations on **Cost**, **Security**, **Reliability**, **Operational excellence**, and **Performance**. *Figure* 5.2 shows the view from the Advisor blade showing different recommendations. In this case, most of the recommendations have been completed, except the **Reliability** recommendations:

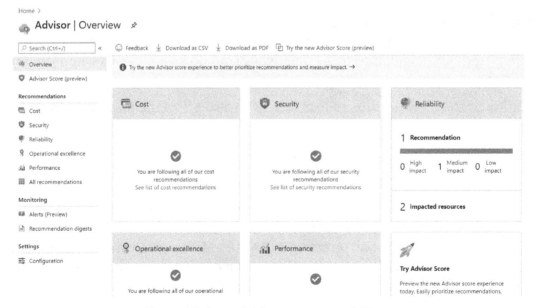

Figure 5.2: Azure Advisor recommendations

These recommendations can be downloaded as CSV or PDF, which you can share with other stakeholders who play vital roles in business decision making.

Analyzing costs using ACM and reviewing the recommendations made by Azure Advisor will help you optimize your workloads in Azure. Now, let's move on to the next phase of our journey, called *Manage & Secure*.

Manage and Secure

In this stage, we will make sure that our migrated resources are secured, and that they are managed correctly. This phase is all about security and data protection and we are going to look at some of the tools that are used to achieve these.

One of the most important pieces of Linux management in Azure is a small component called the **Linux Agent**.

Linux Agent for Azure

Linux provisioning and interaction between the Azure **Fabric Controller** (**FC**) and the virtual machine is managed by the Microsoft Azure Linux Agent, also referred to as waagent or WaLinuxAgent.

The following functionality of Linux on Azure deployments are managed by the Azure Linux Agent:

- Provisioning images
- Network routing and interface naming
- Kernel configuration
- Diagnostics configuration
- Microsoft **System Center Virtual Machine Manager** (**SCVMM**) deployment
- Virtual machine extensions

The agent talks with Azure Service Fabric via two channels. During virtual machine deployment, the agent mounts an **Open Virtualization Format** (**OVF**)-compliant configuration file from a virtual DVD image that contains the required provisioning details. During runtime, communication takes place via the REST API provided by the agent, allowing Azure Fabric to push information and commands to the virtual machine.

When creating your own Linux images or modifying existing images, it is good to remember that the agent is not completely monolithic—it requires the following components from the underlying Linux system:

- Python 2.6+
- OpenSSL 1.0+
- OpenSSH 5.3+
- Filesystem utilities: `sfdisk`, `fdisk`, `mkfs`, `parted`
- Password tools: `chpasswd`, `sudo`
- Text processing tools: `sed`, `grep`
- Network tools: `ip-route`

Even if it is technically possible to run Linux on Azure without the agent, it is highly recommended to always have the agent installed and active in your virtual machine. Without the agent, you cannot run any remote commands to the virtual machine via Azure Fabric. Additionally, Azure would not get any status information about the virtual machine and wouldn't know whether the system was healthy.

All endorsed Linux distributions on Azure come with the agent pre-installed. For your own images, you may install the agent from DEB and RPM packages, as well as using a Python-based installation script.

> **Note**
>
> You should always use the version of the agent distributed with the virtual machine image by your Linux distribution vendor. Only install it manually if there is no official package available for your Linux flavor.

Here are some useful commands for checking that the Azure Linux Agent is installed and updated to the latest version:

- To check whether it is installed and to show the current version number on Ubuntu:

  ```
  apt list -installed | grep walinuxagent
  ```

```
toni@vm1:~$ apt list --installed | grep walinuxagent

WARNING: apt does not have a stable CLI interface. Use with caution in scripts.

walinuxagent/bionic-updates,now 2.2.45-0ubuntu1~18.04.1 amd64 [installed]
```

Figure 5.3: Checking the Azure Linux Agent version number on Ubuntu

Alternatively, you can run waagent --version, which can be used on any distribution without needing to run any package manager-related commands.

- To update the agent or install it in the event that it is missing, run the following command:

```
sudo apt-get install walinuxagent
```

```
toni@vm1:~$ sudo apt-get install walinuxagent
Reading package lists... Done
Building dependency tree
Reading state information... Done
walinuxagent is already the newest version (2.2.45-0ubuntu1~18.04.1).
0 upgraded, 0 newly installed, 0 to remove and 22 not upgraded.
```

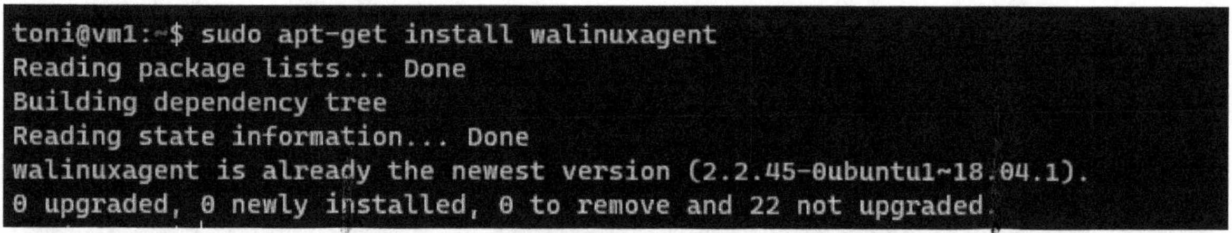

Figure 5.4: Updating the Linux agent on Ubuntu

In our example, the agent was already installed and on the latest version as well.

Azure Linux Agent has a built-in mechanism to update itself. It is good to ensure that it is enabled by editing its configuration file, /etc/waagent.conf:

> **Note**
>
> You can learn more about the technical details of the agent from GitHub as the agent is released as open source: https://github.com/Azure/WALinuxAgent.
>
> Documentation for using the agent can be found here: https://docs.microsoft.com/azure/virtual-machines/extensions/agent-linux.

It is also good to be familiar with cloud-init, a very popular tool for customizing a Linux virtual machine as it boots for the first time. It can be considered an alternative to Azure Linux Agent. You can read more about it here: https://docs.microsoft.com/azure/virtual-machines/linux/using-cloud-init. cloud-init works across Linux distributions and does not depend on the package manager.

Extensions

Azure extensions are tiny helper applications that provide configuration and automation functionality for Azure virtual machines. These extensions can be used once the virtual machine and operating system have been deployed and started. They can also be used during virtual machine deployment using Azure Resource Manager templates.

Extensions are part of the Azure Linux Agent functionality set, but each extension has its own set of features and use cases.

To list all the available extensions for Linux on Azure, you can run the following Azure CLI command:

```
az vm extension image list --location southeastasia --output table
```

```
toni@Azure:~$ az vm extension image list --location southeastasia --output table
Command group 'vm' is experimental and under development. Reference and support levels: https://aka.ms/CLI_refstatus

Name                             Publisher                                            Version
-------------------------------- ---------------------------------------------------- -----------------
AcronisBackup                    Acronis.Backup                                       1.0.33
AcronisBackup                    Acronis.Backup                                       1.0.51
AcronisBackupLinux               Acronis.Backup                                       1.0.33
AlertLogicLM                     alertlogic                                           1.3.0.1
AlertLogicLM                     AlertLogic.Extension                                 1.3.0.0
AlertLogicLM                     AlertLogic.Extension                                 1.4.0.0
AlertLogicLM                     AlertLogic.Extension                                 1.9.0.0
AlertLogicLM                     AlertLogic.Extension                                 1.9.1.0
AgentWinExt                      bmc.ctm                                              9.0.0.1
SCWPAgent                        Brianjac.Symantec.CloudWorkloadProtection            1.0.0.0
ChefClient                       Chef.Bootstrap.WindowsAzure                          11.18.6.2
ChefClient                       Chef.Bootstrap.WindowsAzure                          1207.12.3.0
ChefClient                       Chef.Bootstrap.WindowsAzure                          1210.12.109.1005
ChefClient                       Chef.Bootstrap.WindowsAzure                          1210.12.110.1000
ChefClient                       Chef.Bootstrap.WindowsAzure                          1210.12.110.1001
ChefClient                       Chef.Bootstrap.WindowsAzure                          1210.12.110.1002
ChefClient                       Chef.Bootstrap.WindowsAzure                          1210.13.1.1
ChefClient                       Chef.Bootstrap.WindowsAzure                          1210.13.2.1
ChefClient                       Chef.Bootstrap.WindowsAzure                          1210.13.2.2
ChefClient                       Chef.Bootstrap.WindowsAzure                          1210.13.2.3
```

Figure 5.5: Listing all available extensions for Linux on Azure

The list is quite long and contains extensions from Microsoft and third-party publishers. In this example, we have used Southeast Asia as a location. You should choose your nearest region unless you are working with a specific remote location.

> **Note**
>
> You can explore all the options of the extension image module here: https://docs.microsoft.com/cli/azure/vm/extension/image?view=azure-cli-latest#az-vm-extension-image-list.

Virtual machine extensions can also be found in the Azure portal (see *Figure 5.6*). You can choose **Extensions** under the virtual machine properties and add them using the installation wizard:

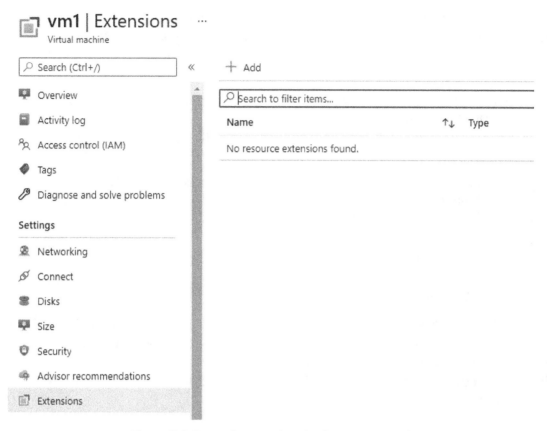

Figure 5.6: Extensions settings in the Azure portal

Extensions are very useful not only for deploying workloads and their configurations, but also during troubleshooting and debugging.

Data protection

In Azure, your data can be protected in multiple ways and in multiple layers. The encryption models supported by Azure are as follows:

- Client-side and server-side encryption
- Azure disks and Azure Storage Service Encryption
- Client-side encryption of Azure blobs
- Various encryption methods for databases and database services
- Encryption of data in transit
- Key management with Key Vault

Depending on your migration workloads and their architecture, you may want to utilize one or more of these encryption features in your project.

For example, if your source virtual machine is using encrypted filesystems, you could migrate it to Azure as-is. However, for performance reasons, it may make sense to turn off the filesystem encryption and to enable encryption on Azure Storage or Managed Disk.

If your entire on-premises storage system is encrypted, the most logical choice is to encrypt at the Azure Storage level as well.

> **Note**
>
> You can read more about the various encryption functionalities in the encryption overview documentation: https://docs.microsoft.com/azure/security/fundamentals/encryption-overview.

Let's take a closer look at the next feature.

Azure Disk Encryption

Azure Disk Encryption for Linux virtual machines uses *DM-Crypt* to provide volume encryption for operating systems and data disks. It is integrated with *Azure Key Vault* to manage and control your encryption keys and secrets. There is also integration with Azure Security Center, which is able to alert you if you have not encrypted virtual machine disks:

VIRTUAL MACHINES RECOMMENDATIONS	TOTAL	
Missing disk encryption	2 of 2 VMs	

Virtual machines

NAME	ONBOARDING	SYSTEM UPDATES	ANTIMALWARE	BASELINE	DISK ENCRYPTION
ASC-VM1	✓	✓	✓	✓	❗
ASC-VM2	✓	✓	✓	✓	❗

Figure 5.7: Azure Security Center

There are certain recommendations and limitations when it comes to using Azure Disk Encryption with Linux virtual machines, and right now there is no direct way of removing encryption from the operating system disks on Linux virtual machines, making the troubleshooting process in the case of "no boot/no ssh" for ADE operating system-encrypted virtual machines quite time-consuming. Currently, the memory requirements shown in *Table 5.1* apply:

Virtual machine	Minimum memory
Only data disks encrypted.	2 GB
Both data and system disks are encrypted. The root filesystem size is under 4 GB.	8 GB
Both data and system disks are encrypted. The root filesystem size is over 4 GB.	2 times the root filesystem size.

Table 5.1: Virtual machines with memory requirements

Note

Once encryption is complete, you may reduce the virtual machine's memory size.

Keep in mind that it is mandatory to have temporary disks enabled in order to use Azure Disk Encryption. On a practical level, this makes virtual machine types Dv4, Dsv4, Ev4, and Esv4 unable to use disk encryption.

Another limitation is that generation 2 virtual machines and Lsv2-series virtual machines are not supported currently. You can find all unsupported scenarios documented here: https://docs.microsoft.com/azure/virtual-machines/linux/disk-encryption-linux#unsupported-scenarios.

The list of supported Linux distributions for Azure Disk Encryption is quite extensive, but it covers only a subset of all endorsed distributions. As the list is updated frequently, we won't include it here, but you can find the up-to-date list in the Azure documentation: https://docs.microsoft.com/azure/virtual-machines/linux/disk-encryption-overview#supported-operating-systems.

Next, let's take a look at how to keep up with updates and security patches for Linux on Azure.

Updating Linux on Azure

Azure provides mechanisms to update all supported Linux distributions. For some distributions, Microsoft has its own update repository mirrored from the official upstream repository, while for others, the updates come directly from third-party vendors' repositories.

Red Hat Enterprise Linux (RHEL) updates are available from Azure directly running Red Hat Update Infrastructure. This update repository is available for PAYG deployments of RHEL. For virtual machines deployed using the **Bring-Your-Own-Subscription (BYOS)** method, you need to use Red Hat's own update servers or your own company's Red Hat Satellite server to download updates.

Read more about RHEL on Azure updates and the Azure RHUI here: https://docs. microsoft.com/azure/virtual-machines/workloads/redhat/redhat-rhui.

> **Note**
>
> If you have a Red Hat Satellite server, you can continue to use it with RHEL on Azure for virtual machines that have been migrated from on-premises to Azure. Satellite can also be used with BYOS installations.
>
> You should not use Satellite with PAYG images as you would be consuming your RHEL client certificates as well as consuming your PAYG subscription and practically paying twice for the RHEL installation.

SUSE Linux Enterprise Server (SLES) has a slightly different architecture for the update servers: your SLES virtual machines will get updates directly from official SUSE-operated repositories. You can find more details on SLES and Azure updates from the SUSE documentation: https://www.suse.com/c/?s=cloud-regionsrv-client.

To update your Linux servers on Azure, you can do it the old-fashioned way by logging in to the servers via SSH and invoking apt-get update or yum update depending on your Linux distribution. Ubuntu on Azure can get also updates from mirrors hosted on Azure. The repository server alias configured by default on Ubuntu images on Azure is azure.archive.ubuntu.com. This host name is resolved to the actual server in the region of your resource group:

```
toni@vm1:~$ sudo apt-get update
Hit:1 http://azure.archive.ubuntu.com/ubuntu bionic InRelease
Hit:2 http://azure.archive.ubuntu.com/ubuntu bionic-updates InRelease
Hit:3 http://azure.archive.ubuntu.com/ubuntu bionic-backports InRelease
Hit:4 http://security.ubuntu.com/ubuntu bionic-security InRelease
Reading package lists... Done
toni@vm1:~$ host azure.archive.ubuntu.com
azure.archive.ubuntu.com is an alias for ubuntu-archive-asm.trafficmanager.net.
ubuntu-archive-asm.trafficmanager.net is an alias for cloud-mirror-lb.southeastasia.cloudapp.azure.com.
cloud-mirror-lb.southeastasia.cloudapp.azure.com has address 20.195.37.151
toni@vm1:~$
```

Figure 5.8: Finding the update server address

In this example, you can see that the nearest Ubuntu update server for me was located in the Southeast Asia region and that its IP address was 20.195.37.151.

Microsoft also provides Azure Update Management, which is an add-on mechanism assisting you in managing updates to Linux servers.

Azure Update Management

To avoid manual repetitive work, you can update one or more servers simultaneously using the Azure Update Management service. This service is part of Azure Automation and supports both Linux and Windows operating systems.

Azure Update Management is not the only tool in Azure for update management. If you are already using Ansible for your update management and automation, Ansible Automation is also available on Azure.

Currently, only some Linux distributions are supported with Azure Update Management. Please refer to the documentation for an up-to-date list: https://docs. microsoft.com/azure/automation/update-management/overview.

You can use the Azure Update Management service to list all available updates and manage the process of installing the required updates for servers. This service uses the Azure Linux Agent to communicate with virtual machines as described earlier in this chapter.

Figure 5.9 illustrates the architecture of the Azure Update Management service:

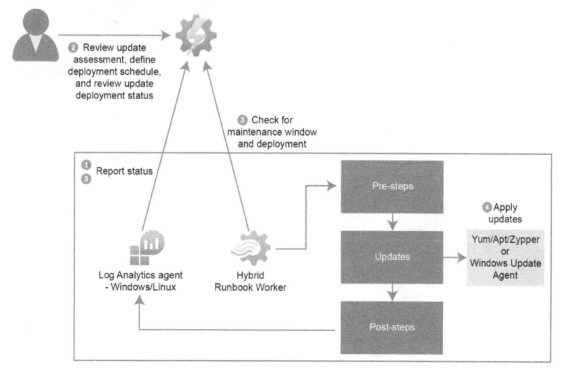

Figure 5.9: Azure Update Management architecture

Azure Update Management does not replace the normal update mechanism or package manager of a Linux distribution, but it issues requests to those to execute the required maintenance tasks. Practically, this means that, for example, the Ubuntu updates are still being installed by the apt tool and, for example, in RHEL, the updates are being managed by yum. The updates are fetched from the repository configured in the Linux installation.

On Linux, the available updates are automatically polled once per hour by Azure Update Management.

Now, let's take a look at the next hands-on lab for managing Linux on Azure to guide you further in your cloud journey.

Hands-on managing Linux on Azure

Linux logs can be ingested into the Log Analytics workspace. In this hands-on exercise, we will see how we can ingest the syslog from our migrated Linux machine into the Log Analytics workspace and analyze it using **Kusto Query Language (KQL)**.

Syslog is an event logging protocol that is widely used in Linux. The messages sent by the applications may get stored on the local machine or delivered to a syslog collector. Using the Linux Log Analytics agent, we will configure the syslog daemon to forward these syslog entries to the agent, and the agent will then send the messages to the Log Analytics workspace, which is part of Azure Monitor. Here, we are using the Log Analytics agent to push the data to the Log Analytics workspace.

Figure 5.10 is a graphical representation of how data is sent to **Azure Monitor** from the Linux machine:

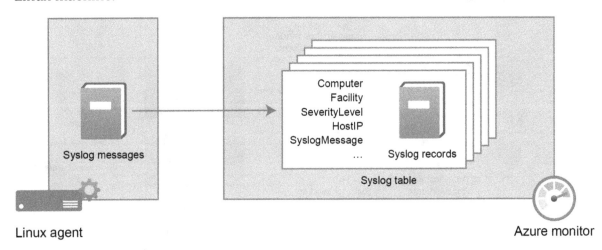

Figure 5.10: Sending syslog messages to Azure Monitor

The syslog collector supports the following facilities:

- kern
- user
- mail
- daemon
- auth
- syslog
- lpr
- news
- uucp
- cron
- authpriv
- ftp
- local0-local7

If you would like to collect any facility outside the list, then you may need to configure a custom data source in Azure Monitor. In our hands-on exercise, we will onboard the LAMP server, which we migrated in *Chapter 4*, *Performing migration to Azure*, to the Log Analytics workspace, and then we will configure it to collect the syslog.

The first step will be to onboard the virtual machine to send logs to the Log Analytics workspace.

Creating a Log Analytics workspace

The process is very simple—we need to create a Log Analytics workspace and connect our virtual machine to the workspace. You can follow the steps outlined here to onboard your virtual machine:

1. Navigate to the Azure portal and search for **Log Analytics workspaces** and click on that. Once you are in the **Log Analytics workspaces** blade, click on the **New** button as shown in *Figure 5.11* to create a workspace:

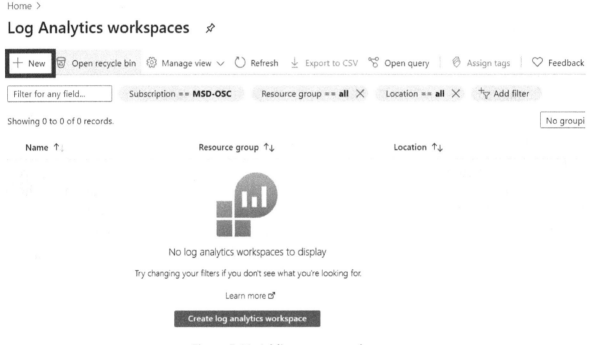

Figure 5.11: Adding a new workspace

2. Clicking on **New** will redirect you to the wizard to create a workspace and the **Basics** tab requires basic information such as **Subscription**, **Resource group**, **Name**, and **Region**. You can complete these details as shown in *Figure 5.12* and proceed to **Pricing tier**:

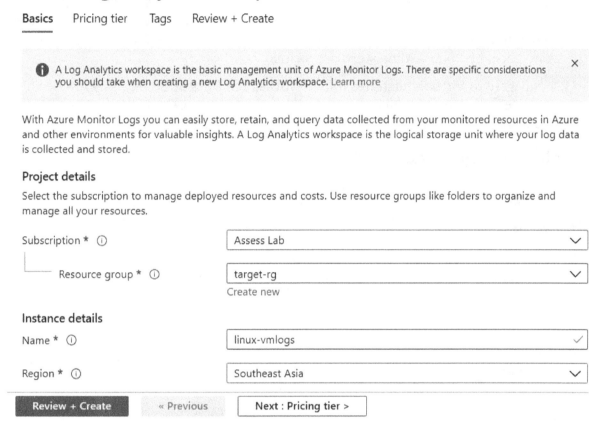

Figure 5.12: Creating a Log Analytics workspace

3. For **Pricing tier**, you can keep the default value: Pay-as-you-go (Per GB 2018). You can also reserve the capacity reservation if required; however, for this hands-on exercise, it is not required.

Finally, you can click on **Review + Create** and the workspace will be created.

Onboarding an Azure virtual machine

Now that you've created the workspace to which the logs will get ingested, the next stage is the virtual machine onboarding. You need to open the workspace we created to onboard the virtual machine. You can search for **Log Analytics workspace** in the top search bar and you will be able to see the name of the workspace. Click on it and open the workspace. The onboarding steps are as follows:

1. Navigate to **Virtual machines** under **Workspace Data Sources** and you'll be able to see the virtual machine that we migrated from on-premises. **Log Analytics Connection** will be shown as **Not connected**, as seen in *Figure 5.13*:

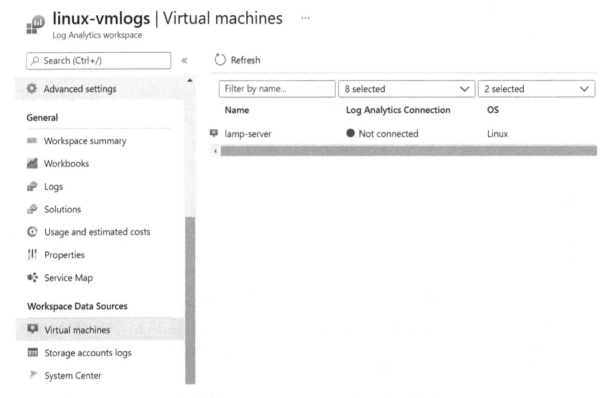

Figure 5.13: Adding data sources to the workspace

2. Click on the virtual machine name and you will be taken to a new page where you will be able to see the **Connect** option, as shown in *Figure 5.14*. Please note that in order for the connect operation to succeed, the virtual machine should be in the running state, otherwise it will fail. Also, make sure that walinuxagent is installed, as already recommended in the *Manage and Secure* section, and that the agent is listed as **Ready** under the **Properties** blade of the virtual machine. Click on **Connect**, after which the extension will be configured on the virtual machine:

Home > Log Analytics workspaces > linux-vmlogs >

lamp-server ⋯
Virtual machine

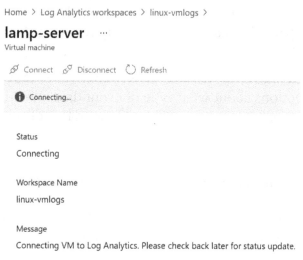

Figure 5.14: Connecting to Log Analytics

3. If you navigate back to the previous **Virtual machines** blade, you will be able to see that the status has been changed to **Connecting**, as is visible in *Figure* 5.15. This process will take some time and Log Analytics extensions will be configured on the selected virtual machine:

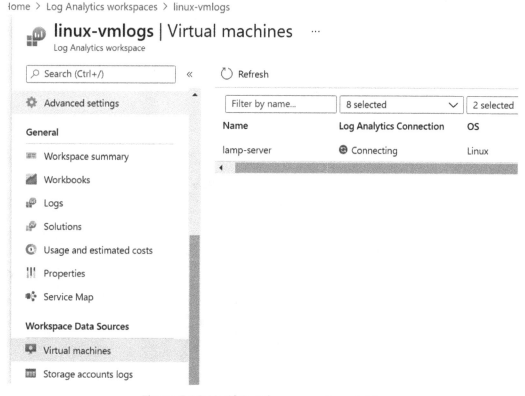

Figure 5.15: Verifying the connection status

4. Once the extensions are installed, the virtual machine is onboarded to the Log Analytics workspace. You can confirm this by verifying that the status of the connection is **Connected**.

Onboarding is complete; however, we still haven't configured that Log Analytics workspace with instructions about what type of event data should be pulled from the virtual machine. In the next section, we will configure data collection.

Data collection

We have onboarded our virtual machine, and the Log Analytics extension is ready to collect the data and ingest it into the Log Analytics workspace. However, we need to set up data collection, that is, we need to specify which datasets we need to pull from the virtual machine. We can configure the collection as follows:

1. Navigate back to the **Log Analytics workspace** we created and select **Agents configuration**, as shown in *Figure 5.16*:

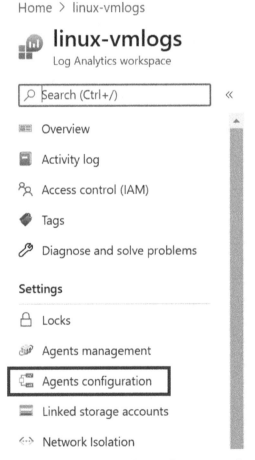

Figure 5.16: Navigating to the data collection configuration

2. Navigate to **Linux performance counters** and add the recommended counters. Azure will present you with a list of recommended performance counter names, as shown in *Figure 5.17*. If you require additional counters, you can click on **Add performance counter** and add it. Once done, click on **Apply** to save the configuration:

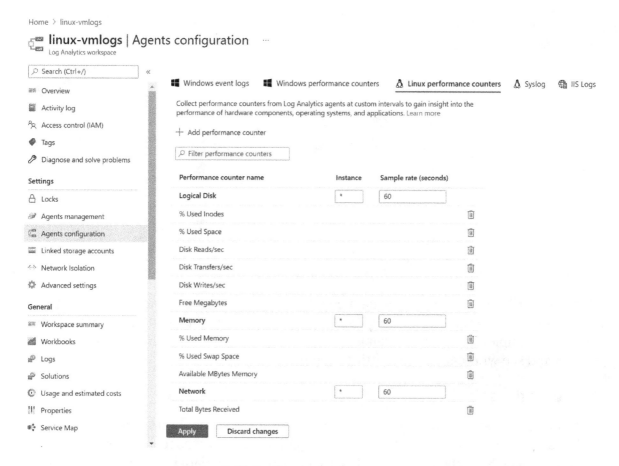

Figure 5.17: Configuring performance counters

3. After configuring the performance counters, you can click on the **Syslog** tab. Clicking on **Add facility** will list all the facilities available to you, including **auth**, **authpriv**, and **cron**. Also, you can specify the logging level for each facility. You can add the following facilities as shown in *Figure 5.18*. Once added, click on **Apply** to save the configuration:

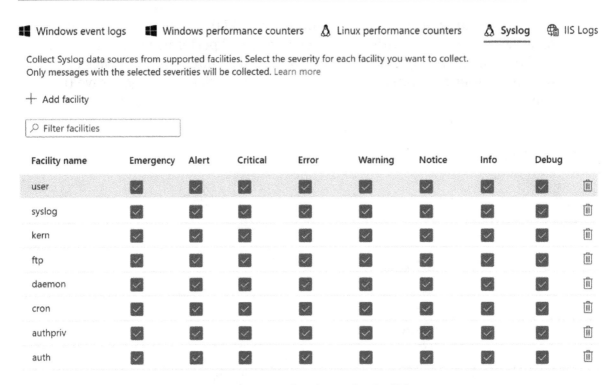

Figure 5.18: Configuring syslog facilities

With that, we have configured the data collection. Now we need to verify whether the data is getting ingested into the Log Analytics workspace, and ingestion will take some time after completing the onboarding. In the next section, we will run some sample queries and see whether we are getting results.

Querying data

In the previous section, we configured several performance counters and syslog facilities that need to be ingested into our Log Analytics workspace. Now, we will query these logs using KQL and verify whether we are getting the data ingested from the virtual machine.

There will be different tables to store the performance, syslog, and other data. You can query the logs of the virtual machine by scoping your queries to the specific virtual machine. If you run the query from the workspace level, logs from all onboarded virtual machines will be returned. Nevertheless, you can change the scope from here, too. In our case, there is only one virtual machine onboarded to the workspace, so querying from the **Virtual machines** blade or the **Log Analytics** blade will be the same. However, let's query from the **Virtual machines** blade to make sure that we are looking at the right scope:

1. Navigate to **Virtual machines** and open the virtual machine we migrated from on-premises in *Chapter 4, Performing migration to Azure.* From **Monitoring**, select **Logs**, as shown in *Figure 5.19*:

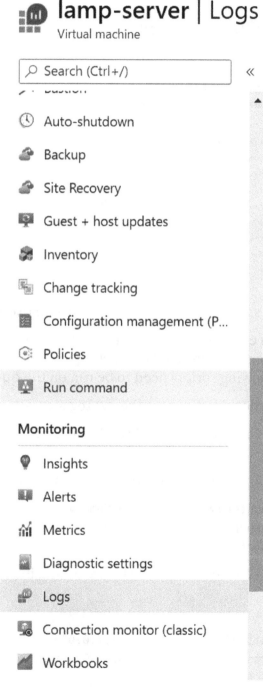

Figure 5.19: Navigating to Logs from the Virtual machines blade

2. To list all the tables in the workspace, you can run a search * | distinct $table, in the **query** window and see the results in the **Results** window. An example is shown in *Figure 5.20*:

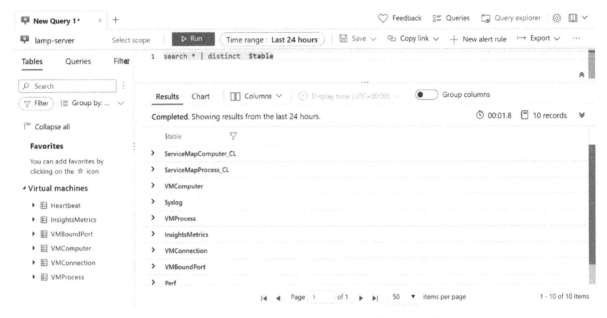

Figure 5.20: Listing all tables in the Log Analytics workspace

3. In the results, you can see multiple tables, such as Syslog, VMProcess, VMBoundPort, VMConnection, and Perf. Let's query some tables and check the results. All the following scripts need to be run on the **query** window.

4. Return all informational logs where the syslog message contains rsyslog:

```
Syslog | where SeverityLevel == "info" and SyslogMessage contains
"rsyslog"
```

5. Render a time chart for the % Used Memory performance counter:

```
Perf | where CounterName == "% Used Memory"
| project TimeGenerated, CounterValue
| render timechart
```

6. Return all external connections made by processes, including the destination IP and port number:

```
VMConnection
| where DestinationIp !startswith "127.0.0"
| distinct ProcessName, DestinationIp, DestinationPort
```

You can run any sort of query using the available dataset. KQL is very powerful, and it can perform wonders on your dataset. With this exercise, we have reached the end of the hands-on lab. In this lab, we onboarded the on-premises virtual machine we migrated in *Chapter 4, Performing migration to Azure*, to the Log Analytics workspace and ingested the performance and syslog into the workspace. Furthermore, we queried the ingested data using KQL to obtain some results and time charts.

Summary

This chapter has covered various details about how to effectively operate Linux on Azure. First, we went through the *Optimize* phase, including the ACM and Azure Advisor tools. Then, we proceeded to the *Manage & Secure* phase, where we spent some time with the data protection functionality as well as the Azure Linux Agent.

Just before the hands-on lab, you also learned how Azure Update Management works in conjunction with various Linux distributions' update mechanisms.

We have now covered all the topics regarding assessing, migrating, and operating Linux on Azure. What happens when something doesn't work as you expect? Let's find out in the next chapter, where we will guide you through troubleshooting Linux on Azure.

6

Troubleshooting and problem solving

Our migration journey started in *Chapter 3, Assessment and migration planning*, where we saw the importance of assessment and its contribution to the overall migration journey.

In *Chapter 4, Performing migration to Azure*, we witnessed the actual migration of Linux workloads to Microsoft Azure Virtual Machines as well as to managed services. *Chapter 5, Operating Linux on Azure*, was more about the post-migration strategies and tools for optimizing and securing workloads in Azure.

At this point, we have our **virtual machine** (**VM**) successfully migrated to Azure. Time to pack your bags and consider the job well done. However, sometimes things don't work the way they should. You might be getting strange errors in your log files or your client might be complaining that the migrated application is behaving incorrectly. You could even find out that your VM doesn't boot at all.

Being able to analyze the problem and debug the affected system yourself is quite important. You don't want to get stuck in the middle of your migration project just because you don't know how to figure out why something doesn't work.

This chapter will help you to learn and understand how to assess, debug, and fix the most common issues in Linux to Azure migration projects. These topics are also useful for newly created Linux VMs on Azure.

In this chapter, you will learn about the following:

- Remote connectivity and VM start issues
- Common Linux runtime challenges
- Azure diagnostics tooling – a summary
- Opening support requests

To get the most from this chapter, you should be familiar with the typical debugging methods for on-premises or hosted Linux servers. On Azure, some aspects of debugging work a bit differently compared to on-premises.

Let's start by discussing the most unwanted problem—a VM you can't connect to.

Remote connectivity and VM start issues

In this section, we'll look at some common problems that can cause your VM to be unreachable via the network, and we'll provide a couple of ways to fix those issues.

The most common problem we have seen is that you can't reach the VM using ssh, as shown in *Figure 6.1*:

```
toni@Toni-SL3:~$ ssh 10.0.0.1
ssh: connect to host 10.0.0.1 port 22: Resource temporarily unavailable
toni@Toni-SL3:~$ |
```

Figure 6.1: SSH connection fails

In this case, the user tried to connect to an Azure VM's private IP address, 10.0.0.1, directly from their laptop. This fails as the private IP addresses on Azure are always in the private IP range and cannot be directly accessed via the public internet. This is a change from your typical on-premises environment where you might have had the ability to directly connect to any VM in your datacenter. The actual error message may differ depending on your operating system and the actual cause of the connection failure.

Azure VMs typically have two IP addresses: the private internal IP and a public external IP. You can get a list of all the IP addresses of a VM from the Azure portal or the command line. With the Azure CLI you can use the `az vm list-ip-addresses` command, as shown in *Figure 6.2*:

```
toni@Toni-SL3:~$ az vm list-ip-addresses --resource-group vm1_group --name vm1 -o table
VirtualMachine     PublicIPAddresses     PrivateIPAddresses
--------------     -----------------     ------------------
vm1                40.65.190.254         10.0.0.4
toni@Toni-SL3:~$
```

Figure 6.2: A list of VM IP addresses

If the connection still doesn't work when using the public IP address, the cause is probably one of the following:

- An Azure network security group is blocking the connection.
- The SSH service is not running on the VM.
- The Linux firewall is blocking the connection.

These are the most common issues we have seen. If your issue is not one of these, you will find more analysis guidance later in this chapter in the *Azure diagnostics tooling – a summary* section.

Network connectivity issues can be analyzed using the Azure Connection Troubleshoot tool found on the Azure portal, as shown in *Figure 6.3*:

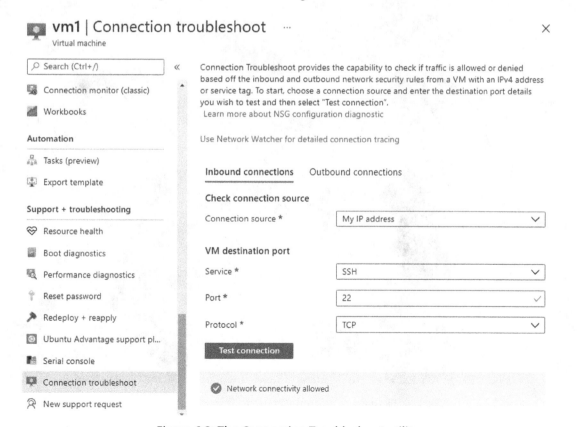

Figure 6.3: The Connection Troubleshoot utility

In this example, we can see that the Azure network connection is working correctly and the problem is not in the network security group settings.

Run commands without a network connection

To tackle problems inside the Linux VM you can use Azure extensions. To start sshd this way you first need to create a local custom.json file with the following content:

```
{
  "commandToExecute": "sudo systemctl start sshd"
}
```

Then invoke a custom extension by using the following command:

```
az vm extension set --resource-group vm1_group --vm-name vm1 \
  --name customScript --publisher Microsoft.Azure.Extensions \
  --settings ./custom.json
```

The result should be successful, as shown in *Figure* 6.4:

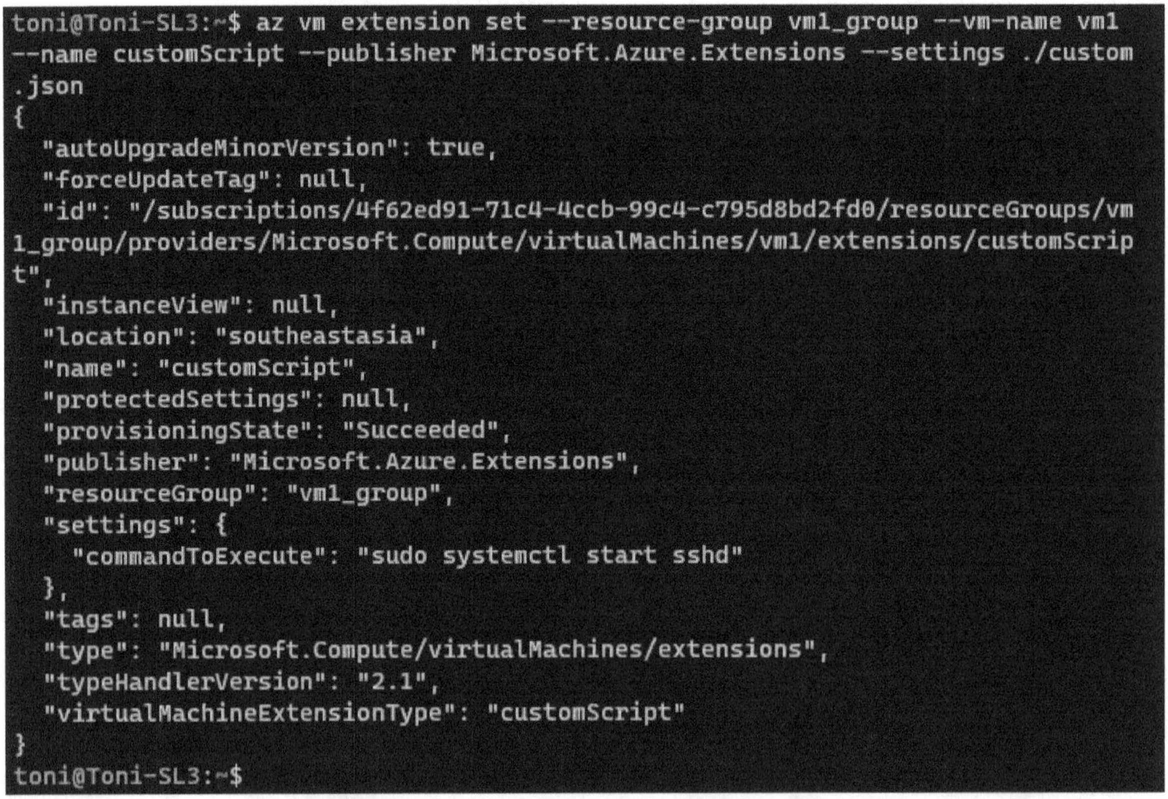

```
toni@Toni-SL3:~$ az vm extension set --resource-group vm1_group --vm-name vm1
--name customScript --publisher Microsoft.Azure.Extensions --settings ./custom
.json
{
  "autoUpgradeMinorVersion": true,
  "forceUpdateTag": null,
  "id": "/subscriptions/4f62ed91-71c4-4ccb-99c4-c795d8bd2fd0/resourceGroups/vm
1_group/providers/Microsoft.Compute/virtualMachines/vm1/extensions/customScrip
t",
  "instanceView": null,
  "location": "southeastasia",
  "name": "customScript",
  "protectedSettings": null,
  "provisioningState": "Succeeded",
  "publisher": "Microsoft.Azure.Extensions",
  "resourceGroup": "vm1_group",
  "settings": {
    "commandToExecute": "sudo systemctl start sshd"
  },
  "tags": null,
  "type": "Microsoft.Compute/virtualMachines/extensions",
  "typeHandlerVersion": "2.1",
  "virtualMachineExtensionType": "customScript"
}
toni@Toni-SL3:~$
```

Figure 6.4: Running a custom extension

You can use the same method to run any commands remotely, for example, to turn off the Linux firewall if you suspect it might be blocking your SSH connection.

The Azure portal also offers a simple user interface to run commands and simple scripts remotely, as shown in *Figure 6.5*:

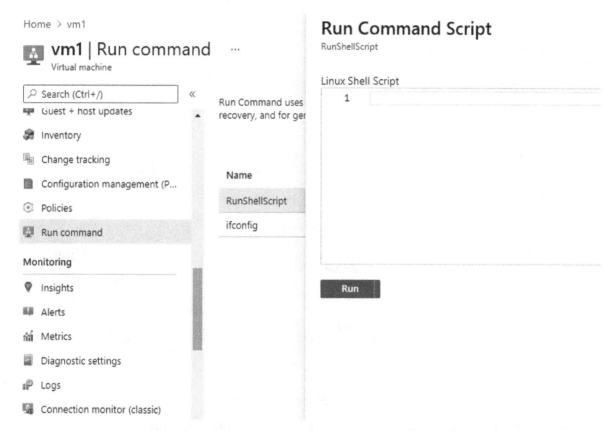

Figure 6.5: Run command functionality in the Azure portal

For the extensions to work, you need to have the Azure Linux Agent installed and running on the VM, as Azure extensions use it to execute commands on the VM.

If the remote SSH connection still doesn't work, the reason could be a bit more serious: your VM might not actually boot properly, and it is not possible to fix this using scripted tools.

Boot diagnostics and serial console access

If you suspect the VM is failing to boot properly, you can easily confirm it by looking at the boot logs using the **Boot diagnostics** tool in the Azure portal, as shown in *Figure 6.6*:

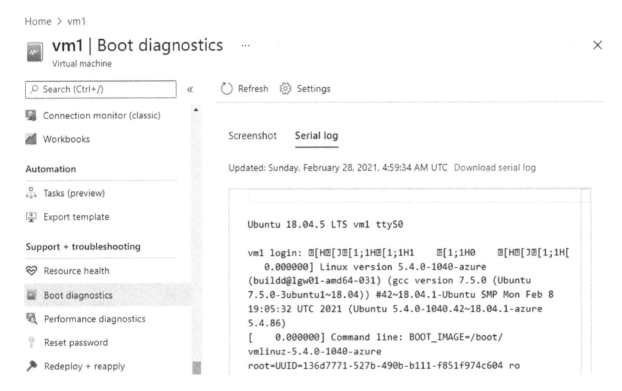

Figure 6.6: Boot diagnostics utility

The system logs are captured from the virtual serial terminal and are read-only. You can use the boot logs to find out about and diagnose problems.

If you need to log in to the system to fix the problem, you can use the Azure **Serial console** functionality, which can be also found in the VM **Support + troubleshooting** section of the Azure portal, as shown in *Figure 6.7*:

Figure 6.7: Using serial console access

In this example, we can see that the Ubuntu server is stuck at the GRUB bootloader screen waiting for interaction from the user. At this point, you can proceed to fix the problem as you would do on any on-premises physical or virtual Linux server. We won't go into the details of fixing this particular problem since it could be caused by a number of issues, ranging from a failed kernel upgrade to a misconfigured partitioning configuration. Instead, let's look at an overview of typical boot failure causes.

Common boot problems

Sometimes your Linux VM doesn't boot at all on Azure. This is quite a rare problem for VMs created from Azure Linux images, but can be quite common if you migrated the VM from on-premises to Azure.

There could be various reasons for a VM not booting. Microsoft has published the following notes regarding Linux on Azure:

- Hyper-V **virtual hard disk (VHDX)** format is not supported. Use fixed VHD instead.
- VirtualBox dynamically allocated disks are not supported. Use fixed size instead.
- The maximum VHD size is 1,023 GB.
- Using **Logical Volume Manager (LVM)** on system disk may cause name collisions. It is recommended to use the standard partition for the system disk and LVM only on data disks.
- UDF file system support is mandatory, so do not disable it. It is used by the Azure Linux Agent.
- Kernel versions before 2.6.37 and Red Hat kernel versions before 2.6.32-504 don't support **non-uniform memory access (NUMA)**. Disable it with the numa=off parameter in grub.conf.
- Do not use the system disk for the swap file. Let the Azure Linux Agent set up the swap on the temporary resource disk.

There are some very common issues with booting Linux on Azure that happen when migrating from **Linux Kernel Virtual Machine (KVM)** or VMware virtualization to Azure. By default, Linux distributions don't include the Hyper-V driver in the ramdisk image. As Azure runs on Hyper-V hypervisors, the hv_vmbus and hv_storvsc kernel modules are necessary for Linux to boot on Azure.

If you encounter this problem, the proper fix is to run these commands on Linux before migrating the VM into Azure:

```
sudo mkinitrd --preload=hv_storvsc --preload=hv_vmbus -v \
-f initrd-'uname -r'.img 'uname -r'
```

Please note that it is not possible to fix this problem on Azure by using this VM directly. Typically, it is better to fix the source image and move it to Azure again. However, the method for fixing this situation on the Azure side would be to mount the disk on a working VM and apply the fixes that way.

Sometimes you may encounter boot issues due the virtual disk size, especially if you have created the disk manually on your source system and have converted a raw disk to VHD. All virtual drives on Azure must use 1 MB size alignment. This can be fixed before uploading the image to Azure, for example by using qemu-img to convert the image:

```
rawdisk="MyLinuxVM.raw"
vhddisk="MyLinuxVM.vhd"
MB=$((1024*1024))
size=$(qemu-img info -f raw --output json "$rawdisk" | \
  gawk 'match($0, /"virtual-size": ([0-9]+),/, val) {print val[1]}')
rounded_size=$(((($size+$MB-1)/$MB)*$MB))
echo "Rounded Size = $rounded_size"
qemu-img resize MyLinuxVM.raw $rounded_size
qemu-img convert -f raw -o subformat=fixed,force_size \
  -O vpc MyLinuxVM.raw MyLinuxVM.vhd
```

After your image is converted correctly, you may upload it to Azure again and start it. Once your server boots properly we can focus on possible runtime issues.

Common Linux runtime challenges

In this section, we will demonstrate how to analyze and fix some common runtime problems. One of the most common issues with applications on Linux is incompatibility with SELinux settings, especially if you migrate your application from one VM to another.

Also, issues with disk space running out or other storage issues such as storage encryption in conjunction with migration may be troublesome. Lastly, some unexpected performance issues may arise when you move workloads from on-premises to Azure. Let's start by looking at how SELinux works in Azure.

SELinux

Security-Enhanced Linux—more commonly known as SELinux—is a security module for the Linux kernel, which provides a mechanism for supporting various access control policies to the operating system. There are some alternatives to SELinux, such as AppArmor, but they are not commonly used currently. SELinux can be considered the standard way of securing Linux installations.

To check the status of SELinux on your Linux VM you can run the sestatus command. It prints out many variables, as shown in *Figure 6.8*:

```
[root@vm2 ~]# sestatus
SELinux status:                 enabled
SELinuxfs mount:                /sys/fs/selinux
SELinux root directory:         /etc/selinux
Loaded policy name:             targeted
Current mode:                   enforcing
Mode from config file:          enforcing
Policy MLS status:              enabled
Policy deny_unknown status:     allowed
Memory protection checking:     actual (secure)
Max kernel policy version:      31
[root@vm2 ~]#
```

Figure 6.8: Output of the sestatus command

In this example, you can see the SELinux status is enabled and the operating mode is enforcing. *Figure 6.8* is taken from a CentOS 8.2.2004 VM installed from Azure Marketplace.

SELinux is available for all the common Linux distributions. However, it may not be enabled by default, or it may be configured in permissive mode by default. The three operating modes for SELinux are:

- enforcing: SELinux security policy is enforced.
- permissive: SELinux prints warnings instead of enforcing the policy.
- disabled: No SELinux policy is loaded.

One of the most common SELinux-related questions is: *How do I disable SELinux?* The correct answer should always be: *You don't.* The recommended operation mode is, for practical reasons, permissive. In the enforcing mode, there is a high probability that many applications from **independent software vendors (ISV)** will stop working or have some unexpected runtime errors. However, if you are running applications developed in house, or are sure the applications are compatible with SELinux in enforcing mode, then naturally the recommendation is to use enforcing mode.

By running SELinux in permissive mode, you can be sure your applications will run and that you can catch possible security problems by auditing the security logs. When developing new applications, it is recommended to use enforcing mode. This way you can be sure your application will run in any production system.

You can learn more about SELinux and the reasons why it should be not disabled in this amazing SELinux coloring book authored by *Dan Walsh* and illustrated by *Máirín Duffy*: https://github.com/mairin/selinux-coloring-book.

On Azure, you can use SELinux in enforcing or permissive mode without problems in most cases. The only time when you need to turn off SELinux completely is when you want to start encrypting a Linux OS disk on Azure. After the encryption is complete, you can enable SELinux again.

If you have SELinux completely disabled or running in permissive mode first, and later decide to switch on enforcing mode, you will probably need to fix the file security labels. The easiest way to do this is by telling SELinux to relabel the filesystem on the next reboot, and then to reboot the server as follows:

```
sudo touch /.autorelabel; sudo reboot
```

After the server is up again, SELinux will have the whole filesystem labeled and the security contexts of the files should be up to date again.

> **Note**
>
> If the system was installed without the selinux-policy package, you will need to make sure SELinux is initialized during system startup. The dracut utility must be run to set SELinux awareness for the initramfs filesystem.
>
> Not doing so will cause SELinux to not start during system boot.

A useful reference for SELinux-related issues can be found via Red Hat: https://access. redhat.com/documentation/red_hat_enterprise_linux/6/html/security-enhanced_ linux/sect-security-enhanced_linux-working_with_selinux-changing_selinux_ modes.

Next, let's take a look at typical storage issues and how to work around them.

Storage configuration issues

In this section, we are going to cover a few things that could go wrong when adding disks. Storage issues are sensitive as they can lead to no-boot scenarios—these errors are mainly due to configuration issues in the /etc/fstab file. Linux administrators know the importance of this file and rectifying misconfigurations of this file can resolve no-boot scenarios related to disk and storage.

The following are some of the common scenarios and the corresponding logs that you would see in the serial console related to fstab. If you see any of these logs in the console, you can determine the root cause easily:

- **A disk mounted using SCSI ID in lieu of UUID**

```
Timed out waiting for device dev-incorrect.device.
Dependency failed for /data.
Dependency failed for Local File Systems.
```

- **An unattached device is missing**

```
Checking file systems…
fsck from util-linux 2.19.1
Checking all file systems.
/dev/sdc1: nonexistent device ("nofail" fstab option may be used to skip
this device)
```

- **Fstab misconfiguration or the disk is no longer attached**

```
The disk drive for /var/lib/mysql is not ready yet or not present.
Continue to wait, or Press S to skip mounting or M for manual recovery
```

- **A serial log entry shows an incorrect UUID**

```
[/sbin/fsck.ext4 (1) – /datadrive] fsck.ext4 -a UUID="<UUID>"
fsck.ext4: Unable to resolve UUID="<UUID>"
[FAILED
```

Other common causes include:

- System crashes
- Hardware or software malfunction
- Buggy drivers
- NFS write errors
- The filesystem not being properly shut down

These other common causes can be sometimes fixed by restarting or often by manually fixing the filesystem. For this, you can use either the serial console access as described earlier in this chapter, or alternatively attach the broken virtual OS disk to another VM as you would do in any on-premises system.

The Azure CLI provides an extension called **vm-repair** that makes it easy to create a repair VM and attach the broken VM disk to it. You can find more information about this extension from here: https://docs.microsoft.com/cli/azure/ext/vm-repair/vm/repair. Note that this extension requires Azure CLI version 2.0.67 or higher.

Disk encryption problems

It is not uncommon to encounter issues with disk encryption on Linux. These problems may arise also on Azure. Here are some typical issues you may face if you are using a customized VM image:

- The filesystem or partitioning doesn't match a customized VM image.
- Some third-party software, such as SAP, MongoDB, Apache Cassandra, and Docker, may be unsupported or not work properly if they are installed before encrypting the disk. Check the setup instructions carefully before installing!
- While a disk is in the middle of encryption initialization, some scripts started by Azure Resource Manager may not work correctly. Serializing encryption and disk encryption will help with these issues.
- SELinux needs to be disabled before starting to encrypt a disk, otherwise the filesystem unmount may fail. Remember to enable it again afterward!
- System disks using LVM cannot be encrypted. Always use normal partitions for system disks, and LVM only for data disks.
- Disk encryption consumes lots of memory. You should have more than 7 GB RAM if you enable encryption.

> **Note**
>
> The Linux system disk encryption process tries to unmount the system drive before running it through the disk encryption process. If it can't unmount the drive, an error message of `failed to unmount after` ... is very likely to appear.

Resizing disks

In case you happen to run out of storage space on your VM's system or data disks, Azure allows you to scale the VMs up and down quite easily, but there are some tasks in the Linux OS to be done to ensure the VM survives the changes.

> **Note**
>
> To test these commands, we recommend you create a new Linux VM on Azure. In the following screenshots we used a CentOS 7.9-based VM image.

First, we need to find out the current VM disk size. The az command is a very powerful tool to query various aspects of a VM:

```
az vm show -g vm1_group -n vm3 \
  --query "[storageProfile.osDisk.diskSizeGb, \
  storageProfile.osDisk.name, hardwareProfile.vmSize]"
```

This command lists the operating system disk size, unique name, and the VM size parameters, as shown in *Figure 6.9*:

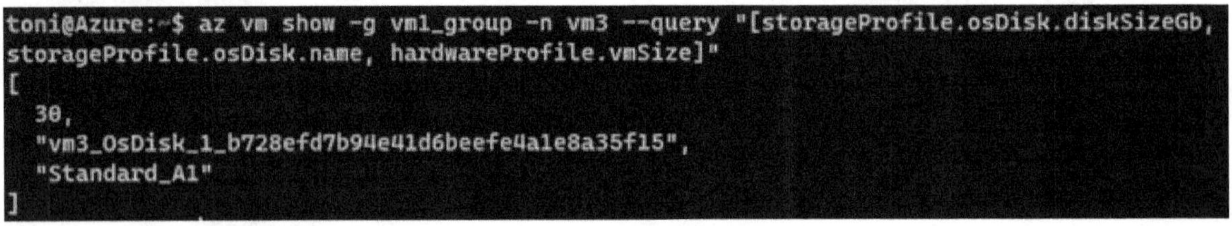

```
toni@Azure:~$ az vm show -g vm1_group -n vm3 --query "[storageProfile.osDisk.diskSizeGb,
storageProfile.osDisk.name, hardwareProfile.vmSize]"
[
  30,
  "vm3_OsDisk_1_b728efd7b94e41d6beefe4a1e8a35f15",
  "Standard_A1"
]
```

Figure 6.9: Output of the az vm show command

If you get an error, it is quite possible that the VM is not running. Start it and try again.

In our example the disk size was 30 GB and the VM is of the Standard_A1 type. The disk name is vm3_OsDisk_1_b728efd7b94e41d6beefe4a1e8a35f15.

To modify the disk the VM needs to be deallocated—just stopping it is not enough. After the VM has been deallocated we can proceed to increasing the system disk size.

> **Note**
>
> Currently, you cannot shrink disks in Azure. When increasing disk size, only add the space you will need.

To set the new size to 50 GB, do the following:

```
az disk update -g  vm1_group \
  -n vm3_OsDisk_1_b728efd7b94e41d6beefe4a1e8a35f15 --size-gb 50
```

This should output the new parameters for the disk after successful modification, as shown in *Figure 6.10*:

```
"name": "vm3_OsDisk_1_b728efd7b94e41d6beefe4a1e8a35f15",
"osType": "Linux",
"provisioningState": "Succeeded",
```

Figure 6.10: Successful disk resize

If you would like to verify that the change was implemented, you can show the actual disk size as follows, even when the VM is not running:

```
az disk show -g vm1_group \
 -n vm3_OsDisk_1_b728efd7b94e41d6beefe4a1e8a35f15 \
 --query "diskSizeGb"
```

This will print out the size in gigabytes and should show 50 in this case. Now we have successfully resized the disk on the storage system side, but at this point Linux thinks the disk size is 30 gigabytes.

Next, you will need to start the VM and log in to Linux with SSH. Now, in the Linux terminal, you can proceed to check whether you need to manually increase the volume size and filesystem size as you would do on any other Linux server.

Since there are numerous different ways to do these tasks, we will not be addressing them all. Azure doesn't set any limitations on how you manage the disks from within the Linux operating system.

In our test system, CentOS 7.9, it seems that the virtual disk size change on the sda2 device was automatically recognized by the operating system at boot time, as you can see in *Figure 6.11*.

You can run the lsblk command to see the block device sizes on your VM:

```
[root@vm3 ~]# lsblk
NAME        MAJ:MIN RM   SIZE RO TYPE MOUNTPOINT
sda           8:0    0    50G  0 disk
├─sda1        8:1    0   500M  0 part /boot
├─sda2        8:2    0    49G  0 part /
├─sda14       8:14   0     4M  0 part
└─sda15       8:15   0   495M  0 part /boot/efi
sdb           8:16   0    70G  0 disk
└─sdb1        8:17   0    70G  0 part /mnt/resource
```

Figure 6.11: Block devices list

To see if the filesystem has also noticed the increase in the block device size, you can run the df -hT command. Our system demonstrated that the XFS filesystem on the sda2 disk was automatically resized:

```
[root@vm3 ~]# df -hT
Filesystem       Type      Size  Used Avail Use% Mounted on
devtmpfs         devtmpfs  830M     0  830M   0% /dev
tmpfs            tmpfs     842M     0  842M   0% /dev/shm
tmpfs            tmpfs     842M  9.0M  833M   2% /run
tmpfs            tmpfs     842M     0  842M   0% /sys/fs/cgroup
/dev/sda2        xfs        50G  1.6G   48G   4% /
/dev/sda1        xfs       494M   65M  430M  14% /boot
/dev/sda15       vfat      495M   12M  484M   3% /boot/efi
/dev/sdb1        ext4       69G  2.1G   64G   4% /mnt/resource
tmpfs            tmpfs     169M     0  169M   0% /run/user/1000
```

Figure 6.12: List of filesystems

For many years, Linux administrators had to manually resize block devices and filesystems after the physical or virtual storage size was changed. Nowadays, some Linux distributions can resize the system disk automatically for you at boot time or even at runtime. Data disks still require you to manually grow the partition or volume size and to grow the filesystem size as well.

For data disks, the process is very similar. The biggest difference is that you can do it while the VM is running. To do this you practically need to unmount the disk and detach it from the VM before you modify the virtual disk size. Consider taking backups before modifying partitions, volumes, or filesystems manually—there is a risk of data loss if you make even a small error in the process.

Performance issues and analysis

Performance counters in Linux are useful for providing insights into the performance of hardware components, operating systems, and applications. With Azure Monitor, you can collect performance counters from Log Analytics agents at frequent intervals for **Near Real-Time (NRT)** analysis. You also get aggregated performance data for longer-term analysis and reporting.

To set up performance counters, you can use the Azure Log Analytics workspace user interface or the command line.

As there are massive numbers of metrics we could collect from a Linux VM, we are not going into detail at this point. However, it is worth mentioning that the typical data sources are:

- Syslog
- CollectD
- Performance counters
- Custom logs

You can find details about data collections supported by the Log Analytics agent here: https://docs.microsoft.com/azure/azure-monitor/agents/agent-data-sources.

This documentation will give you a good set of tools you can use to analyze the performance of your VM.

In on-premises environments, it is a common practice to use tools such as dd to see how the storage is performing. In Azure however you should not rely on the results of this command. Instead, you should use a tool called **fio**, available from most Linux distribution repositories. It gives reliable results when analyzing the actual disk performance, measured as **input/output operations per second (IOPS)**.

To use fio, you will first need to create a new file called `fiowrite.ini` with the following content:

```
[global]
size=30g
direct=1
iodepth=256
ioengine=libaio
bs=4k
numjobs=1
[writer1]
rw=randwrite
directory=/
```

The last parameter tells us which directory or mount point we want to use for testing. In this case, we are using the system disk, which is mounted on the root directory.

To start the test, run the following command, which starts a test that runs for 30 seconds:

```
sudo fio --runtime 30 fiowrite.ini
```

You should get an output like the one in *Figure 6.13*:

```
Starting 1 process
writer1: Laying out IO file (1 file / 30720MiB)
Jobs: 1 (f=1): [w(1)][0.1%][eta 08h:32m:19s]
writer1: (groupid=0, jobs=1): err= 0: pid=28941: Sun Feb 28 13:15:10 2021
  write: IOPS=265, BW=1062KiB/s (1087kB/s)(35.9MiB/34654msec); 0 zone resets
    slat (usec): min=3, max=3528.7k, avg=3426.34, stdev=81575.04
    clat (usec): min=268, max=8415.6k, avg=960238.53, stdev=1444497.63
     lat (usec): min=679, max=8421.5k, avg=963665.87, stdev=1446247.47
    clat percentiles (msec):
     |  1.00th=[   11],  5.00th=[   13], 10.00th=[   16], 20.00th=[   20],
     | 30.00th=[   29], 40.00th=[   53], 50.00th=[  134], 60.00th=[  376],
     | 70.00th=[ 1028], 80.00th=[ 2232], 90.00th=[ 3205], 95.00th=[ 3540],
     | 99.00th=[ 6342], 99.50th=[ 6342], 99.90th=[ 6342], 99.95th=[ 7886],
     | 99.99th=[ 8423]
   bw (  KiB/s): min=    7, max=10536, per=100.00%, avg=2965.46, stdev=2799.57, samples=24
   iops        : min=    1, max= 2634, avg=741.21, stdev=699.87, samples=24
  lat (usec)   : 500=0.01%, 750=0.01%
  lat (msec)   : 2=0.01%, 10=0.74%, 20=20.68%, 50=17.70%, 100=7.59%
  lat (msec)   : 250=7.94%, 500=8.27%, 750=3.66%, 1000=1.90%, 2000=11.26%
  lat (msec)   : >=2000=20.23%
  cpu          : usr=0.13%, sys=0.58%, ctx=192, majf=0, minf=13
  IO depths    : 1=0.1%, 2=0.1%, 4=0.1%, 8=0.1%, 16=0.2%, 32=0.3%, >=64=99.3%
     submit    : 0=0.0%, 4=100.0%, 8=0.0%, 16=0.0%, 32=0.0%, 64=0.0%, >=64=0.0%
     complete  : 0=0.0%, 4=100.0%, 8=0.0%, 16=0.0%, 32=0.0%, 64=0.0%, >=64=0.1%
     issued rwts: total=0,9199,0,0 short=0,0,0,0 dropped=0,0,0,0
     latency   : target=0, window=0, percentile=100.00%, depth=256

Run status group 0 (all jobs):
  WRITE: bw=1062KiB/s (1087kB/s), 1062KiB/s-1062KiB/s (1087kB/s-1087kB/s), io=35.9MiB (37.7MB)
, run=34654-34654msec

Disk stats (read/write):
  sdb: ios=147/9255, merge=0/11, ticks=212/6986463, in_queue=6982406, util=1.60%
```

Figure 6.13: Disk performance output

We have highlighted the IOPS line in yellow. In this case, the average IOPS number was 741.21. We used a standard SSD disk and the Standard A1 VM type with 1 vCPU and 1.72 GiB memory. The system disk was 30 GB with the nominal maximum IOPS being 500.

The storage encryption on this server used server-side encryption with a platform-managed key.

There are various guides available for optimizing the storage performance for Linux on Azure users. One very good (although slightly old) guide is this blog post: https:// docs.microsoft.com/archive/blogs/igorpag/azure-storage-secrets-and-linux-io-optimizations.

The blog post covers many details about performance tuning and is worth reading even if you don't have performance problems currently. It is always worth optimizing performance.

Next, let's take a look at what tools Azure provides to analyze and debug VM problems.

Azure diagnostics tooling – a summary

In the Azure portal, on the VM's **Diagnose and solve problems** screen, you can find all the official guides and tools to learn more about troubleshooting various VM-related problems. *Figure 6.14* shows a partial list of common scenarios documented:

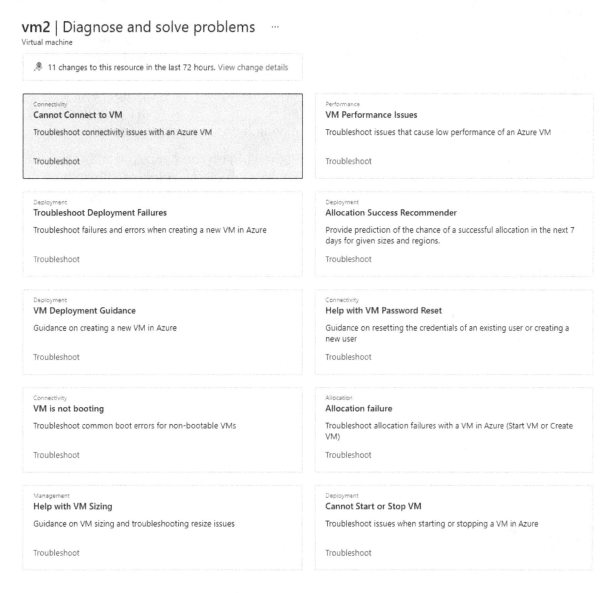

Figure 6.14: Common scenarios list

These guides should give you decent tools to analyze and fix most of the problematic situations you might encounter after you have migrated a Linux VM into Azure. These are also applicable for all VMs created directly on Azure.

Let's not forget there are also various ways to ask for help from Microsoft if you have problems with Azure.

Opening support requests

Just like any other issue with Azure, you can open support requests for Linux on Azure as well. It only makes sense up to a certain point to try to analyze or fix the problem yourself. The best part is both Red Hat and SUSE offer integrated co-located support. This benefits customers as they don't have to open multiple cases—opening a single case with support would suffice. In fact, the Red Hat and SUSE Support Engineers sit in the same office as the Microsoft Support Team, which ensures faster resolution.

The **New support request** feature (shown in *Figure* 6.15) on the Azure portal is easy to use and can guide you through opening the request with all the relevant information. This helps the support staff to get a clear picture of the problem from the beginning.

You can find the request tool in the left-hand menu for the VM that you are having an issue with, shown as follows:

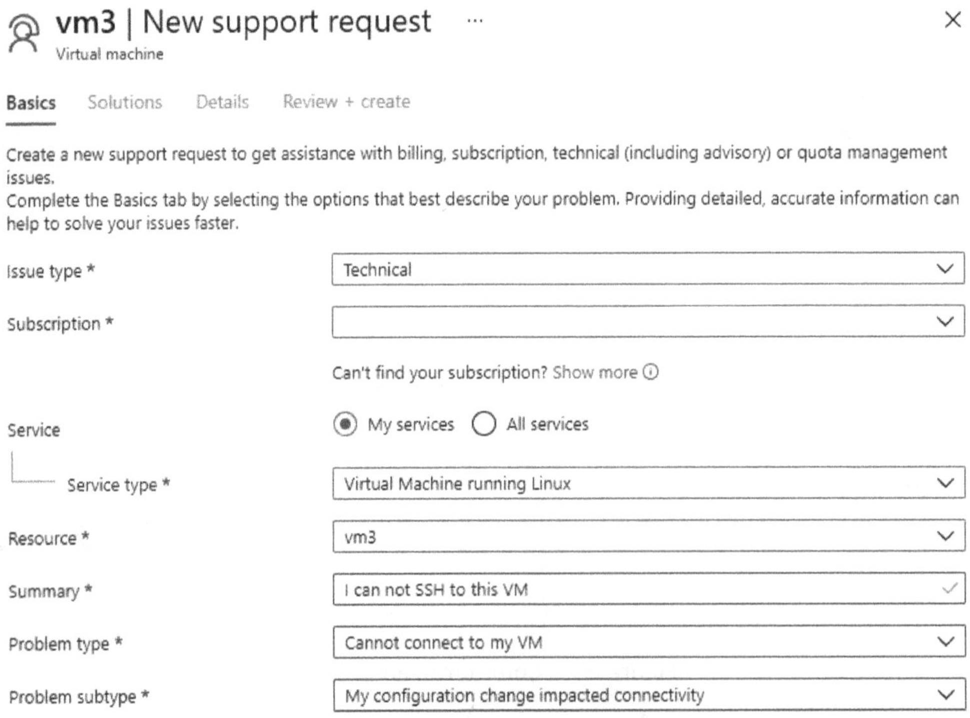

Figure 6.15: New support request

In this example, our problem is described as **I can not SSH to this VM**, and the **New support request** tool was able to suggest a couple of possible problem types. We selected **Cannot connect to my VM** for the **Problem type** option, and **My configuration change impacted connectivity** for the **Problem subtype** option.

In the **Solutions** tab, we will find a possible solution to the problem:

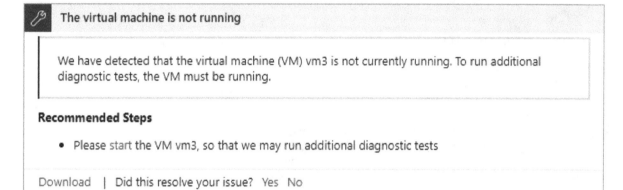

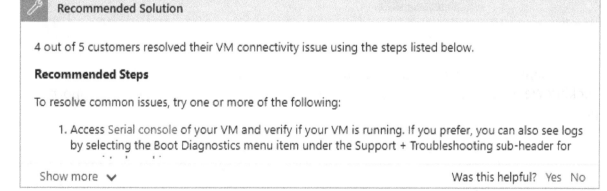

Figure 6.16: List of possible solutions

In many cases, these automatic suggestions can guide you through fixing the issue. As you can see in this example, it appears the VM is not running–probably because the Azure Linux Agent is not reachable. The system recommends you use the previously mentioned serial console method to connect to the server.

Sometimes you may need assistance from Microsoft Technical Support, or you may have found an actual bug in Azure or one of the supported Linux distributions. In that case, you will be presented with the option to open a support ticket or ask for help from the Azure Community.

The availability of Microsoft Technical Support depends on your contract with Microsoft:

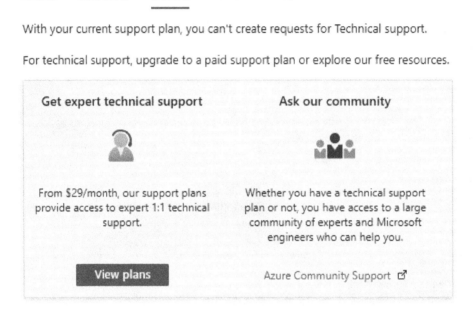

Figure 6.17: Support options

In our example, we used a subscription that does not include technical support. By clicking **View plans** (shown in *Figure 6.17*), we can see the various technical support plans:

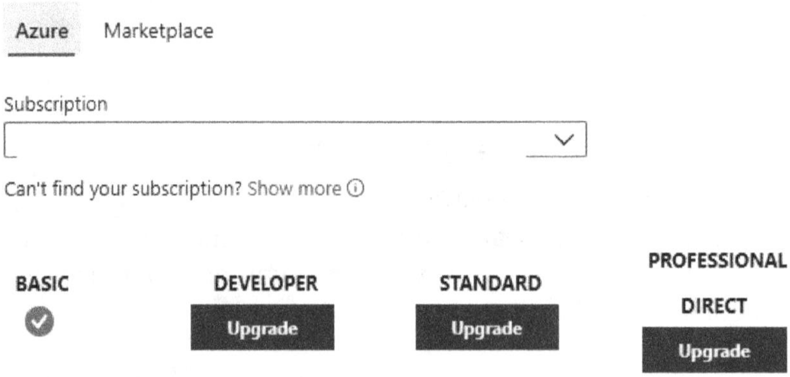

Figure 6.18: Microsoft Technical Support plans

Which plan is best for you depends on many factors. A Microsoft sales representative can provide you with further guidance if you are unsure about choosing a plan.

Additionally, there is support available from Linux vendors via Azure Marketplace. As shown in *Figure 6.19*, by clicking on the **Marketplace** tab, you can see all available Linux support plans that are valid for this specific VM:

Azure   Marketplace

Subscriptions

Can't find your subscription? Show more ⓘ

SUBSCRIPTION	SUBSCRIPTION ID	UBUNTU ADVANTAGE IN...	
Toni	████████████████████	No support plan exists	Purchase

Figure 6.19: Marketplace support plans

In this example, the Linux distribution installed on this VM was Ubuntu. Canonical, the company publishing Ubuntu, offers a support plan called **Ubuntu Advantage Infrastructure Support**, as shown in *Figure 6.19*. As you can see in this case, we have not purchased the plan.

All commercial Linux vendors have their own support packages available for purchase or offered already bundled in the enterprise subscription.

Summary

Having completed this chapter, you should be able to debug and fix some of the most common issues with Linux on Azure. In this chapter, we talked about remote connectivity issues and how to solve these problems if your VM does not let you log in. We also discussed the typical boot problems and discovered the Azure tools that can help in resolving these situations. SELinux- and storage-related issues are quite common runtime problems, which were also covered in this chapter. We also addressed Linux on Azure performance analysis. Finally, we explained how to find support for Linux on Azure from Microsoft Technical Support and Azure Marketplace partners.

This book took a holistic approach to migrating Linux workloads from on-premises infrastructure to Azure. Starting from the planning, assessment, service dependency building, replication, and testing migration, to a complete cutover from on-premises to Azure, the hands-on labs we developed for you should have provided a quick start to your first real migration project. We have shared some of the best practices and vital points that need to be incorporated while migrating Linux workloads to Azure. Consider these recommendations and adopt them in your migration projects. It will accelerate them and contribute to the success of the migration, along with saving a lot of time.

At this point, we would like to congratulate you on learning many new useful skills. We have spent quite a long period of our lives working with Azure, Linux, and many other open-source technologies, many of which have been discussed on the pages of this book. We hope you have enjoyed reading the book as much as we enjoyed writing it. Certain things you cannot learn by reading books or documentation or even by following official training courses. Those things can be only learned by trying and doing things yourself.

For further reading we recommend reading about the Microsoft **Cloud Adoption Framework (CAF)** for Azure: https://docs.microsoft.com/azure/cloud-adoption-framework/. It is a collection of best practices, tools, documentation, and other useful proven guidance from Microsoft designed to accelerate your cloud adoption journey.

Now it is your turn to do good—teach others about what you have learned. Take the information from this book, be successful in your Linux to Azure migration projects, and do not forget to share your knowledge with others!

New horizons for Linux in Azure

In this book, we started with the tagline "Microsoft ♡ Linux", announced by Microsoft CEO Satya Nadella. That was indeed a milestone in Microsoft's history. In the earlier days, Microsoft Azure was known as Windows Azure, which created the impression that Azure was meant for Windows workloads and was not optimized for running Linux workloads. Under Satya Nadella's leadership, Microsoft started to embrace Linux and contribute to other open-source projects, and in 2016, they joined the Linux Foundation.

The change was not only about Linux. Microsoft also released the Edge browser, Visual Studio Code, and Microsoft Teams for Linux, actions that indicated their readiness to welcome and fully embrace Linux. In 2018, Microsoft developed their own Linux flavor called **Azure Sphere**, which is used in IoT devices. With the recent update of Windows 10, Microsoft shipped a full Linux kernel, which opened the doors for developers who are working on Linux development as well as cross-platform. Very soon, the usage of Linux increased and outshone Windows usage in Microsoft Azure. The anti-Microsoft ideology that was present among Linux users is long gone. Looking at all the progress, it is obvious that Microsoft truly loves Linux. All of Microsoft's open-source contributions to the community can be found at https://opensource.microsoft.com/.

Many organizations now use Linux for running a variety of workloads, varying from workstations to SAP clusters, and the features and support offered by Linux on Azure welcomed them to the benefits of the cloud. Administrators can administer their Linux workloads as they normally manage on-premises Linux computers. Azure now provides tools like Azure Migrate, Azure Site Recovery, and Azure Database Migration Service, which accelerate the migration of workloads to Azure.

Organizations that initially believed that cloud computing is expensive have now started to explore the benefits, savings, and features of the Azure cloud. Since these organizations have license subscriptions from popular vendors like RedHat and SUSE, it is easy for them to reuse the same license subscription in Azure as well, without the need to spend extra for licensing in the cloud. Apart from the cost perspective, scaling and high availability are far better than what organizations could achieve in their on-premises infrastructure. Also, it's worth mentioning the security and governance features that Azure provides for running Linux workloads. If you have workloads that are hosted on-premises, outside Azure, due to compliance reasons, then Azure Arc-enabled servers provide you with the ability to manage them natively from the Azure portal.

As we speak, Microsoft is developing new Azure features, pushing updates to preview, and promoting updates to general availability. If you look at the Azure Updates page (https://azure.microsoft.com/updates/?query=Linux), you will be able to see all the new Linux-related updates coming to Azure. The updates are in chronological order, and looking at the number of updates coming in, you will realize the dominance of Linux on Microsoft Azure. It is 2021 and today, even if it may sound a little absurd to some people, the fact is that Microsoft is really an open-source organization.

Index

About

All major keywords used in this book are captured alphabetically in this section. Each one is accompanied by the page number of where they appear.

A

accelerate: 62, 70, 184-185
access: 24, 39, 48, 98, 122, 129, 166-169, 171-172
account: 25, 36, 44, 47, 68, 73, 105-106
acquired: 30-31
acquisition: 30-31
Actions: 80, 185
add-ons: 55
address: 1, 37, 80, 83-84, 113, 122-123, 129, 146, 162-163
admin: 122, 128
adopt: 62, 69, 184
Advisor: 35, 138-139, 159
agent: 33, 72, 91-94, 100, 139-142, 147-148, 152, 159, 165, 168, 177, 181
Agent-based: 71-72, 90-91
agentless: 71-72, 90
agent-linux: 141
allocate: 14
analysis: 13, 59, 71-72, 75, 90, 94, 99, 136, 163, 176, 183
Analytics: 13, 33, 72, 90-91, 94, 148-154, 156, 158-159, 176-177
Ansible: 30, 34, 147
Apache: 7, 10, 13, 19, 28, 33, 36, 59, 75, 173
APIs: 11, 72, 137
AppArmor: 169
application: 7-8, 15, 21, 23, 34, 58-59, 63-64, 66-69, 73, 75-76, 99, 109-110, 113, 138, 161, 169-170
apps: 76, 137

apt-get: 141, 146
Arc-enabled: 185
architecture: 11-12, 19, 22-23, 35-36, 59-60, 64, 66, 68-69, 75, 95, 143, 146-147
assemble: 5, 19
Assessing: 57-58, 70, 75, 77, 95, 159
assessment: 45, 55, 57-59, 67-68, 70-72, 75-76, 78-79, 85-90, 94-95, 97-101, 105, 135, 161, 184
auditing: 170
authenticate: 48, 81
AzCopy: 62
azps-: 54
Azure: 1-2, 5, 11, 13-14, 16-25, 27-29, 31-49, 54-55, 57-58, 60-77, 79-82, 84-90, 93-95, 97-101, 104-110, 112-113, 116-118, 120-133, 135-150, 152, 155, 157, 159, 161-185

B

back-end: 8, 23
balancer: 8
Bash: 4, 47, 122-123, 132
binaries: 9
bind-address: 128
bin-logs: 128
blade: 76-77, 136, 138, 150, 152-153, 156-157
BLFS: 5
blobs: 143
block-level: 20
blog: 178

boot: 5, 144, 161, 165-169, 171, 175-176, 183
bootloader: 167
breakdown: 75, 89, 136
budgets: 137
bug-free: 4
build: 24, 137
bulbs: 24
BYOS: 24, 39, 146

C

Cache: 60
CAF: 62, 66-67, 184
Canonical: 5, 18, 29-30, 34-35, 50-52, 55, 183
CapEx: 24
Cassandra: 173
catalyst: 68
CentOS: 5-6, 18, 24, 28, 31-32, 37-38, 46, 59, 75, 170, 173, 175
Chainsaw: 117
chpasswd: 140
Cisco: 64
Client-side: 143
cloud: 1-2, 6, 8, 11, 13-17, 20-21, 23-24, 27-30, 32-33, 39, 41-42, 44-46, 55, 58, 61-69, 71, 73, 90, 98-100, 105, 122, 125, 129, 133, 135-136, 138, 148, 184-185
cloud-access: 39
CloudForms: 30, 34
CloudFoundry: 31
cloud-init: 33, 141
cloud-native: 68, 98
CloudOps: 66

cluster: 12, 19-20, 61, 82-83
collection: 61-62, 72, 154, 156, 184
collisions: 168
compliance: 185
compute: 9, 11, 15, 37-39, 45, 54, 61, 89, 107, 121
conf: 141, 168
configure: 80, 92, 103, 106, 120-121, 128, 130, 148-149, 154
connection: 16, 72, 84, 104, 122-123, 125, 128-129, 152-154, 162-165
consumers: 6, 16
container: 2, 6, 9-10, 12-13, 32, 34
Controller: 139
CoreOS: 30, 46
cost: 3, 14-16, 24, 37-39, 41-45, 67, 69, 71, 73-74, 87, 89, 95, 136-138, 185
Couchbase: 60
CouchDB: 60
CounterName: 158
CounterValue: 158
CPU-based: 23
credentials: 33, 48, 82-84, 125
cron: 149, 155
cross-region: 99
CUBRID: 60
curl: 47
custom: 33, 35, 39, 149, 164, 176
custom-made: 16
customScript: 164
Cygnus: 30

D

daemon: 4, 148-149
dashboards: 33, 137
data: 2, 8, 13, 15-16, 20-21, 23, 33, 58-60, 62, 72, 74, 80, 89, 94, 100, 106-107, 114, 117, 120, 122-126, 130, 132, 136-137, 139, 143-144, 148-149, 152, 154, 156, 159, 168, 171, 173, 176-177
database: 7-8, 19, 60, 62-63, 95, 97, 99, 117-118, 120-133, 135, 143, 185
datacenter: 11, 14-16, 21-22, 64, 73, 135, 162
dataset: 124, 130-131, 159
DDoS: 16
deadlines: 67-68
deallocate: 14, 43, 69
Debian: 28, 31-32, 46
debug: 161-162, 179, 183
dependencies: 68, 72, 91, 94
deploy: 9, 11, 21-22, 35, 50, 58, 60, 62, 66, 72, 79, 99, 111, 117
deployments: 11, 17, 31, 33, 135, 139, 146
Derby: 60
Diagnose: 166, 179
directory: 33, 177
disable: 168, 170
disk: 4, 20, 33, 65, 68, 89, 99, 107, 144-145, 168-169, 171-178
distribution: 4, 12, 23, 28-31, 36, 59, 65, 140-141, 146, 148, 177, 183

distros: 5-6, 24-25, 32, 37, 46, 55
DM-Crypt: 144
Docker: 10, 173
docs: 20-24, 34, 44-46, 54, 62, 66-67, 112, 128, 138, 141-142, 144-147, 172, 177-178, 184
Domains: 21
DRBD: 20, 22
dynamic: 59-60

E

eastus: 50, 52
egress: 37
encounter: 128, 168-169, 173, 180
encryption: 143-145, 169, 171, 173, 178
environment: 11, 15, 33, 45, 58, 63, 67-68, 71-72, 75, 79-80, 90, 94, 135, 162
ESXi: 59
event: 22, 98, 141, 148, 154
explore: 78, 142, 185
ExpressRoute: 65
extension: 31, 33, 142, 152, 154, 164, 172

F

factors: 69, 87, 89, 183
failovers: 109
failure: 19, 68, 162, 167
features: 2, 16, 18, 20, 23-24, 27, 33, 55, 137-138, 142-143, 185
Fedora: 5-6, 59
filesystem: 4, 21, 140, 144, 171-173, 175-176

fiowrite: 177
Firebird: 60
firewall: 122-123, 163, 165
Flatcar: 32
floppy: 4
forensic: 15
Foundation: 18, 184
FQDN: 84
framework: 62, 99, 184
fsck: 172
fstab: 171-172
Functions: 137

G

gateways: 65
gigabytes: 175
github: 99, 109, 141, 170
Glassfish: 7
GlusterFS: 20
governance: 66, 185
grep: 140
group: 3, 19, 71, 77,
    88, 105-106, 112,
    115, 118, 146, 150,
    163-164, 174-175
grub: 167-168
GUIs: 6

H

Hadoop: 13
HANA: 21
hands-on: 54-55, 58-60,
    67, 72, 75-76, 80, 95,
    97-99, 116-117, 133,
    148-149, 151, 159, 184
hardware: 9, 14, 21-23,
    63, 73, 117, 172, 176
Hashicorp: 34
HDInsight: 13
high-end: 24

high-level: 12
holistic: 184
host: 5, 8-9, 11, 14-15,
    34, 59, 62, 75,
    79-80, 82-84, 94,
    97, 104, 116, 146
HPFS: 21
HSQLDB: 60
HTML: 59, 171
HTTP: 112
Hybrid: 16, 24, 30, 36,
    38-41, 44-45, 61, 87, 118
Hyper: 90
Hyper-V: 8, 59, 67, 71,
    75, 79-80, 82-83, 94,
    97, 99-102, 104-105,
    116, 132, 135, 168
hypervisors: 8-10, 33, 168

I

IaaS: 17, 60, 68, 99, 117
Identity: 48, 63
image: 9, 19, 29, 32,
    34-35, 39, 46, 48-50,
    52-55, 139-140,
    142, 168-169, 173
implement: 13-15, 18, 61
import: 80, 83, 125
include: 5, 8, 10, 17, 35, 55,
    60-61, 72-73, 87, 136,
    138, 145, 168, 172, 182
incorporate: 62
INCREMENT: 117, 123
incur: 117
information: 2, 22, 48,
    63, 66, 69, 73, 79-80,
    85, 92, 139-140,
    150, 172, 180, 184
ingest: 33, 72, 148, 154
initial: 3, 17, 69, 112
initramfs: 171

initrd-: 168
InkTank: 30
insights: 33, 176
install: 8-9, 11-14, 17,
    19, 35, 46, 59, 71-72,
    81, 91-94, 100, 102,
    117, 133, 140-141
instance: 8, 35, 43,
    46, 52, 68, 117-118,
    120, 132, 136, 138
integrate: 137
Intel: 3
interface: 6, 39, 46,
    139, 165, 176
intervals: 176
inventory: 58, 67-68,
    70, 86, 100
invoke: 137, 164
iodepth: 177
ioengine: 177
IOPS: 21, 177-178
ip-route: 140

J

Java: 7, 30-31, 36, 58
JBoss: 7, 30-31, 34
Jetty: 7
json: 49, 164, 169

K

kernel: 4-5, 28, 35,
    139, 167-169, 185
Kubernetes: 12, 17, 31
Kusto: 33, 72, 94, 148

L

labels: 171
labor: 74
labs: 31, 97, 133, 184

LAMP: 58-60, 75, 91, 95, 99, 109, 117, 149
landing-zone: 66
latency: 22
legacy: 22, 65
level: 29, 61, 136, 144-145, 155-156
leverage: 137
license: 14, 28, 37-39, 45, 69, 73, 87, 185
limitation: 20, 145
Linux: 1-6, 8-9, 11-13, 17-20, 22-25, 27-37, 39, 42, 44, 46, 55, 57-63, 65-66, 72, 75, 92, 95, 97-99, 122, 133, 135-136, 139-142, 144-148, 155, 159, 161-165, 167-171, 173, 175-178, 180-185
list: 5, 13, 28, 31-33, 36, 49-50, 52-54, 63-64, 70-71, 83, 94, 122, 140, 142, 145, 147, 149, 155, 158, 162-163, 175-176, 179, 181
list-offers: 50
load: 8, 19, 23, 94
local: 33, 46, 122, 148-149, 164, 171
location: 50-52, 106, 118, 142
logging: 39, 47, 123, 146, 148, 155
logic: 7-8, 137
login: 33, 47, 81, 122-123, 125
logs: 33, 72, 148-149, 152, 156-158, 166, 170-171, 176
lsblk: 175
LucidDB: 60

M

machine: 4, 12, 14, 33, 80, 92, 98-99, 114, 122, 125, 139-142, 144-145, 148-150, 152-154, 156-157, 159, 161, 168
machines: 2, 8, 28, 71-72, 74, 86, 89-90, 104, 114, 136, 138, 141, 144-147, 152-153, 156-157, 161
macOS: 6, 20
main: 3-4, 15, 61-62, 75, 89
maintenance: 22, 117, 148
Makara: 30
manage: 11-12, 14, 17, 19, 60, 62, 67, 70, 75, 135-136, 139, 144, 147, 152, 159, 175, 185
managed: 13, 20, 48, 60, 62, 66, 99, 120, 139, 144, 148, 161
ManageIQ: 30
management: 12, 14-15, 17, 24, 31, 33, 62-63, 65-68, 97-98, 117, 136-137, 139, 143, 147-148, 159
Manager: 15, 20, 33, 36, 65, 80, 139, 141, 148, 168, 173
managing: 15, 33, 98, 147-148
manual: 105, 147, 172
mapping: 43, 70, 129
MariaDB: 8, 60
Marketplace: 18-19, 23, 32-33, 39, 46, 49, 55, 170, 183
master: 12, 93
MaxDB: 60

mechanism: 141, 147-148, 169
memory: 8, 14, 144-145, 158, 168, 173, 178
Mesos: 10
message: 20, 84, 104, 129, 158, 162, 173
metadata: 76
method: 39, 72, 117, 146, 165, 168, 181
methods: 57, 117, 143, 162
metrics: 33, 72, 138, 176
microservice: 12
Microsoft: 1-2, 8, 14, 16-25, 28, 32-37, 39, 42-47, 54-55, 60-62, 66-67, 72-73, 79, 93, 98, 100, 112, 117, 120, 128, 132, 137-139, 141-142, 144-147, 161, 164, 168, 172, 177-178, 180, 182-185
Migrate: 5, 18, 27, 39, 57-58, 60, 62, 64-66, 70-72, 75-77, 79-82, 84-86, 89-90, 94-95, 97-100, 105, 107, 109-110, 112-114, 116-117, 120, 126, 132-133, 135, 144, 169, 185
migrated: 24-25, 58, 66-68, 89, 98-99, 105, 115, 117, 122-123, 129-130, 133, 135-136, 138-139, 146, 148-149, 152, 157, 159, 161, 167, 180
migrating: 1-2, 16-18, 24, 58, 61-62, 67, 71, 73, 97-99, 105, 109, 114, 116-117, 120, 124, 126, 133, 159, 168, 184

migration: 1-2, 16-18, 23, 27, 43, 45, 55, 57-60, 62-63, 65-71, 73, 75-76, 78, 80, 86, 89, 95, 97-102, 105, 109-118, 120, 122, 125-127, 130-133, 135-136, 143, 149, 157, 159, 161-162, 169, 184-185

migrations: 18, 23, 27, 63, 66, 76, 97-98, 117

mkfs: 140

mkinitrd: 168

mode: 66, 118, 170-171

model: 8, 23, 28, 36-39, 41-45, 120

models: 28, 36, 44-46, 55, 143

Modernize: 75

modes: 118, 170-171

modify: 84, 174, 176

module: 54, 142, 169

modules: 5, 35, 55, 168

MongoDB: 8, 60, 173

Monitor: 11, 33, 67, 71-72, 137, 148-149, 176

Monitoring: 72, 136, 157

monolithic: 12, 140

mount: 168, 177

mounted: 20-21, 62, 171, 177

mounting: 20, 172

MyLinuxVM: 169

MySQL: 8, 10, 19, 36, 59-60, 62, 97, 99, 117, 120-129, 132-133, 135, 172

mysqld: 128

mysqldump: 124

mysql-rithin: 125

N

Nadella: 1, 184

navigate: 76, 91, 100, 110, 112-113, 116, 122, 126, 150, 152-155, 157

NetApp: 20-21

netstat: 72

network: 11, 16-17, 19-23, 33, 36-37, 39, 63-65, 72, 80, 105-106, 111, 119-120, 139-140, 162-164

networking: 4, 14, 65, 73, 95, 119, 125

NGINX: 9-10

no-boot: 171

--nodata: 124

--no-data: 124

node: 20, 36, 61

nodes: 12, 20, 23, 61

nofail: 172

non-uniform: 168

NoSQL: 60

NULL: 117, 123

NYSE: 30

O

OCFS: 20

official: 4, 35, 132, 140, 145-146, 179, 184

offline: 49, 117-118, 126

onboard: 93, 149-150, 152

onboarded: 154, 156, 159

onboarding: 152, 154, 156

on-premises: 2, 5-6, 8, 13-15, 17-18, 20-25, 33, 57, 60-63, 67, 69-71, 73-74, 79, 86, 100, 107, 109, 116-118, 121-125, 128-130, 135, 144, 146, 152, 157, 159, 162, 167, 169, 172, 177, 184-185

open: 18, 28-29, 47, 60, 80, 85, 89, 139, 141, 152, 157, 180, 182

OpenShift: 12, 17, 30-31, 34

opensource: 18, 185

open-source: 1, 5, 18, 27-28, 30, 55, 60, 184-185

OpenSSH: 140

OpenSSL: 140

OpenStack: 11, 31

openSUSE: 31-32

operate: 15, 133, 159

operates: 16, 66

operating: 2-3, 5-6, 9, 11, 16-17, 24, 27, 30-32, 35, 46, 75, 133, 135, 141, 144, 147, 159, 161-162, 169-170, 174-176

operation: 23, 152, 170

operational: 15, 36, 138

operations: 54, 66, 177

OpEx: 24

optimal: 68

optimization: 35, 45, 67, 136, 138

Optimize: 16, 45, 68, 70, 75, 135-136, 138-139, 159

optimized: 14, 62, 73, 135, 184

optimizing: 16, 136, 161, 178

Oracle: 32, 46, 60

orchestrator: 30

organization: 3, 5, 13-15, 24, 32, 36, 46, 67, 73, 185

OrientDB: 60
OsDisk: 174-175
os-release: 44
other: 4-5, 7-8, 15-16, 19, 28-29, 31, 34-36, 38, 44, 59-60, 62, 64, 67-71, 73, 75, 89-90, 94, 117, 132-133, 136, 139, 156, 169, 172, 175, 180, 184
others: 6, 60, 62, 79, 145, 184
outlined: 80, 115, 150
output: 47, 50-53, 74, 170, 174, 177-178
--output: 142, 169
outsourced: 66
Outsourcing: 15
overview: 55, 90, 122, 128, 144, 147, 167

P

PaaS: 17, 30, 60, 68, 99, 116-117
package: 9, 35, 65, 140-141, 148, 171
packages: 10, 33, 59, 61, 140, 183
pane: 41, 43, 118, 122, 128-129
parameter: 49-51, 124, 168, 177
Password: 48, 80, 128, 140
paths: 68
pattern: 66
PAYG: 24, 36-39, 41-45, 137-138, 146
perform: 13, 47, 54, 67, 70-73, 84, 86, 109-110, 113-114, 117, 159

performance: 19, 21, 35, 61, 65, 67, 73, 121, 136, 138, 144, 155-156, 158-159, 169, 176-178, 183
Performing: 61, 71, 75, 97, 109, 135, 149, 157, 159, 161, 177
Perl: 59
permissions: 35, 61, 76
phase: 33, 55, 63, 67, 71, 75, 78, 99-100, 136, 138-139, 159
phpMySQLapp: 99, 109
planning: 44-45, 50, 55, 57-58, 62-67, 75, 97-99, 126, 135, 161, 184
platform: 2, 7, 11, 17, 21, 30-31, 34, 59-60, 67, 76, 79, 101, 105
platforms: 67, 90, 94, 117, 132-133
plethora: 55, 60, 117
port: 128, 158
portability: 23
portal: 43, 46, 71, 76, 81-82, 84-85, 88, 92-93, 104, 120, 136, 142-143, 150, 162-163, 165-166, 179-180, 185
portals: 71
ported: 4, 10, 22
ports: 72
PostgreSQL: 8, 60, 62
PowerShell: 54, 79
practical: 57, 95, 97, 133, 145, 170
practices: 35, 62, 66, 184
pre-designed: 66
--preload: 168

Premium: 20, 117-118
preparations: 63, 95
prepare: 27, 67
prepay: 36, 38, 42, 44-45
Pre-project: 63, 95
Prerequisite: 81
preview: 72, 118, 120, 185
price: 29
pricing: 3, 16, 36-37, 39, 42, 73, 87, 117-118, 121, 150-151
private: 11, 64, 162
process: 1, 14, 33, 41, 47, 58, 60, 70, 73, 75, 79, 81, 84-85, 92, 95, 99, 102-105, 108-109, 115-116, 118, 120-121, 125-126, 135, 144, 147, 150, 153, 173, 176
ProcessName: 158
processors: 73
product: 31, 34, 39, 43-44, 66, 69
production: 30, 34, 36, 55, 63, 109, 170
products: 18, 31, 34, 60
project: 3, 5, 24, 57-58, 63-67, 70-71, 75-80, 85, 90, 95, 97-101, 104-105, 112, 116, 120, 122, 125-127, 133, 143, 158, 161, 184
projects: 5, 18, 31, 63, 65, 97-98, 162, 184
prompt: 47, 103
Protected: 108, 143
protection: 136, 139, 143, 159
protocol: 20, 61, 64, 102, 148

provider: 14-16, 36, 64, 66, 100-102, 135
providers: 16, 39, 65, 90, 99-100, 105, 133
proxy: 103
PSCore: 54
public: 2-3, 11, 16, 23-24, 28-30, 37, 41, 65-66, 112-113, 115, 129, 162-163
--publisher: 164
publishers: 46, 50, 142
publishing: 183
push: 72, 80, 85, 139, 148
Python: 36, 59, 140
Python-based: 140

Q

QEMU: 8
qemu-img: 169
query: 33, 49, 72, 148, 156, 158-159, 174, 185
--query: 174-175
Qumranet: 30
Quoting: 3

R

ramdisk: 168
ramp: 47
Rancher: 12, 31
randwrite: 177
range: 36, 55, 162
RavenDB: 60
rawdisk: 169
RDMA-based: 23
read-only: 166
Real-Time: 176
real-world: 58, 121
rearchitect: 68-69
re-architect: 68
reboot: 171

rebooted: 22
rebuild: 69
rebuilding: 69
recalculate: 89
recommended: 49-50, 62, 68, 73, 140, 152, 155, 168, 170
recompile: 4
reconnect: 123
Recovery: 99-103, 172, 185
recreating: 68
redeploy: 41
redeployment: 39
redhat: 34, 39, 146, 171, 185
redhat-rhui: 146
redirect: 150
redirected: 80, 130
Redis: 60
Refactor: 68
refactoring: 55
region: 50, 72, 89, 101, 106, 142, 146, 150
register: 76, 80-81, 102-103
registration: 41, 67, 82, 102-104
Rehost: 68
released: 4, 31, 123, 141, 185
Reliability: 138
replicate: 104-105, 107-108, 110
replicated: 68, 99, 106, 109-110, 114
Replicating: 105, 108
replication: 68, 101, 105-106, 108-109, 117, 133, 184
repo: 99

repositories: 4-5, 145-146, 177
repository: 145-146, 148
request: 44, 180-181
requests: 8, 23, 148, 162, 180
requirements: 8, 24, 32, 46, 55, 61, 87, 121, 144-145
re-run: 89
reservation: 151
reservations: 20, 43-45
Reserved: 42-43, 45, 138
Reset: 128
resolution: 35, 55, 180
resource: 9, 14, 33, 61, 77, 105-106, 112, 115, 118, 120, 136, 141, 146, 150, 168, 173
resources: 9, 11, 14, 16, 19, 37, 66, 73, 98, 101, 105-106, 111-113, 115, 133, 136-139
response: 49
revalidation: 84
review: 61, 69, 75, 80, 89, 94, 108, 120, 122, 130, 138, 151
Reviewing: 89, 102, 115, 139
RHEL: 5, 31-32, 34, 37, 39-42, 44-45, 66, 146, 148
RHEV: 8
RHUI: 146
robocopy: 62
routing: 65, 139
rsyslog: 158
runtime: 10, 139, 162, 169-170, 176, 183
--runtime: 177
Russinovich: 17

S

SaaS: 16-17, 69
sbin: 172
scalability: 16, 61, 69
scalable: 23
scale: 12, 14-16, 173
scaling: 14, 24, 61, 185
schema: 124-125, 133
scope: 28, 31, 35-36, 55, 68, 98, 156
script: 33, 47, 117, 124, 140
scripted: 165
scripts: 79, 93, 158, 165, 173
SCSI: 20, 171
SCVMM: 139
search: 36, 49, 54, 58, 76, 118, 120, 150, 152, 158
Secure: 14, 70, 75, 135-136, 139, 152, 159
secured: 139
security: 14-16, 33, 35, 65-67, 98, 122, 129, 135-136, 138-139, 144-145, 163-164, 169-171, 185
self-hosted: 2
self-service: 14
SELinux: 65-66, 169-171, 173
SELinux-: 183
seqNum: 64
serial: 166-167, 171-172, 181
-series: 145
server: 5, 7-9, 11-12, 14, 20-21, 23, 30-33, 39, 58-62, 66, 68-69, 71, 74-75, 78-80, 83, 85-86, 89-92, 94, 97, 99-103, 105, 108, 117, 120-126, 128-130, 132, 135, 138, 146, 149, 167, 169, 171, 175, 178, 181
servername: 124-125
servers: 2, 5, 7-9, 14-17, 20-21, 24, 29, 39, 44, 58, 60-61, 67-68, 70-73, 75-79, 85-86, 88-92, 94-95, 97-101, 105, 108-110, 113-117, 130, 133, 135, 138, 146-147, 162, 185
server-side: 143, 178
service: 9-10, 12, 16-17, 20-21, 29, 48, 58-60, 62, 66, 68, 71-72, 76, 90, 97, 99, 117-120, 126, 128, 133, 135, 139, 143, 147, 163, 184-185
services: 5, 7-9, 11, 13-14, 16-19, 39, 58, 60, 66, 68, 76, 100, 109, 118, 122, 129, 135-136, 138, 143, 161
sestatus: 170
Setting: 20, 67, 76, 80, 87, 90, 128
settings: 80, 105-107, 130, 143, 164, 169
--settings: 164
setup: 4, 173
setups: 22
sfdisk: 140
SFTP: 92
Shell: 4-5, 46, 122, 125
sign: 29, 33, 48, 82
SKUs: 52
Slackware: 31
SLES: 31-32, 37, 39, 43-44, 146
software: 1, 3-5, 7-10, 14-16, 19-20, 22, 27-31, 39, 42-45, 55, 66, 69, 100-102, 170, 172-173
solution: 8, 14, 20-21, 23-24, 36, 66-69, 71, 99, 117, 181
solutions: 2, 7-8, 11, 17-18, 20-23, 25, 60, 64, 68, 71, 116, 181
source: 5, 18, 28-29, 60, 67, 72, 86, 105, 119, 124, 126, 128-130, 141, 144, 149, 168-169
sources: 117, 152, 176
Splunk: 13
SQLite: 60
sshd: 164
stack: 11, 59, 95
stage: 4, 6, 40, 69-71, 73, 75, 100, 103, 109, 130, 136, 139, 152
stakeholders: 63, 65, 69, 75, 90, 139
status: 108, 112, 130-131, 140, 153-154, 170
storage: 8, 11, 15, 17, 19-21, 23, 30, 34, 37, 39, 61-63, 73-74, 80, 89, 95, 105-106, 121, 143-144, 169, 171, 173, 175-178
store: 59-61, 71, 76, 156
stored: 83, 148
storvsc: 168
strategies: 16, 55, 75, 161
Subnet: 106
subscribe: 29
subscription: 19, 23-24, 29, 37, 39-42, 44, 65, 76-77, 90, 98, 106, 118, 129, 136, 146, 150, 182-183, 185
subset: 6, 60, 145
subtype: 181

sudo: 35, 47, 93, 140-141, 164, 168, 171, 177

SUSE: 5, 18, 23-24, 29-31, 34-35, 41-42, 44-46, 55, 146, 180, 185

Synapse: 13

sync: 114

syntax: 124-125

sysadmin: 20

sysadmins: 2, 17

syslog: 148-149, 155-156, 158-159, 176

syslogs: 33

systemctl: 164

T

technical: 18, 23, 27, 29, 34-36, 55, 57, 60, 63, 65, 141, 182-183

technologies: 1, 6, 13, 36, 39, 60, 65, 184

technology: 1, 20, 30, 65, 67

templates: 33, 41, 141

terms: 15-16, 22-23, 29, 73, 81, 89, 117, 138

test: 109-113, 115, 173, 175, 177

testing: 8, 38, 45, 177, 184

tier: 117-118, 121, 150-151

tiers: 20-21, 117-118

tool: 34, 36, 71, 98, 105, 129, 136-138, 141, 147-148, 163, 166, 174, 177, 180-181

tooling: 62, 70, 75, 98-99, 135, 162-163, 179

toolkit: 30

tools: 3-4, 12-13, 17-18, 20, 30, 33, 55, 57-58, 62, 66-67, 70-72, 75,

78, 88, 95, 98-101, 110, 113, 122, 136, 139-140, 159, 161, 165, 177, 179-180, 183-185

toolset: 105

two-step: 102

Two-tier: 8

U

Ubuntu: 5-6, 18, 24, 29-32, 34-35, 37-38, 46-47, 50, 59, 75, 135, 140-141, 146, 148, 167, 183

UbuntuServer: 52

Unix: 2-3

upgrade: 20, 167

usage: 33, 39, 41, 70, 185

username: 48, 124-125

users: 3, 5, 11, 17-18, 30, 33, 59, 63-64, 76, 178, 185

utilities: 4-5, 140

utility: 163, 166, 171

utilize: 33, 39, 42, 143

util-linux: 172

uucp: 149

UUID: 171-172

V

validate: 81, 94

validation: 81, 84, 120

varchar: 117, 123

variables: 27, 170

variants: 24

vCores: 44

vCPU: 37, 43, 121, 178

vCPUs: 43, 79

vendors: 12, 18, 29-30, 34-36, 42, 46, 55, 67,

71, 145, 170, 183, 185

verification: 132

verified: 84

verify: 55, 58, 69, 84-85, 99, 132, 138, 156, 175

Verifying: 85, 88, 108, 113, 132, 153-154

version: 3-5, 20, 30-31, 44, 46, 53, 93, 120, 140-141, 172

--version: 141

versions: 3-4, 28, 31, 35, 44, 46, 52-53, 98, 168

vhddisk: 169

VHDX: 168

view: 17, 33, 54, 64-65, 67, 94, 98, 137-138, 142, 182

viewing: 89, 110

virtual: 2, 8, 14, 28, 80, 98-99, 105-106, 111, 119-120, 136, 138-142, 144-147, 149-150, 152-154, 156-157, 159, 161, 166-169, 172, 175-176

VirtualBox: 8, 168

virtualized: 67

virtual-size: 169

VM-based: 19

VMBoundPort: 158

vmbus: 168

VMConnection: 158

VM-hosting: 17

--vm-name: 164

VMProcess: 158

VM-related: 179

vm-repair: 172

vmSize: 174

VMSSs: 49

VMWare: 8, 59, 71-72, 79, 90, 94, 168

vSphere: 72, 79

W

waagent: 139, 141
walinuxagent: 139-141, 152
Webserver: 75
wget: 92-94
window: 47-48, 77,
    87, 102-103, 158
Windows: 2, 5-6, 8, 12, 20,
    39, 46, 65, 72, 79-80,
    92, 122, 147, 184-185
WordPress: 19, 36
workload: 5, 14,
    43, 62, 71, 97
workloads: 1-2, 5, 8, 18,
    23-24, 31, 33-35, 44,
    55, 57-58, 61-62, 67-69,
    73-74, 94-95, 98-99,
    133, 135-139, 143, 146,
    161, 169, 184-185
workspace: 33, 72,
    90-94, 148-152, 154,
    156, 158-159, 176
workstation: 6, 30, 46
workstations: 6,
    13, 20, 185

X

Xbox: 16

Z

zdnet: 17

www.ingramcontent.com/pod-product-compliance
Lightning Source LLC
Chambersburg PA
CBHW080527060326
40690CB00022B/5047